STRUCTURAL CHANGES IN
U.S. LABOR MARKETS

STRUCTURAL CHANGES IN
U.S. LABOR MARKETS

Causes & Consequences

Edited by

Randall W. Eberts and Erica L. Groshen

M.E. Sharpe Armonk, New York • London, England

Available in the United Kingdom and Europe from M. E. Sharpe, Publishers,
3 Henrietta Street, London WC2E 8LU.

Library of Congress Cataloging-in-Publication Data

Sturctural changes in U.S. labor markets:
causes and consequences / edited by Randall W. Eberts and Erica L. Groshen.
p.   cm.
Includes bibliographical references and index.
ISBN 0-87332-825-6
1. Compensation management—United States—Congresses.
2. Wages—United States—Congresses.
3. Labor market—United States—Congresses.
I. Eberts, Randall W.
II. Groshen, Erica L., 1954–
HF5549.5.C67S77   1991
331.12′0973—dc20
91-11478
CIP

Printed in the United States of America
The paper used in this publication meets the minimum requirements of
American National Standard for Information Sciences—
Permanence of Paper for Printed Library Materials,
ANSI Z 39.48-1984.

MV   10   9   8   7   6   5   4   3   2   1

Contents

Foreword

Policymakers face an ever-changing economic environment that affects the way in which they formulate policy, as well as the way in which their policy decisions impact the economy. During the decade of the 1980s, dramatic structural changes in labor markets complicated the task of policymakers. We observed relatively sluggish wage growth during the initial stages of the expansion of the 1980s. Even as the economy gathered steam to generate the longest peacetime expansion in modern times, the subsequent tightness in the labor markets (as measured by the low unemployment rates) did not exert the upward pressure on wages that past experience would have suggested.

For those of us concerned about inflation, the apparent lack of significant upward wage pressure was welcomed. However, the lack of a firm understanding of the changes in labor-market behavior was unsettling as we attempted to chart a policy course to keep inflation in check. Was the relatively low wage inflation during much of the 1980s a temporary phenomenon or the reflection of a more permanent shift in the way wages are determined? Moreover, to what extent are changes in compensation practices revealed in the way we measure changes in wages?

The Federal Reserve Bank of Cleveland sponsored a conference in October 1989 to identify and analyze recent developments in personnel policy and worker compensation practices. These practices may have led to less wage inflation during the 1980s and may continue to affect wage behavior in the 1990s. We also considered what, if any, consequences these changes might have on the formulation of macroeconomic policy. A distinguished group of researchers and practitioners from academia and private industry explored these issues. In addition, two prominent macroeconomists commented on how this body of research may influence our thinking about the workings of the macroeconomy.

The papers and discussion during the two-day conference were very insightful, and we hope that this volume of papers will prove useful to readers interested in important changes in U.S. labor markets.

W. Lee Hoskins
President
Federal Reserve Bank of Cleveland

Acknowledgments

The success of a volume that attempts to deal with current issues depends on the dedication and cooperation of the contributing authors and discussants to provide the most up-to-date information available and then to carry through expeditiously in preparing their research for publication. We have been very fortunate to enlist the participation of a group of economists and labor-relations practitioners with these qualities. We owe an enormous debt of gratitude to all the authors involved.

One participant deserves special thanks. Sharon Smith's enthusiasm for the research topic and her counsel in preparing the agenda kept the project moving forward. We are most grateful for her encouragement and participation.

This book represents the joint efforts of many individuals, in addition to the authors and discussants. Several of the authors have acknowledged the assistance of their colleagues and staff in footnotes at the end of the respective chapters. The editors are indebted to the management of the Research Department for sponsoring the conference and to their colleagues for advice and support in planning the conference. Also, the editors would like to thank William Murmann for copyediting the manuscript and helping with its production; Jane Sardelle for her assistance in organizing the conference; Connie Jones for helping to type the final manuscripts; and Liz Hanna for typesetting the book. We would also like to thank Richard Bartel and the fine editorial staff at M.E. Sharpe for their assistance in producing the volume.

Finally, the authors of each chapter and the editors wish to state that the views expressed in this book are their own and do not necessarily reflect the views of the institutions with which they are associated.

STRUCTURAL CHANGES IN
U.S. LABOR MARKETS

1

Overview

Randall W. Eberts and Erica L. Groshen

Despite apparently tight labor markets, wage inflation in the late 1980s was much lower than most observers anticipated. *The Wall Street Journal* quoted one noted economist as saying, "The most interesting phenomenon in the United States today is the existence of enormous labor shortages in some areas accompanied by no upward pressure on wages."[1] The article went on to state that the reasons for this phenomenon raise doubts about forecasts that wage pressures would soon contribute to inflation.

Several explanations were offered at that time for the slow nominal wage growth that occurred during the second half of the decade. Chief among the factors cited was a reversal in labor–management psychology about wage increases, brought on in part by productivity declines, a severe economic downturn, and increased foreign competition. The common perception was that during the 1970s, workers, with the consent of management, felt entitled to automatic wage increases that were at least in line with inflation. The demand for "3 percent plus cost of living" was a common refrain around many negotiating tables. This mindset evaporated as workers saw massive job losses during the twin recessions of the early 1980s and as managers faced mounting foreign competition that eroded market share and placed downward pressure on domestic prices. Instead of focusing on wage increases, negotiations centered on wage concessions in exchange for job security.

In addition to a change in the psychology of wage-setting behavior, institutional changes were also cited as possible causes of sluggish wage growth. Mitchell (1989), in comparing the wage pressures of the 1980s with those of the 1960s, concludes that recent changes in labor-market institutions have pushed wage-setting in a more competitive direction. With the decline of the proportion of employment in the union sector and in big firms, jobs are less likely to be cushioned from labor-market forces by union contracts and bureaucratic personnel practices.

Changes in demographics, particularly the greater participation of women in the labor force, were also said to figure into the moderate wage growth that occurred during the 1980s. To the extent that women are less attached to the labor force than are men, they could provide a buffer by filling vacancies during tight labor markets and by leaving the labor force during slack periods.

The questions that faced many policymakers and analysts during this period were twofold: What was really behind this apparent change in wage behavior, and was the change permanent or temporary? To provide a better understanding of these issues, the

1

Federal Reserve Bank of Cleveland commissioned a set of papers by prominent labor economists to provide a careful and comprehensive analysis of some of the important developments that took place in the labor market during the 1980s. The research focuses primarily on labor-market behavior and industrial relations practices that could explain the macroeconomic relationship between unemployment and wages and the effect of this relationship on output and employment stability. Four of the six papers included in this volume deal with compensation practices, the use of lump-sum and profitsharing payments and fringe benefits, and the structure of union contracts. The remaining two studies examine the effects on wages of increased pressure from international competition and changing labor-force demographics.

I. Comparisons Across the Last Three Decades

Was wage behavior different during the 1980s than during the preceding two decades? This brief section argues that this may indeed have been the case. Many analysts have noted that nominal wage growth during the expansion of the 1980s fell far short of the wage growth experienced during the expansions of the 1970s and even those of the 1960s (Table 1). The same relatively sluggish growth rates of the 1980s are also evident for the broader measure of compensation per hour, which includes fringe benefits, a growing component of employee compensation. This casual observation alone might tempt one to conclude that fundamental changes in the structure of wage determination and worker compensation during the 1980s dampened the upward pressure on wages.

However, leaping to that conclusion ignores differences in economic conditions across the past three decades. Although observers in the 1980s generally perceived labor markets to be extremely tight (particularly during 1988 and early 1989), typical measures of labor-market tightness do not support this view. In fact, the minimum unemployment rate during the 1980 expansion (5.2 percent) was higher than that of the expansions of the previous two decades (3.4 percent during the 1960s and 4.8 percent during the 1970s). In addition, the maximum rate of capacity utilization was lower during the 1980 expansion than during the expansions of the 1960s and 1970s (84.4 percent versus 91.6 percent and 87.3 percent, respectively). Therefore, it is not clear whether the slow wage growth that occurred during the 1980s resulted from structural changes in wage-setting practices or simply from differences in business conditions.

One way to partially disentangle these effects is to ask the conceptual question: What would have happened to wages if the expansions of all three decades had shared the same economic conditions and differed only in the way wages responded to changes in the economic environment? We use a simple econometric technique to estimate the wage behavior separately for each of the last three decades. These estimates record how wages responded to economic conditions in each decade, and are then used to simulate the net nominal wage change that would have taken place if the wage behavior unique to each decade had responded to alternative economic conditions.

Table 1:   Economic Conditions in Previous Decades

	1960 expansion	1970 recession	1970 expansion	1980 recession	1980 expansion
Average hourly earnings	5.21	6.93	7.38	7.66	3.39
Compensation per hour index	6.36	9.01	8.35	9.10	4.26
Consumer Price Index	3.41	8.45	6.94	10.04	3.68
Output per hour, private business sector	2.41	−0.38	1.82	0.18	1.70
Real GNP, 1982 dollars	4.21	−0.18	3.47	−0.25	3.65
Unemployment rate	4.06	5.37	6.42	8.17	7.02
Unemployment rate, male, age 25 and up	2.31	2.99	3.78	5.81	5.39
Capacity utilization	87.80	80.99	80.78	75.93	79.99

NOTE: The 1960 expansion is defined as the period between 1961:QI and 1969:QIV. The 1970 recessions include the periods 1970:QI to 1970:QIV and 1973:QIV to 1975:QI. The 1980 recessions include the periods 1980:QI to 1980:QII and 1981:QII to 1982:QIV.
SOURCES: Average hourly earnings in the private business sector, the compensation per hour index, output per hour in the private business sector, unemployment rates, and the Consumer Price Index are obtained from the Department of Labor, Bureau of Labor Statistics. Hourly earnings, compensation per hour, and output per hour are shown as annual percentage changes averaged over the respective time periods. The Consumer Price Index and the unemployment rates are average rates over the respective time periods. The capacity utilization rate for manufacturing is obtained from the Board of Governors of the Federal Reserve System and is the average rate for the time period. Real GNP is obtained from the Department of Commerce, Bureau of Economic Analysis. It is shown as the average annual percentage change over the time period.

We follow a variant of the wage-change model used recently by Wachter and Carter (1989) and earlier by Gordon (1982). Annual changes in average hourly nominal earnings are explained econometrically by annual changes in the unemployment rate, capacity utilization, labor productivity (measured by output per hour), the GNP implicit price deflator, and the Consumer Price Index (CPI, all items for urban workers). Other specifications of the wage-change model are possible, and many have been posited and estimated. This simple specification is based on the premise that wages respond to pressures in the labor market and to inflation expectations. Therefore, changes in the unemployment and capacity utilization rates proxy changes in the tightness of labor and product markets. The CPI reflects workers' expectations of price inflation. Labor

Table 2: Explaining Annual Changes in Nominal Average Hourly Earnings

	1960	1970	1980
Intercept	0.465	6.022	0.473
	(0.63)	(7.43)	(2.11)
Consumer Price Index (percentage change, lagged one quarter)	0.887	0.082	0.325
	(2.07)	(1.18)	(5.70)
Unemployment rate (percentage change)	−0.018	0.027	0.051
	(−1.74)	(1.84)	(6.09)
Capacity utilization rate (percentage change)	0.045	0.150	0.142
	(0.63)	(2.66)	(6.19)
Labor productivity (percentage change)	0.286	−0.221	0.002
	(2.07)	(−2.70)	(0.03)
GNP implicit price deflator (percentage change)	0.271	0.138	0.498
	(0.77)	(1.12)	(5.60)
Recession (variable = 1 for quarters marked by recession)	−0.387	−0.674	−0.138
	(−1.10)	(−1.80)	(−0.43)
R^2	0.89	0.52	0.99

NOTE: Observations are quarterly and percentage changes are year over year. Separate regressions are run for each decade. T-ratios are in parentheses.
SOURCE: Authors' calculations.

productivity changes measure workers' contribution to production and, consequently, employers' ability to grant higher wages. The GNP implicit price deflator captures changes in producer prices, which also reflect employers' ability to pay higher wages.

These relationships are estimated separately, using quarterly observations for each decade. A variable that takes the value of one during quarters marked by national recessions is also included in the regression to account for business-cycle effects.

Since our main interest in this exercise is to demonstrate wage behavior under similar economic conditions, we do not dwell on the estimates of individual coefficients. Suffice it to say, however, that most of the variables in Table 2 appear to have the expected effect on nominal wage changes. For the most part, higher nominal wage increases are associated with higher inflation expectations, increased capacity utilization, gains in labor productivity, and higher producer prices. However, the relationship between changes in nominal wages and unemployment rates is not what one would normally expect, showing a positive correlation in the 1970s and 1980s. These results are consistent with periods of stagflation during the 1970s and with the long, gradual recovery of the 1980s, when the rate of wage increase declined as inflation moderated and unemployment rates fell.

Table 3:   Simulations of Annual Nominal Earnings Changes

		Structure (relationship between conditions and wages)		
		1960	1970	1980
	1960	5.41	6.17	3.65
Explanatory variables (economic conditions)	1970	9.52	7.51	6.97
	1980	6.43	6.65	4.24

NOTE: The values are the average annual percentage changes in nominal hourly earnings during the decade. Simulations are performed by multiplying the explanatory variables for a given decade by the coefficients for the appropriate decade. The values on the diagonal (i.e., for the same decade) are identical to the actual annual wage changes.
SOURCE: Authors' calculations using estimates from Table 2.

The net effects of these differences in the relationship between nominal wage changes and changes in economic conditions are shown in Table 3. The bottom row is of primary interest. The first entry in that row is the average annual nominal wage change that would have taken place in the 1980s if labor during that period had responded to economic conditions in the same way it did during the 1960s. In this hypothetical case, wages would have increased 6.43 percent annually on average during the 1980s. Subjecting the wage behavior that prevailed during the 1970 expansion to 1980 economic conditions yields a slightly higher annual growth rate of nominal wages of 6.65 percent. Both of these growth rates are substantially higher than the 4.24 percent increase that actually took place during the 1980s.

It is also interesting to note that if wages responded to economic conditions during the 1960s as they did during the 1980s, wage growth would have been considerably lower in the earlier decade than it actually was—3.65 percent versus 5.41 percent. The same holds true for the 1970s. The actual annual wage increase was 7.51 percent, compared with an annual rate of 6.97 percent when the 1980 wage structure is used.

Therefore, this simple analysis suggests that something did take place during the 1980s that dampened the responsiveness of wages to economic conditions, such as changes in unemployment rates and price levels. The chapters that follow explore the various changes that have taken place, assessing the extent of these developments and their implications for wage behavior and ultimately for the behavior of the U.S. economy.

II. Why the Slow Wage Response in the 1980s?

A. Four Possible Explanations

The explanations for the slow wage growth during the 1980s explored in this volume can be classified around four reasons for the change in the wage–unemployment relationship. The first category considers increased competition within product markets, particularly that resulting from greater penetration of foreign imports into domestic markets. Under this scenario, pressures to keep prices in line with those of foreign competitors would place a cap on wage increases. Chapter 2 addresses this issue.

The second category is the substitution of job security for wage growth. The reordering of worker preferences toward job security is rooted to a large extent in labor's experience during the 1982-1983 recession. Proponents of this view suggest that the severe job losses incurred at that time prompted workers to seek job security in exchange for minimal wage increases and, in some cases, wage concessions. Chapter 2 also addresses this issue in conjunction with an analysis of the effect of unemployment rates on wage growth. Chapters 3 and 4 consider wage concessions as one reason for an increase in alternative payment schemes, such as lump-sum and profitsharing payments.

The third class of explanations relates to institutional changes in firms' wage-setting practices. Prompted by two key economic events of the 1980s—a deep recession and significantly lower price inflation—workers were willing to accept alternative payment schemes (chapters 3 and 4), a reduction in fringe-benefit coverage (chapter 5), and the elimination of cost-of-living clauses from their union contracts (chapter 6). All three changes reduced the fixed component of labor costs. If firms can adjust wages, as well as employment, in response to economic conditions, employment should be less sensitive to business-cycle fluctuations. Of course, this explanation may be linked to the trade-off between wages and job security, if workers consciously accepted the new arrangements in order to enhance their employers' chances of survival.

Finally, changes in wage behavior could be related to differences in the demographic composition of the labor force, because demographic groups may differ in their responses to labor-market conditions. Thus, when a group's representation in the labor market changes significantly, the behavior of the labor market may be altered. Chapter 7 considers the impact of an increase in female participation on cyclical fluctuations in labor-market tightness.

B. Summary of the Research Reported in this Volume

The essay by Vroman and Vroman (chapter 2) offers a very useful overview of the major determinants of wage changes. Although the chapter focuses primarily on the effect of increased international trade on money-wage growth, it also considers other key factors, such as inflation expectations and the composition of unemployment. The focus on international trade as a significant contributor to sluggish wage growth is well supported by the events of the 1980s. Since the 1960s, the U.S. economy has become increasingly open to foreign trade with respect to both imports and exports. As imports increasingly penetrate domestic product markets, one would expect labor markets to also become more competitive, placing downward pressure on domestic nominal wage growth.

Vroman and Vroman present two sets of estimates to test this hypothesis. The first is based on a time-series analysis of a modified Phillips curve, which shows the trade-off between nominal wage growth and unemployment. The second is based on a longitudinal study of more than 2,000 collective-bargaining agreements in the manufacturing sector between 1959 and 1984. Both sets of estimates show that developments in international trade in the 1980s contributed to the slowdown in money-wage inflation, with nonpetroleum import prices and real nonpetroleum import share registering the most significant effects. The authors are quick to point out, however, that international trade accounted for only a small part of the slowdown, at most 18 percent in selected years. This contribution would have been even smaller for the entire private business sector, since international trade should have the largest effect on manufacturing, but manufacturing directly involves only one-fifth of U.S. workers.

Vroman and Vroman also explore other possible explanations for the moderate wage growth of the 1980s, most importantly inflationary expectations and the composition of unemployment. They conclude that a reduction in inflationary expectations during the latter half of the decade was the primary factor in the wage-inflation slowdown, accounting for at least half of the total reduction. The unusually high rate of unemployment among prime-age males also exerted a restraining effect on money-wage growth, equaling the effect of international trade.

By extending the scope of inquiry beyond the international trade question, the Vroman and Vroman essay provides a convenient basis for examining in greater detail the issue of inflationary expectations and the question of how these expectations are manifested in wage-setting practices and bargaining contracts. Their analysis also puts into perspective the effect on wages of demographic changes in the labor force.

A common theme among the next three papers (chapters 3, 4, and 5) is that developments in wage-setting processes may have reduced the trade-off between wage inflation and unemployment. These studies examine alternative ways of compensating workers that may promote flexibility in firms' employment decisions. Bell and Neumark (chapter 3) consider the growth of lump-sum payment schemes in union firms to determine whether the spread of this alternative compensation arrangement contributed to the decline in wage inflation during the 1980s.

Lump-sum payments may reduce wage inflation in at least three ways. First, such payments signal a change in the labor–management environment toward either a strengthened management stance or a worker preference for this form of compensation. The second possibility is simply the result of a change in accounting: Some labor costs are shifted out of wages and salaries and into other forms of compensation. Finally, lump-sum payments increase labor-market flexibility by tying compensation more directly to worker productivity and firm profits. Profit sharing provides employers with the ability to respond to shocks in the product market. Since profitsharing payments are not counted as part of an employee's base salary, adjustments in either direction can be made quickly in response to changes in business conditions. The increased wage flexibility has led some economists, including Weitzman (1984), to advocate profit sharing as a means of stabilizing employment and output.

To analyze these effects, Bell and Neumark examine more than 5,000 union contracts negotiated in 1,200 private-sector establishments between 1975 and 1988. Within this sample, they find a dramatic increase in the number of contracts with lump-sum payment provisions. Within only one year, between 1983 and 1984, the percentage of workers signing contracts with lump-sum payments skyrocketed from 5.9 to 69.5. The authors do not believe that this increase is related to concessionary behavior on the part of labor. Rather, their evidence shows that unions exhibited some preference for this alternative form of compensation.

Applying the Phillips-curve framework to the trade-off between nominal wage growth and unemployment, Bell and Neumark find that the prevalence of lump-sum payments is associated with a reduction in wage inflation. They estimate that a 10 percentage point increase in the share of workers covered by lump-sum contracts reduces the annual rate of wage inflation by 0.3 or 0.4 percentage points. The authors reject all but one of the aforementioned explanations for the dampening effect of lump-sums on wage growth. They dismiss the accounting explanation of a shift from base wages with evidence that lump-sums also reduce the percentage increase in total labor costs of firms. They also find little support for the flexibility explanation. In fact, their estimates are inconsistent with the hypothesis; firms offering lump-sum payments exhibit *less* employment flexibility in response to changes in demand for their products. The authors conclude that something in the labor–management environment must have changed during the 1980s.

Kruse (chapter 4) picks up where Bell and Neumark leave off by exploring the effect of another particular form of nonwage payment—profit sharing—on wage growth. He is quick to point out that even this somewhat narrow type of compensation takes several different forms, such as profit-related bonuses, deferred pension plans, or some combination of the two. Results of his study show that a steady growth in deferred profitsharing plans occurred during the 1980s, when the percentage of the private wage and salary work force covered by such plans increased from 13.3 percent in 1980 to 18.4 percent in 1986. Although profitsharing plans cover a relatively small proportion of the work force, they appear to be concentrated in industries that historically have demonstrated fairly downwardly rigid wage behavior, such as manufacturing.

Kruse concentrates on increased labor flexibility to explain the negative relationship that he finds between profit sharing and wage growth, a relationship that is similar to the one between lump-sums and wages described in chapter 3. He finds little agreement among the nine previous empirical studies that have examined the connection between profit sharing and employment stability.

Kruse pursues his own empirical test using deferred pension plans as a measure of profit sharing. His analysis yields some, albeit weak, support for the position that firms do not view profitsharing payments as part of the short-run cost of labor. Rather, they see such payments as a distribution of profits to labor after other costs (including base labor costs) have been taken into account. In this way, the firm's employment decisions are not influenced by profitsharing payments, since these are not considered a part of base wages. For 586 U.S. publicly traded companies, Kruse finds little trade-off between higher profitsharing payments and employment. On the other hand, he finds the typical trade-off between base wages and employment. The author concludes from these results that profit sharing is not simply "disguised wages," but is indeed a more flexible form of employee compensation.

Although wage growth may have been reduced by flexible payment schemes in the 1980s, the fringe-benefit component of labor compensation continued to escalate, claiming an increasing share of total labor costs. Between 1983:QI and 1990:QII, wages and salaries increased by 33.1 percent, while fringe-benefit costs rose 45.6 percent, pushing up total compensation per hour by 35.5 percent. Woodbury and Bettinger's analysis (chapter 5) suggests that this increase would have been even greater if fringe-benefit coverage had not fallen during the decade. The percentage of workers included in employer-provided pension plans dropped from 60 percent in 1979 to 55 percent in 1988. During the same period, the inclusion of workers in employer-provided group health insurance plans fell slightly, from 74 percent to 72 percent. Thus, the findings suggest that the moderate wage growth in the 1980s was not necessarily the result of large compensating increases in benefit coverage.

From a very detailed analysis of the determinants of fringe-benefit coverage, Woodbury and Bettinger conclude that the decline in coverage during the 1980s resulted both from the decrease in marginal tax rates on personal income during the middle of the decade and the steady drop-off in union representation throughout the decade. The decline in the manufacturing sector, shifts in occupational mix, and aging of the work force had little to do with the decrease in coverage, according to the authors' estimates.

The most significant determinant of fringe-benefit coverage was the lowering of marginal tax rates in 1986, which induced workers to trade fringe benefits for increased wages. However, employees' willingness to substitute wages for fringes was not uniform across all types of voluntary benefits. Woodbury and Bettinger estimate that workers were more willing to trade wages for employer-provided pensions than for employer-provided health coverage. The authors interpret the decline of benefit coverage as a tendency for a reduction in the fixed component of worker compensation and a move toward a more "spot market" type of compensation.

Wage moderation in the 1980s was disproportionately concentrated in the union sector, which experienced lower wage growth in the latter half of the 1980s (14.2 percent) than did the nonunion sector (23.9 percent). In contrast, in every year between 1976 (when data first became available) and 1982, union wage increases outpaced nonunion wage changes. After 1982, however, when the economy began to recover from the high unemployment brought on by the twin recessions that inaugurated the decade, many unions placed job security above wage growth as the top priority in their bargaining rounds. This reordering of priorities is certainly evident in union nominal wage increases.

Bils (chapter 6) examines two changes in the structure of labor contracts that could have led to slower wage growth in the union sector: reductions in indexation and reductions in contract length. For all union contracts settled in the private sector, the percentage of workers with inflation escalator clauses declined from an average of 55.2 between 1980 and 1983 to an average of 36.8 percent between 1984 and 1988. However, the length of contracts remained virtually the same over the decade, averaging slightly more than 31 months.

An extensive body of theoretical papers supports the view that the length of contracts and the inclusion of indexation reflect the degree of uncertainty facing workers and employers. To explore this proposition, Bils examines a detailed longitudinal set of major collective bargaining agreements reached between 1955 and 1985 in the manufacturing sector. Surprisingly, his results for contract length contradict the generally accepted wisdom that increased uncertainty should shorten contracts. Instead, he finds that contracts are longer in industries that face more uncertainty (durable goods, for example). Bils suggests that these findings are consistent with the notion that longer contracts are written in order to reduce strikes.

With respect to indexing, Bils finds that the percentage of contracts with cost-of-living escalator clauses is positively related to increases in inflation and inflation uncertainty. This result is consistent with the generally accepted view that escalator clauses protect workers from unanticipated price inflation. However, he also finds that the decision to index is closely related to high wage growth, a result he considers odd.

The final explanation for the moderate wage growth in the 1980s covered in this volume is related to one aspect of demographic changes. Korenman and Okun (chapter 7) consider the effect of female participation in the work force on cyclical unemployment. Women, by purportedly being less attached to the labor force than are men, provide a pool of workers who move freely in and out of the labor force, depending on the stage of the business cycle. This procyclical participation pattern of a large group of workers weakens the use of unemployment rates as a measure of labor-market tightness. Consequently, fluctuations in wages and our standard measures of unemployment rates associated with business cycles are dampened.

The major issue that Korenman and Okun explore, therefore, is whether women are indeed less attached to the labor force than are men. Their analysis shows that while women are still less attached, their connection to the labor force grew during the 1980s. Although these results might suggest that cyclical unemployment should rise in response to increased labor-force attachment among women, further analysis shows no association between these two factors. The authors attribute this latter finding to the disparate distribution of men and women across industries and occupations. Women are largely concentrated in growth industries that demonstrate little cyclical fluctuation, while men are concentrated in industries with the opposite characteristic. Thus, although Korenman and Okun's results do not rule out the possibility that the increase in female labor supply during the 1980s reduced wage growth by reducing labor-market tightness, their findings suggest little, if any, change in the long-run cyclical behavior of the economy as a result of the increased labor participation of women.

III. Implications for Macroeconomics

We asked two prominent macroeconomists, Olivier Blanchard and Finn Kydland, to comment on whether the findings summarized above alter the way in which labor markets figure into their view of the workings of the macroeconomy. In particular, we were interested in whether the trend toward more flexibility and risk-sharing in wage-setting practices would alter their theories and policy recommendations. Their comments are contained in chapter 8.

Blanchard focuses his remarks primarily on the macroeconomic implications of lump-sum bonuses and profitsharing. He sees both schemes as ways of lowering the risk of bankruptcy among firms, and notes an interesting tension between the implications of increased risk-sharing in labor contracts and increased risk-sharing in recently introduced financial arrangements, such as high-yield "junk" bonds. The former generally provides increased stability by reducing the likelihood of bank-ruptcy, while the latter increases the risk of a firm going under.

Blanchard sees the reduction in bankruptcy risks leading to three macroeconomic effects: 1) stabilization of employment in the short run, 2) alteration of the factors determining labor mobility, and 3) modification in the specification of the Phillips-curve trade-off between inflation and unemployment. The first effect results from the simple fact that firms will not be as likely to close their doors during downturns, and through wage adjustments, will be able to retain workers longer. This should reduce employment swings during business cycles. The second effect is related to labor adjustments that follow sectoral shocks. If wages are rigid, then unemployment is the only signal that leads workers to leave declining sectors. However, if wages vary, then both wages and job security enter a worker's decision. Finally, an increase in wage flexibility breaks the link between tightness in the labor markets, as measured by unemployment rates, and price inflation.

Kydland frames his remarks in terms of implications surrounding business cycles and business-cycle theory. He notes that researchers interested in this line of inquiry have changed their methodology from the system-of-equations approach popular in the 1960s to one based on the neoclassical growth model. Under the former framework, models were constructed around a set of equations that described economic behavior such as wage rates, unemployment rates, household consumption, and firm investment. The current approach, based on the neoclassical growth model, instead stresses empirical knowledge organized around the parameters of technology, preferences, and institutional arrangements. Consequently, this transition is important in determining how questions are posed and data are organized.

Kydland finds that research presented in this volume is, for the most part, organized around the former methodology—that is, based on estimates of behavioral equations. He stresses that in order to bridge the gap, questions posed in the business-cycle framework will have to be translated into the behavioral-equation framework, and vice versa. Therefore, business-cycle researchers, who pursue issues concerning the main sources of shocks that lead to business-cycle fluctuations, may either have to ask slightly different questions or else organize the information contained in this volume in a different way.

IV. Conclusion

The research presented in this volume underscores the thinking of many observers and market analysts who, during the latter half of the 1980s, perceived that developments were taking place in labor markets that altered to some extent certain basic relationships between wage behavior and economic performance. These essays suggest that the increased adoption of more flexible pay schemes during the latter half of the decade led to lower labor costs, perhaps to more flexibility for firms in their employment decisions, and, in general, to more stability in employment (at least in the short run). Thus, evidence indicates that these more flexible pay schemes might well be able to accommodate relatively lower unemployment rates without igniting serious wage inflation.

Although some observers argue that this increased flexibility, which resulted from the adoption of lump-sum payments and profitsharing arrangements, was simply a way to obscure wage concessions, the research presented here finds little support for this view. The fairly widespread acceptance of these arrangements by workers and managers suggests that the shift in the relationship between labor markets, unemployment, and price inflation observed in the 1980s may extend well into the 1990s. This structural change, along with other changes noted in the volume, may be welcomed by policymakers who are attempting simultaneously to contain inflation and stabilize output.

Note

1. "Wage Increases Are Sluggish Despite a Scarcity of Workers," *The Wall Street Journal,* p. A1, September 1, 1987.

2

International Trade and Money Wage Growth in the 1980s

Susan Vroman and Wayne Vroman

I. Introduction

The United States' economy experienced seven years of continuous expansion between 1982 and 1989, during which real gross national product (GNP) grew 31 percent, from $3,159 billion in the fourth quarter of 1982 to $4,134 billion in the second quarter of 1989. During this period, the unemployment rate declined by half, from 10.7 percent of the civilian labor force to 5.3 percent. The sustained expansion in real output and the associated decline in unemployment has not yet provoked large-scale increases in the rates of wage and price inflation. Inflation indicators remained in the 4 to 5 percent range even in 1988 and 1989, when most observers would describe the economy as operating close to, or even above, full employment.

This paper examines recent developments in the labor market to determine whether special factors have been operative in restraining money-wage inflation. Major attention is focused on the economy's foreign-trade sector and its performance during the present expansion. The expansion in real output since 1982 has been accompanied by foreign-trade deficits of a scale not previously witnessed in the post–World War II period. Using both aggregate time-series data and microdata for manufacturing bargaining situations, we estimate wage-change equations that include international trade variables. At the same time, however, we also consider three other factors operative in the 1980s: inflationary expectations, unemployment demographics, and declining union strength. Our principal conclusion is that these other factors have been quantitatively much more important than international trade in explaining the sluggish behavior of money wages in the 1980s.

At the outset, two major limitations in the scope of the paper should be noted. First, this is not a complete treatment of the inflation process, as we do not undertake a separate investigation of price inflation. Instead, actual and expected price inflation are taken as given in an analysis of money-wage growth. Papers by Mitchell (1989) and Wachter and Carter (1989), as well as our own earlier papers (Vroman and Vroman [1987] and Vroman and Abowd [1988]), provide ample precedent for focusing solely on labor-market inflation. Second, international trade has effects on domestic employment levels both in import-competing and export industries. We do not attempt to estimate the employment

Table 1:   Wage Inflation, Price Inflation, and Unemployment, 1965 to 1989 (percentages)

	Wage inflation[a]			Price inflation		Unemployment rate	
	Hourly earnings index	Emp. cost index wages	Emp. cost index comp	All items CPI[a]	GNP deflator[b]	All persons 16 and older	Men aged 25-54
Time period:							
1965 to 1969	5.4	N.A.	N.A.	3.8	4.2	3.8	2.0
1970 to 1974	7.2	N.A.	N.A.	6.7	6.8	5.4	3.0
1975 to 1979	7.7	7.6[c]	N.A.	8.2	7.6	7.0	4.4
1980	9.3	9.0	9.7	12.5	9.9	7.1	5.2
1981	8.1	8.8	9.8	8.9	8.7	7.6	5.5
1982	6.1	6.2	6.4	3.8	5.2	9.7	8.0
1983	3.8	5.0	5.7	3.8	3.6	9.6	8.2
1984	3.2	4.1	4.9	3.9	3.4	7.5	5.9
1985	3.2	4.1	3.9	3.8	3.1	7.2	5.6
1986	2.0	3.1	3.2	1.1	2.6	7.0	5.6
1987	2.7	3.3	3.3	4.4	3.0	6.2	5.0
1988	3.3	4.1	4.9	4.4	4.0	5.5	4.4
1989	N.A.	4.2	5.0	6.1	4.3	5.2[d]	4.0[d]

a. Consumer Price Index. December to December changes. For 1989, the annualized change from December 1988 to June 1989 is shown.
b. Fourth quarter to fourth quarter changes. For 1989, the annualized change from 1988 fourth quarter to 1989 second quarter is shown.
c. 1976 to 1979.
d. January to June 1989.
N.A. Data not available.
SOURCES: All data from the U.S. Department of Labor or the National Income Accounts.

effects of trade. In the microanalysis, employment effects on wage adjustments are estimated, but the sources of employment changes are not identified.

II. Background Data

Table 1 presents descriptive data on wage inflation, price inflation, and unemployment, with particular attention to developments of the 1980s. At the start of the decade, wage inflation was growing at a 9 to 10 percent annual rate according to both the hourly earnings index (HEI) and the employment cost index (ECI). Between 1981 and 1984, all three wage-inflation series in the table decelerate by nearly 5 percentage points, reach bottom in 1986, and then accelerate moderately during 1987 to 1989.

Throughout the 1980s, the HEI grows more slowly than the ECI, mainly due to the different occupational coverage of the two surveys. For the six-year period 1983 to 1988, the cumulative growth in money wages was 19.7 percent for the HEI and 28.9 percent for the ECI. When ECI wage growth is measured using the occupational mix of the HEI, that is, using fewer white-collar workers and more blue-collar workers, the two show nearly identical growth rates in the 1980s.[1] With the discontinuation of the HEI in 1989, the ECI will become the primary wage series for future time-series, wage-inflation research.

From the two ECI series in the table, it is also clear that compensation has generally grown more rapidly than wages in the 1980s. The data for 1988 and 1989 repeat a pattern that was present in the first half of the decade, as well as in earlier years.[2] Although not shown separately in the published ECI reports, employer-provided health insurance costs rose rapidly in 1988, causing overall fringe-benefit costs to rise by 6.8 percent for the year. A continuation of the wages-fringe-benefit growth differential is apparent in 1989 as well.

The price-inflation data in Table 1 show about the same pattern in the 1980s as money-wage growth; rapid deceleration between 1980 and 1983, low rates thereafter, reaching their lowest rates in 1986, and accelerating modestly after 1986. The effect of the volatile energy component in the consumer price index (CPI) is important both in 1986 and in the first half of 1989. When food and energy are removed from the CPI, the remainder of the index advanced at a 4.9 percent annual rate in the first half of the year. Expected price inflation as measured in the Livingston survey and the University of Michigan survey has also remained quite low. Twelve-month expectations about CPI inflation have remained close to 5 percent into mid-1989.[3]

The generally low rates of wage and price inflation have persisted while the economy has approached, many would say reached, full employment. The overall unemployment rate has been less than 6.0 percent in every month since November 1987 and has remained continuously below 5.5 percent since September 1988. Table 1 also displays the prime-age male unemployment rate. It too has trended downward sharply since 1983, reaching an average of 4.0 percent in the first half of 1989. One unusual aspect of the labor market in the current expansion has been the persistence of relatively high unemployment among prime-age men. Their relative unemployment rate in the first half of 1989 was 0.77 times the overall rate. To anticipate a later result, we find that high unemployment among prime-age men has contributed to the moderate pace of wage inflation in the mid-to-late 1980s.

Since our paper focuses primarily on the link between foreign trade and money-wage growth, Table 2 displays several nominal- and real-trade variables for the 1965 to 1989 period. Nonpetroleum merchandise import price inflation grew at an annual rate of 7.0 percent or more in each year of three periods: 1972 to 1974, 1977 to 1980, and 1986 to 1988. Major appreciation in both the real and nominal exchange rate of the dollar is apparent during 1981 to 1984, followed by depreciation from 1985 to 1987. Dollar appreciation was again occurring in the first half of 1989.

The export and import trade-share variables, percentages of real gross domestic

Table 2: Import Price Changes, Exchange Rates, and Trade Shares, 1965 to 1989 (percentages)

Time period	Nonpetroleum import price changes	Nominal exchange-rate change	Real exchange-rate change	Net export share	Real international trade measures		
					Export share	Import share	Nonpetroleum import share
1965 to 1969	3.3	0.4	0.7	-0.8	6.5	7.3	6.0
1970 to 1974	11.4	-3.7	-3.3	-1.2	8.2	9.4	7.1
1975 to 1979	6.6	-2.6	-0.8	-0.3	10.1	10.5	7.2
1980	10.2	1.9	-0.2	1.8	12.4	10.6	8.0
1981	-0.5	17.8	12.6	1.5	12.3	10.8	8.5
1982	-2.2	15.1	10.0	0.8	11.6	10.8	8.8
1983	-1.1	6.5	1.8	-0.6	10.8	11.4	9.5
1984	-1.0	12.6	8.5	-2.4	10.8	13.2	11.3
1985	-0.3	-13.0	-9.8	-2.9	10.3	13.2	11.5
1986	7.0	-17.6	-13.7	-3.5	10.8	14.3	12.2
1987	7.1	-14.3	-11.3	-3.0	11.8	14.8	12.8
1988	7.2	1.2	-0.3	-1.9	13.3	15.1	13.0
1989[a]	0.0	15.7	13.1	-1.3	14.1	15.4	13.2

NOTE: All series are averages of quarterly changes or levels measured at annual rates.

a. First six months of 1989.

SOURCES: Nonpetroleum import price changes—National Income and Product Accounts, Table 7.15 from 1967 to 1988, derived by authors prior to 1967. Nominal exchange-rate change—Federal Reserve series for 10 countries. Real exchange rate—Morgan Guaranty series for 15 countries. Real international trade measures—National Income and Product Accounts, Table 4.2. Real trade shares are measured as a percentage of real GDP. Real petroleum imports prior to 1967 were assumed to equal 0.1815 of total real imports (0.1815 was the 1967 to 1968 average).

product (GDP), document the gradual opening up of the U.S. economy that has been occurring over the last 25 years. Real export shares and real import shares in the late 1980s are more than twice their respective levels of the late 1960s. In these aggregate data, the falloff in net exports during the first half of the present expansion, 1983 to 1986, is obvious. Also, the recovery of exports in 1987 to 1989 has been so vigorous as to cut the 1989 (first-half) net export deficit to about one-third of its 1986 level, that is, 1.3 percent versus 3.5 percent of real GDP. The strong appreciation of the dollar in 1989, coupled with the large continuing federal budget deficit, probably imply that the real net export share will not continue this pattern of improvement.

Of the various trade variables in Table 2, the exchange rates and real net export shares display more variability in the 1980s than in the previous 15 years. The growth in export shares and import shares during the 1980s represents a continuation of trends apparent in earlier years. Import price inflation has actually been lower in this decade than in earlier periods covered by the table. We next turn to the linkage between foreign trade and money-wage growth.

III. A Selective Review of Time-Series Literature

Only a limited number of studies have used time-series data to estimate the effect of foreign trade on money-wage adjustments in the United States. Part of the reason for the paucity of such studies is undoubtedly the small size of the foreign-trade sector prior to the 1980s. Further, if the effects of trade on wages operate more strongly through imports and exports,[4] then much of the rapid growth in the real import share has been a phenomenon of the present decade, particularly the growth of nonpetroleum imports. Note in the final column of Table 2 that the real nonpetroleum import share grew by only two percentage points between 1965 to 1969 and 1980, from 6.0 percent to 8.0 percent, but it then increased to 13.2 percent by the first half of 1989.

Earlier studies have often incorporated trade variables within a modified Phillips-curve specification, that is, money-wage changes as a function of the unemployment rate and the expected rate of price inflation. An early study by Nordhaus (1972) examined wage growth in the United States and six other developed economies. One set of estimated equations explained the annual growth in manufacturing hourly earnings from 1955 to 1971 with a fixed lag distribution of import price changes from the current year and the two previous years (with declining weights of 0.50, 0.33, and 0.17). He reported a coefficient of 0.384 with a t-ratio of 3.3 for the United States. Although the paper did fit modified Phillips curves, the investigation of import-price effects was conducted using simple regressions in each country. Therefore the independent effect of import-price changes, holding constant the effects of unemployment and price inflation, cannot be assessed from his reported results.

Robert Gordon has undertaken several investigations of wage and price dynamics. Many of his studies have appeared in the *Brookings Papers on Economic Activity*. In work through the late 1970s, he estimated separate wage and price equations. By the early 1980s, however, when his specifications began to incorporate international trade variables, he began to use a vector autoregression analysis of price dynamics. Based on causality tests, he concluded that wage inflation exerted no separate effect on the inflation process (Gordon [1982]; and Gordon and King [1982]). The two trade variables that have entered his analysis are import price inflation (the deviation from overall inflation as measured by the GNP deflator) and the exchange rate of the dollar. In equations explaining quarterly private nonfarm compensation growth from 1954:Q2 to 1980:Q4 (Gordon [1982, Table 6]), he employed the nominal exchange rate (current and lagged three quarters) in the set of explanatory variables. Its coefficient was negative as expected in three reported equations, but significant in only one of the three.

McClain (1984) examined changes in private nonfarm hourly compensation from 1964:Q3 to 1984:Q3 and included in the set of explanatory variables the change in the real exchange rate, current and lagged one quarter, along with unemployment, price changes, incomes policy dummies, and social insurance tax rates. His specifications closely resemble those used earlier by Gordon. Both real exchange-rate terms entered significantly with the expected negative signs in equations fitted through 1984:Q3, but not in equations that stopped in 1978:Q3. The coefficients implied that the contemporaneous effect was about twice the size of the lagged effect. One can question the timing of the real exchange-rate effects in these estimates. Wages are traditionally viewed as responding slowly to product price changes, so that a large contemporaneous effect is implausible. The difference in results for the two estimation periods may reflect a spurious correlation between the increase in the real exchange rate and money-wage deceleration of the 1981 to 1984 period.

In a paper that examines both the theoretical and empirical effects of international trade on the domestic economy, Dornbusch and Fischer (1986, Table 8.9) report results of modified Phillips-curve estimates. They explain growth in hourly earnings in manufacturing from 1962:Q4 to 1983:Q3 with unemployment, past inflation, and a lagged trade variable. Three trade variables are tested: import-price inflation, changes in the nominal exchange rate, and changes in the real exchange rate of manufactured goods. Distributed lags of 1 to 4 quarters are used on import prices and of 1 to 6 quarters on exchange rates. In separate equations, each of the three trade variables was significant with coefficients ranging from 0.108 to 0.141 and with t-ratios ranging from 3.1 to 3.3. The performance of the exchange-rate variables was almost identical to that of import-price changes.

Vroman and Abowd (1988, Table 2) fitted quarterly wage-growth equations for the private nonfarm economy for the period from 1964:Q2 to 1987:Q4. In addition to significant effects of unemployment and lagged price inflation, they found that a four-quarter distributed lag on import-price changes entered significantly with a coefficient of 0.10. Since a direct extension of that work is to be reported in the next section, the earlier paper will not be discussed further here.

The final paper to note is a comparative analysis of money-wage growth in Organisation for Economic Co-operation and Development (OECD) countries completed recently by Prywes (1989). He examined the growth in wages and salaries per worker in the private sectors of 13 countries and the growth in manufacturing average hourly earnings in four countries. The United States was included in both samples. His principal interest was in the sensitivity of output prices to shocks from the foreign sector and in how greater price sensitivity cushions the effects of external shocks. In semiannual private-wage-growth equations for the United States fitted from 1964 second half to 1986 second half, Prywes did not find important output price effects (Prywes [1989], Appendix Table 1), nor important terms of trade effects (Appendix Table 2). The modified Phillips curves in manufacturing estimated from 1967 first half to 1986 second half tested for effects of both export-price changes and import-price changes. For the United States, he reported (Appendix Table 3) a significant coefficient of 0.22 and a t-ratio of 5.5 for the effect of current import-price changes. This import-price coefficient is about twice the size of most other estimates, except for those reported by Nordhaus (1972). Since both Prywes and Nordhaus used current import-price changes in their equations, there is a likely problem of simultaneity.

In all the papers discussed above, the international trade variables tested have been limited to import-price changes, to (real and/or nominal) exchange-rate changes, and to Prywes' use of export-price changes. No U.S. time-series study reviewed here used real-trade-share variables such as those shown in Table 2, but studies using detailed industry data (Freeman and Katz [1987]) and microdata (Vroman and Abowd [1988]) have examined the effects of trade shares on money-wage adjustments. The previous studies have used a variety of lag patterns on the trade variables, from current measures to lags of up to two years. The question of lags and the comparative length of lags for different trade variables merits some additional discussion.

In considering how international trade variables affect money-wage adjustments, it would seem that exchange-rate changes should have the longest lags. A change in an exchange rate, caused by, for example, a monetary disturbance, would take some time to affect import prices. Recent work by Hooper and Mann (1989) shows vividly that exchange-rate changes are not followed by immediate and full pass-through to import prices. Margins can fluctuate sharply in the short run. Their empirical work on U.S. manufacturing import-price changes experimented with lags of up to 12 quarters and found that the best fits were obtained in equations with lags of from 5 to 7 quarters. (See their reported equations [10], [11], and [12].) They reported a short-run exchange rate pass-through of only about 20 percent and a long-run pass-through of only about 60 percent.

After import (and export) prices are affected by a change in the exchange rate, there is undoubtedly a lag before real trade-flow variables fully respond to the price changes. This suggests that the effects of real trade-flow variables on wage adjustments are shorter than the effects of import (and export) price changes. Given the sluggish behavior of money wages, however, even real-trade variables would be expected to operate with a lag. In the later empirical specifications, we employ lags on all trade variables, and the longest lags are used on exchange-rate changes.

A second specification issue of importance is the possible asymmetry of the money-wage response to equal-sized changes in imports and exports. Earlier findings reported by Freeman and Katz (1987), using detailed industry data, and by Vroman and Abowd (1988), using microdata for bargaining units, strongly suggest that imports affect money wages much more than exports. If this holds generally, then attention to import variables (both prices and quantities) is much more important than attention to the corresponding export variables. Empirical results to be reported later in the paper suggest strongly that import variables are indeed more important than export variables.

IV. Earlier Work with Microdata

Vroman and Vroman (1987) used a longitudinal data file covering 2,767 major collective-bargaining settlements in manufacturing to analyze the effect of import competition on union wages in manufacturing over the period 1957 to 1984. The specification used included a dummy variable for the 1980s, a dummy variable for import-sensitive industries, and an interaction of the two dummies. It also included 1) the inverse of the unemployment rate for prime-age males; 2) expected inflation at the time the contract was signed (based on the Livingston Index); 3) the inflation surprise over the contract (the difference between actual inflation measured by the CPI and the expected inflation) interacted with dummies for contracts with uncapped escalators and for those with capped escalators; 4) the annual percentage wage increase in the last auto or steel contract (whichever was later); and 5) after-tax industry profits (the four-quarter average, lagged one quarter).

Both the dummies for the 1980s and for import-sensitive industries were found to have negative and significant coefficients. If the worsening U.S. trade position had particularly affected import-sensitive industries, one would expect the interaction dummy to have a negative sign. It was found to be positive, but insignificant. Thus, while import-sensitive industries had lower union-wages growth over the entire period, on the basis of this study it does not appear that the slowdown in the growth of union wages in the 1980s was due primarily to import competition.

Vroman and Abowd (1988) augmented the longitudinal contract data set by adding industry-specific trade variables. This reduced the sample size to 2,718 and the sample period to 1959 to 1984, but allowed for a richer set of hypotheses to be tested. Their basic specification included explanatory variables representing four factors that in-fluence wage inflation. The first two factors are: 1) aggregate labor-market condi-tions—the prime-age male unemployment rate, the change in this unemployment rate, and the most recent wage settlement in the auto or steel industry (whichever was later); and 2) aggregate price inflation expectations and realizations—expected inflation (measured by predicted annual inflation of the CPI and by the Livingston Index), inflation surprise over the life of the current contract interacted with dummies for capped and uncapped escalator clauses, and lagged inflation surprises or "catch-up" effects interacted with dummies for unescalated contracts, capped escalators, and uncapped escalators. The remaining factors are: 3) product-market controls—the change in industry prices, the weighted change in domestic consumption, the weighted change in industry exports, the weighted change in the import penetration ratio, all measured over the previous contract; and 4) labor-cost controls—the change in the nominal wage, and the change in employment, both measured over the previous contract.

They found that the import-penetration ratio had the expected negative sign and was highly significant. Its coefficient was six times the size of the coefficient on apparent domestic consumption, indicating that the effect of import penetration far exceeds the simple effect of lost output. They also found that wage settlements in the 1980 to 1984 period were predicted well by the same determinants that explained wages over the previous 20 years. Thus, the recent slowdown in wage settlements does not appear to reflect a deviation from historic patterns. Lowered expectations of price inflation and smaller key agreements in autos and steel made the largest contributions to the reductions in wage settlements. To determine if the effects of import penetration were heterogeneous by industry, the estimated equations were simulated for various two-digit industries. While wages in all industries were slowed by imports, the effects were found to be largest in the leather, primary metals, apparel, tobacco, and lumber industries.

Because very few studies using microdata have been completed to date, it would probably be premature to try to identify their most significant findings. From the two studies reviewed above, it seems that increased import penetration reduces union-wage adjustments and by an amount that exceeds the direct loss in domestic sales of import-competing industries.

V. Time-Series Regression Results

The time-series analysis examines quarterly changes in fixed-weight indices of average hourly earnings. There were two estimation periods (1964:Q2 to 1979:Q4 and 1964:Q2 to 1988:Q4) and two dependent variables (hourly earnings indices for the entire private nonfarm economy and for manufacturing). The HEI data were chosen in preference to ECI data because of their earlier starting date. Quarterly changes are available from 1964:Q2, as opposed to 1975:Q4, for the ECI. The estimation periods were selected to test for the sensitivity of results to inclusion and exclusion of the 1980s, the period of rapid money-wage deceleration. Since manufacturing is much more closely linked to the international economy than most other industrial divisions, it seemed advisable to focus separately on manufacturing-wage adjustments. Detailed input-output data by industry show manufacturing import shares and export shares to be about three times the size of the corresponding all-industry averages.[5]

Our approach uses specifications that add international trade variables to modified Phillips curves. The equations employ the level of the unemployment rate after tests showed that the level performs better than a nonlinear formulation using the inverse of unemployment. Expected price changes are proxied with a 12-quarter distributed lag on the All-Items CPI, lagged one quarter to avoid the problem of simultaneity. The CPI was selected in preference to the consumer expenditures deflator because it enters cost of living adjustment (COLA) payment formulas of unionized wage adjustments. Equations fitted using the consumer expenditures deflator yielded results similar to those to be reported.

Labor-market-demand conditions were represented by the unemployment rate for men aged 25 to 54. This measure performed much better than the overall unemployment rate, particularly in equations that included the 1980s. Because prime-age male unemployment rates have remained relatively high throughout the 1980s, this unemployment series indicates that the labor market is further from full employment than does the series for all persons aged 16 and older. Recall from Table 1 that men aged 25 to 54 had an unemployment rate of 4.4 percent in 1988, the same average rate as during 1975 to 1979. Overall unemployment during 1975 to 1979, however, was 1.5 percentage points higher than in 1988 (7.0 percent versus 5.5 percent). Later in the paper, we discuss some possible reasons for the change in the demographics of unemployment in the 1980s.

Table 3 displays the basic time-series regressions and then the results when international trade variables are added. The basic equations explain 70 to 80 percent of wage variation, with both unemployment and price inflation making highly significant contributions. Except for the larger price inflation coefficients in manufacturing, essentially unity versus 0.81 in the private nonfarm equations, the estimated slope coefficients are similar across the four regressions.

The superior performance of the prime-age male unemployment rate vis-a-vis the overall rate can be illustrated by comparing the values of R^2 of equations that differ only in the specification of the unemployment rate. For the four basic equations, the R^2 values were uniformly lower (by 0.030, 0.058, 0.016, and 0.065, respectively) in regressions that used the overall unemployment rate. Fitted values from regressions using the overall unemployment rate were larger, particularly in the 1980s. The regressions in Table 3 explain the wage slowdown since 1981 as the result of lower inflationary expectations and high unemployment among prime-age men.

To illustrate the contribution of high prime-age male unemployment to the low growth in money wages, data from 1988 are pertinent. The first equation from Table 3 projected average money-wage growth of 4.051 percent for the year. Recall from Table 1 that the prime-age male unemployment rate in 1988 was 4.4 percent, 0.80 times the overall rate of 5.5 percent. If their relative unemployment rate of 1975 to 1979 had prevailed in 1988 (0.63 times the overall rate), adult men would have had an unemployment rate of 3.5 percent for the year. Replacing a 4.4 percent unemployment rate with a 3.5 percent rate would have caused the equation to project 0.705 percentage points of additional money-wage inflation in 1988, 17.4 percent more than actually projected by the equation.

Each of the basic regressions in the top half of Table 3 was then reestimated adding international trade variables. The results of six different specifications, each with a different trade variable, appear in the bottom half of the table. Coefficients and t-ratios are displayed for the sum of the distributed lag effects of trade variables. The trade variables were all lagged one quarter to reduce simultaneity.

Changes in nonpetroleum import prices enter all equations significantly with

Table 3: Aggregate Time-Series Equations, Changes in Hourly Earnings

	Private nonfarm		Manufacturing	
	1964:Q2- 1979:Q4	1964:Q2- 1988:Q4	1964:Q2- 1979:Q4	1964:Q2- 1988:Q4
Basic regressions: Constant	4.95 (11.2)	5.25 (15.1)	4.45 (7.5)	4.79 (11.3)
Unemployment rate	−0.81 (4.2)	−0.87 (10.5)	−0.68 (2.7)	−0.87 (8.5)
Price inflation, 12Q lag	0.81 (9.1)	0.81 (17.9)	0.99 (8.4)	0.98 (17.9)
Adjusted R^2	0.682	0.809	0.723	0.820
Standard error	0.97	1.00	1.29	1.22
Durbin Watson	1.77	1.71	1.83	1.53

International Trade Variables, Added Individually to the Regressions:

Nonpetroleum import price change, 4Q lag expected sign, pos.	0.109 (2.3)	0.068 (2.4)	0.131 (2.1)	0.066 (1.9)
Change in nominal exchange rate, 8Q lag expected sign, neg.	0.014 (0.3)	0.008 (0.5)	0.012 (1.2)	0.029 (1.4)
Change in real exchange rate, 8Q lag expected sign, neg.	−0.069 (1.5)	−0.003 (0.1)	−0.103 (1.6)	−0.018 (0.6)
Real net export share, 4Q lag expected sign, pos.	−0.329 (1.5)	0.017 (0.2)	−0.416 (1.3)	−0.043 (0.3)
Real import share, 4Q lag expected sign, neg.	0.318 (2.0)	−0.032 (0.5)	0.440 (2.1)	−0.082 (1.1)
Real nonpetroleum import share, 4Q lag expected sign, neg.	0.376 (1.3)	−0.091 (1.3)	0.446 (1.2)	−0.171 (2.0)

SOURCE: All regressions based on the hourly earnings index, not seasonally adjusted. Additive seasonal dummies included in each regression. Unemployment refers to men, aged 25 to 54. Price changes measured with the All-Items Consumer Price Index. All trade- and price-change variables enter as polynomial distributive lags (PDLs). Beneath each coefficient is the absolute value of its t-ratio.

coefficients ranging from 0.131 to 0.066 and t-ratios ranging from 2.4 to 1.9. Note in equations estimated through 1988 that the coefficient in the manufacturing sector is not larger than for the private nonfarm economy as a whole, even though trade is much more important to manufacturing. Note also that the coefficients are smaller when data from the 1980s are included. Tests with longer lags did not find larger import price effects. Using the overall import price deflator with the same lag pattern as the nonpetroleum price index yielded a more significant coefficient, but this was due mainly to the petroleum price run-up of 1973 to 1974. The most direct interpretation for an effect of import prices is that wages (and probably prices as well) in import-competing industries can rise more rapidly when import prices rise because the product market is under less restraint from import competition.

Neither of the two exchange-rate variables make significant contributions, although the coefficients for the real exchange rate have the expected negative signs and t-ratios of 1.5 to 1.6 in equations fitted through 1979. The table shows results when eight-quarter lags are used, but the same results were obtained in equations with lags of four and six quarters. No evidence of significant exchange-rate effects was found.

The bottom three equations show results when real-trade-share variables (percentages of real GDP) were tested. The real-net-export shares and real-import shares have incorrect signs (negative and positive, respectively) in equations estimated through 1979, and two import-share coefficients have t-ratios of at least 2.0. When the 1980s are included, the import-share coefficients are negative and generally small. But, in manufacturing, the nonpetroleum import share has a coefficient of –0.171 and a t-ratio of 2.0. Very similar results for the trade variable were obtained when changes in trade penetration (lagged one quarter) were entered. Also, attempts to find separate effects of export shares and import shares did not yield significant findings. One implication of specifications in which the level of import penetration affects wage adjustments is that increased openness in future years would exert an even larger restraining effect on money wages than at present.

The main result of the time-series estimation is the generally weak performance of the international trade variables. Of the various trade variables tested, the nonpetroleum import price change performed the best, but even its coefficients were uniformly small.

As a factor in the decline of money-wage adjustments in the mid- to late 1980s, import price changes make only a modest net contribution. Recall from Table 2 that nonpetroleum import price changes were negative from 1981 to 1984, the period of the dollar's appreciation, but then positive from 1986 to 1988. We performed a simulation using the private nonfarm-wage equation fitted through 1979, but replacing actual nonpetroleum import price changes with a time series that equaled CPI price changes in each quarter. The effects on annual money-wage increases of the import price change deviations were reductions of –0.13, –0.59, –0.88, –0.61, –0.48, –0.68 percent, respectively, for the years 1980 to 1985. From 1986 to 1988, the import-price deviations added 0.21, 0.37, and 0.42 percent, respectively, to money-wage growth. The largest estimated annual effect due to the deviation of import-price changes from overall price changes in these nine years occurred in 1982, a reduction of 0.88 percentage points, which was 15 percent of actual wage changes for the year. Import price effects have the same time-series pattern, but are only about half as large in the equations estimated through 1988.

The other large contribution of an international trade variable to wage-growth moderation from the Table 3 regressions was found in the manufacturing equation fitted through 1988, using the real nonpetroleum import share. Multiplying its coefficient of −0.171 times the 1980 to 1988 growth in the real import share, 5.0 percentage points (from 8.0 percent to 13.0 percent), yielded an estimate of 0.86 percentage points of wage-growth moderation in 1988 due to increased nonpetroleum imports. Since actual money-wage growth in manufacturing for the year averaged only 2.456 percent, this estimated effect represents 35 percent of actual money-wage growth for the year. All other estimated effects of international trade from the Table 3 regressions are much smaller.

Recall from Table 1 that the total slowdown in money-wage inflation between 1980 to 1981 and 1984 to 1988 was about 5 percentage points. All of the time-series regression results suggest that developments in international trade in the 1980s have accounted for less than one-fifth of the slowdown. Since many economists would not be persuaded by results based only on time-series regressions such as the equations of Table 3, we next turn to an alternative data source to estimate the effects of international trade on money-wage adjustments.

VI. Microdata Analysis

In this section, we report the results of the estimation of wage equations using longitudinal bargaining unit data. The data set is the same as that used in Vroman and Abowd and covers 2,718 major collective bargaining settlements in manufacturing over the period 1959 to 1984. The basic specification is similar to that in Vroman and Abowd. Thus the model includes four sets of variables: aggregate labor-market variables, price-inflation expectations and realizations, product-market controls, and labor-cost controls. In addition, incomes-policy dummies are added to test for an effect of these policies on wage settlements. A dummy variable for the Reagan Administration is also included to test whether the "antiunion" climate of the Reagan Administration had a negative effect on union wage settlements. Results are presented for the entire sample, and for two subsamples—industries with an average import share about 8 percent and those with an average import share below 8 percent—to see if the effect of changes in import penetration was greater in those industries that have a greater exposure to imports. We also split the sample period into two subperiods, before 1973 and after 1973, to see if the change to flexible exchange rates affects the results.

We find that import penetration has a negative effect on wage settlements for the entire sample. As in Vroman and Abowd, we find that the effect of import penetration exceeds the effect that would be predicted solely on the basis of the lost output. We also find that the effect of import penetration is much larger in those industries that have a higher average import share over the sample period. The results when the sample period is split at 1973 indicate that the effect of import penetration is the same in both subperiods, although the effects of other variables differ. We proceed by first describing the variables that are used and then reporting the results.

The dependent variable is the annualized rate of wage change over the life of the contract. The variables representing aggregate labor-market conditions are 1) the unemployment rate for prime-age (25-54) males and 2) the most recent settlement in the auto or steel industry (whichever is later).

The inflation expectation variables are based on data from the Livingston survey of economists. The expected rate of inflation is the annual inflation rate from the Livingston Index just prior to the contract settlement. Also included is the inflation surprise over the life of the current contract. This is measured as the annualized excess of the actual inflation (measured by the CPI) over the expected rate of inflation. Inflation surprises should only have an effect on wage changes in contracts that have escalator clauses and the effect should be greater in contracts that have uncapped escalator clauses. Therefore this variable is interacted with escalator dummies—one for uncapped escalators and one for capped escalators. The final set of inflation variables are the lagged inflation surprise, that is, the inflation surprise over the previous contract. Inflation surprises over the previous contract may give rise to demands for "catch-up" wage gains. These should be lower if the previous contract included an escalator clause, so the lagged inflation surprise variable is interacted with dummies for 1) unescalated contracts, 2) contracts with uncapped escalators, and 3) contracts with capped escalators.

The product-market variables include the annual rate of change of industry prices as measured by the value of the product shipments deflator from the Annual Survey of Manufactures and a set of measures reflecting the decomposition of the value of shipments. The decomposition of shipments is given by:

$$dlnS = \frac{(S-X)}{S} \, dlnD + \frac{X}{S} \, dlnX - \frac{D}{S} \, dIPR \, ,$$

where S is shipments, D is apparent domestic consumption, X is exports, and IPR is the import penetration ratio (imports divided by apparent domestic consumption).[6] We use the weighted change in apparent domestic consumption, the weighted change in exports, and the weighted change in the import-penetration ratio.

Finally, we include the nominal wage change from the previous contract and the annual rate of change in employment in the bargaining unit over the life of the previous contract. Table 9 shows the means and standard deviations of all the variables for the sample.

Table 4 gives the results for the basic specification over the entire sample period, as well as the results for the bargaining units with an average import share (imports/shipments) below 8 percent and for those above 8 percent. Table 5 presents results when incomes policy dummies are added.

These are:

> KJD = guidepost dummy (1 for April 1962 to June 1966; 0, otherwise);
> NIXD1 = Nixon Controls dummy, Phase II (1 for Dec. 1971 to Dec. 1972; 0, otherwise);
> NIXD2 = Nixon Controls dummy, Phases III and IV (1 for Nov. 1978 to Dec. 1979; 0, otherwise);
> CARD1 = Carter Controls dummy, Phase I (1 for Nov. 1978 to Dec. 1979; 0, otherwise) ;
> CARD2 = Carter Controls dummy, Phase II (1 for Jan. 1980 to Aug. 1980; 0, otherwise).

This specification also includes a dummy variable for the Reagan Administration. This variable is one for 1981 to 1984 and zero otherwise.

The unemployment rate has the expected negative sign in all three columns of Table 4, but is insignificant and has a smaller coefficient for the high-import industries. The effect of the most recent auto or steel wage settlement is highly significant in all three columns and has a greater impact on the high-import settlements.

Since a number of settlements in transportation equipment (SIC 371) and primary metals (SIC 331) are included in the high-import sample, we were concerned that the key settlements coefficient could be affected by simultaneity. We were also concerned that the effect of import penetration might be underestimated since the steel and auto industries have come under increased import competition in the 1980s. To test for the stability of the import coefficient, the key settlements variable was removed from equation (3) of Table 4. The main effects of the change were to lower the R^2 modestly (to 0.57) and to raise the coefficient on expected inflation from 0.44 to 0.82 (with a t-ratio of 11.5). The import penetration coefficient remained –0.11 with a t-ratio of 2.5. From this, we infer that the effects of import penetration are not underestimated when key settlements are included in the specification.

The effect of expected inflation is positive and highly significant in all columns, and this variable appears to have a similar effect regardless of the level of the import share. The same is true of the inflation surprise in the current contract for contracts with uncapped escalator clauses. The current-contract inflation surprise has an insignificant coefficient for contracts with capped escalators in the high-import sector, which reflects the scarcity of such escalators in this sector.[7] The lagged inflation surprise has a positive coefficient for all contracts. For contracts with uncapped escalators, the coefficient is significant and virtually identical in all columns. For unescalated contracts, the coefficient is smaller and less significant for high-import industries, as is the coefficient for contracts with capped escalators. This again probably reflects the difference in escalator coverage between the two sectors.

Lagged wage change and the change in employment both have positive and significant coefficients for the entire sample and for the low-import sector. Neither is significant in the high-import sector. Of the product-market variables, only the

Table 4:   Determinants of Wage Settlements in U.S. Manufacturing, 1959 to 1984

Variable	All bargaining units (1)	Below 8% (2)	Above 8% (3)
Constant	2.24 (16.3)	2.23 (14.7)	2.27 (7.5)
U rate	−0.155 (4.9)	−0.18 (5.0)	−0.11 (1.6)
Key settlements	0.18 (11.6)	0.14 (8.3)	0.26 (8.0)
Expected inflation	0.44 (15.6)	0.44 (13.9)	0.44 (6.9)
Inflation surprise:			
uncapped contracts	0.62 (19.1)	0.63 (17.9)	0.64 (7.9)
capped contracts	0.23 (4.6)	0.26 (4.9)	0.11 (0.8)
Lagged inflation surprise:			
unescalated contracts	0.24 (7.9)	0.28 (8.3)	0.13 (1.9)
Uncapped contracts	0.22 (6.0)	0.23 (5.7)	0.22 (2.3)
Capped contracts	0.38 (6.9)	0.44 (7.4)	0.22 (1.5)
% Δ industry prices	0.01 (1.2)	0.01 (1.8)	0.00 (0.3)
wtd. % Δ App Dom Cons.	0.02 (3.1)	0.02 (3.1)	0.01 (1.1)
wtd. % Δ exports	−0.02 (1.0)	−0.01 (0.4)	−0.03 (0.8)
wtd. Δ import pen	−0.10 (3.1)	−0.05 (0.6)	−0.11 (2.8)
Lagged wage change	0.16 (8.6)	0.20 (9.4)	0.07 (1.7)
Δ log (employment)	0.72 (2.8)	0.74 (2.5)	0.53 (1.0)
Adj. R^2	0.64	0.67	0.59
Number of contracts	2,718	2,023	695

SOURCE: Listings in *Current Wage Developments,* U.S. Department of Labor. T-statistics are in parentheses.

weighted change in apparent domestic consumption and the weighted change in import penetration are significant for the entire sample. These have the expected sign. As in Vroman and Abowd, the coefficient on import penetration is close to six times as large in absolute value as the coefficient on domestic consumption, indicating that the effect of import penetration substantially exceeds the effect one would predict solely on the basis of the lost output. The effect of domestic consumption is positive for both low-import and high-import settlements, although it is not significant for the high-import sector.

The most interesting result is the difference in the effect of the weighted change in the import penetration rate for the two sectors. In the low-import sector, the coefficient is negative but insignificant. In the high-import sector, the coefficient is larger and significant. The import penetration coefficient in the high-import sector is eight times the size of the coefficient on domestic consumption. Thus, as might be expected, the effect of import penetration is concentrated among the bargaining units that have had a higher import share over the sample period.

Table 5 presents the results when the incomes-policy dummies and the Reagan Administration dummy have been added. The incomes-policy dummies are significant and have the expected negative coefficients for the entire sample and for the low-import sector. In the high-import sector, they have negative coefficients, but are insignificant. The dummy for the Reagan Administration is insignificant in all three columns, but it does have the expected negative sign.

Table 6 displays results when the sample period is split at 1973 to reflect the change to flexible exchange rates. On the basis of three estimates, it appears that the effect of import penetration on wage settlements was similar in both periods. Both coefficients are negative and significant and they are roughly equal in magnitude.

While there is little difference between the periods in terms of the effect of import penetration, a number of other variables have quite different effects in the two periods. Most notable is the prime-age male unemployment rate. It has the expected negative sign in the early period, but has a positive and significant coefficient in the later period. This probably reflects the unusual stagflation period in the mid-1970s when both inflation and unemployment were above historic levels. This period may also account for the difference in the coefficients on expected inflation. The lower coefficient in the second period may be the result of the very high levels of expected inflation after 1973 and the fact that wage settlements failed to adjust completely to such high levels.

The results for the inflation-surprise variables are also interesting. The coefficients on the inflation surprise in the current agreement for contracts with uncapped escalators are quite similar in both periods—indicating that escalator yields were similar. The catch-up effects are larger and more significant in the earlier period. This may also reflect the fact that the inflation surprises were very large in the later period and that consequently unions were unable to gain as much of a catch-up.

In sum, the results using microdata indicate that import penetration reduces wage gains for unions in manufacturing industries and that this effect is particularly strong in industries with a high average import share. However, the findings do not indicate that import penetration is a major factor in explaining the recent slowdown in union wage growth. The effect of import penetration appears to have been equally strong prior to 1973.

To estimate the effects of increased import penetration and the other major variables in the 1980s, we used equation (1) of Table 4, along with changes in the variables, to simulate their individual contributions to the wage slowdown. Expected price inflation and key agreements, each important indicators of the inflationary environment surrounding union wage setting, contributed about 3.2 percentage points to the slowdown of 5.9 percentage points that occurred between 1980 and 1984. In contrast, increased import penetration accounted for at most 0.7 percentage points, even for settlements reached in 1985 and 1986, when lagged changes in import

Table 5:   Determinants of Wage Settlements in U.S. Manufacturing, 1959 to 1984

Variable	All bargaining units (1)	Below 8% (2)	Above 8% (3)
Constant	2.53 (15.0)	2.55 (13.7)	2.51 (6.5)
U rate	−0.20 (5.3)	−0.22 (5.3)	−0.15 (1.8)
Key settlements	0.17 (7.4)	0.14 (5.4)	0.25 (4.9)
Expected inflation	0.51 (12.0)	0.50 (10.8)	0.50 (5.1)
Inflation surprise:			
uncapped contracts	0.60 (18.4)	0.61 (17.1)	0.63 (7.6)
capped contracts	0.21 (4.1)	0.23 (4.4)	0.09 (0.6)
Lagged inflation surprise:			
unescalated contracts	0.19 (5.9)	0.22 (6.3)	0.10 (1.3)
Uncapped contracts	0.19 (4.8)	0.18 (4.3)	0.20 (2.0)
Capped contracts	0.34 (6.1)	0.39 (6.4)	0.19 (1.3)
% Δ industry prices	0.00 (0.6)	0.01 (1.1)	0.00 (0.2)
wtd. % Δ App Dom Cons.	0.02 (3.5)	0.02 (3.4)	0.02 (1.1)
wtd. % Δ exports	−0.02 (1.1)	−0.01 (0.4)	−0.03 (0.8)
wtd. Δ import pen	−0.10 (3.1)	−0.03 (0.3)	−0.11 (2.7)
Lagged wage change	0.16 (8.3)	0.20 (9.3)	0.06 (1.4)
Δ log (employment)	0.73 (2.8)	0.72 (2.5)	0.59 (1.0)
Dummies:			
Kennedy-Johnson	−0.45 (3.6)	−0.51 (3.7)	−0.30 (1.0)
Nixon I	−0.51 (2.0)	−0.61 (2.1)	−0.21 (0.4)
Nixon II	−0.83 (4.2)	−0.92 (4.3)	−0.44 (0.9)
Carter I	−0.89 (3.6)	−0.84 (3.0)	−1.04 (1.9)
Carter II	−0.80 (2.7)	−0.88 (2.7)	−0.27 (0.4)
Reagan	−0.35 (1.3)	−0.43 (1.5)	−0.19 (0.3)
Adj. R^2	0.65	0.67	0.59
Number of contracts	2,718	2,023	695

SOURCE: Listings in *Current Wage Developments,* U.S. Department of Labor.

Table 6:   Determinants of Wage Settlements in U.S. Manufacturing, 1959 to 1984

Variable	Before 1973 (1)		After 1973 (2)	
Constant	1.33	(5.4)	−0.16	(0.2)
U rate	−0.10	(1.9)	0.25	(3.5)
Key settlements	0.08	(3.5)	0.33	(8.1)
Expected inflation	0.82	(9.6)	0.39	(6.8)
Inflation surprise:				
uncapped contracts	0.66	(11.5)	0.58	(12.9)
capped contracts	0.13	(1.8)	0.23	(3.2)
Lagged inflation surprise:				
unescalated contracts	0.54	(7.5)	0.12	(2.6)
Uncapped contracts	0.36	(3.4)	0.20	(3.7)
Capped contracts	0.51	(4.6)	0.27	(3.3)
% Δ industry prices	0.00	(0.6)	−0.02	(1.6)
wtd. % Δ App Dom Cons.	−0.00	(0.0)	0.07	(6.0)
wtd. % Δ exports	−0.03	(1.1)	0.02	(0.7)
wtd. Δ import pen	−0.14	(3.5)	−0.12	(2.5)
Lagged wage change	0.24	(9.9)	0.08	(2.8)
Δ log (employment)	0.24	(0.9)	1.29	(2.7)
Adj. R^2	0.62		0.46	
Number of contracts	1,594		1,124	

SOURCE: Listings in *Current Wage Developments,* U.S. Department of Labor.

penetration would have been largest. For agreements reached in other years, the effects of international trade would be smaller.[8]

Given the consistency of results in the time series and in the microdata, we are left with the original question: Why has money-wage growth been so low during this period of sustained economic expansion? We believe a large part of the answer lies in the labor-market experiences of adult men in the present decade.

Figure 1: Overall Unemployment Rates and Relative Unemployment Rates for Men Aged 25-54, 1954 to 1988

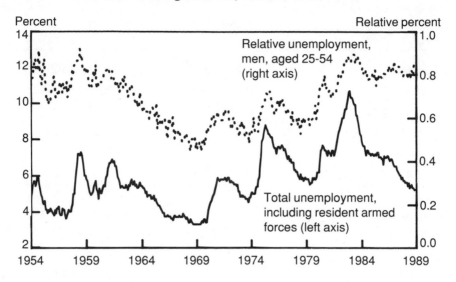

SOURCE: Based on unemployment data published by the U.S. Department of Labor.

VII. Unemployment Demographics of the 1980s

The U.S. labor market of the 1980s can be described as providing differential employment and earnings opportunities for subgroups of labor-force participants. Among the major developments have been the measurable gains in earnings realized by women relative to men, increased rates of return to college education, coupled with decreased returns to high school and lower levels of educational attainment, and the low earnings gains for unionized workers.[9] Employment growth since 1982 has been unusual in the degree to which it has been concentrated in the service industries. The economic expansion since 1982 has also been unusual in the persistence of relatively high unemployment rates among prime-age male workers. Since prime-age men earn so much more than other labor-force groups, reviewing their experiences in the 1980s may help in understanding why money-wage growth has been so moderate.

Some salient facts about overall unemployment and the relative unemployment of men aged 25 to 54 over the past 35 years are illustrated in Figure 1. Note that in recession years like 1958, 1975, and 1982, the spikes in the overall unemployment rate are mirrored by spikes in the relative unemployment rate for prime-age men. In periods of economic expansion, the relative unemployment rate for these men declines.

A major contrast is apparent in Figure 1 between the sustained periods of expansion of the 1960s and the 1980s. Between 1961 and 1969, when the overall rate declined by nearly half, from 6.7 percent to 3.5 percent, the relative rate for prime-age men declined from 0.753 to 0.465. Although the overall unemployment rate also declined sharply between 1982 and 1988 (from 9.7 percent to 5.5 percent), the relative rate for prime-age men was comparatively stable, declining from 0.827 to 0.791. In the expansion of the 1980s, unemployment rates for adult men have declined at about the same pace as the average of other unemployment rates.

The industrial pattern of employment growth in the 1980s has been unusual in the small share of employment gains that have been realized by manufacturing industries. Table 7 summarizes data on private nonfarm employment growth by industry in the 1960s and 1980s, with attention to major demographic groups. Industry employment data from the 1980 Decennial Census are displayed for all persons, women, men, and men aged 25 to 54. The Census detail for men aged 25 to 54 is then used to provide estimates for this group in the 1982 establishment survey data shown in the right side of Table 7, Panel 1. Percentage employment distributions are then shown in the second panel of the table. About half of men (all men and men aged 25 to 54) work in the first five industrial divisions (mining, construction, durables, nondurables, and transportation), but only about one-fourth of women work in these divisions.

Table 7, Panel 3, shows industry employment growth rates for six-year intervals in the 1960s and 1980s. For the periods covered by these data, overall employment growth was somewhat higher in the 1960s, 22.7 versus 19.6 percent. The only industry to grow much more rapidly in the 1980s was construction. Note also that retail trade, finance, and services each had about the same growth rate in the two periods. Dramatic employment growth slowdowns in the 1980s occurred in mining and in durables and nondurables, with noticeable slowdowns also apparent in transportation and wholesale trade. Slower rates of employment growth in the 1980s have been heavily concentrated in industries that employ above-average percentages of male workers. The concentration of employment growth in service industries is due to the lack of employment growth elsewhere, not to an unprecedented employment growth in trade, finance, and services per se.

To the extent that workers may not be fully mobile between industries in the short run, the lower employment growth rates in industries like manufacturing and mining during the 1980s could have adverse consequences for overall male employment. To help assess the contrast between the 1960s and the 1980s, demographically weighted employment-growth indices were constructed. For each demographic group, its 1982 employment distribution was used to weight the industry employment growth rates in the two periods. The resulting growth indices in the bottom-right section of Table 7, Panel 3, show that the industry distribution of employment growth favored women in both decades, but that the differential for women was larger in the 1980s. The female index for the 1960s was 2.2 percentage points higher than the all-worker index (26.6 percent versus 24.4 percent but 3.6 percentage points higher in the 1980s.

The more favorable industrial distribution of female job growth in the 1980s is further illustrated in the bottom row of Table 7, Panel 3, which shows ratios of demographically weighted employment growth indices from the 1980s to their

Table 7: Private Nonfarm Employment Changes in the 1960s and 1980s (Panel 1)

Industry Division	Employment by industry 1980 Decennial Census				Employment by industry 1982 Establishment Survey			
	Total	Men	M2554	Women	Total	Men	M2554[a]	Women
Mining	1,031	904	621	127	1,128	994	683	134
CON[b]	5,730	5,260	3,466	480	3,905	3,527	2,324	378
DMFG[c]	13,218	9,814	6,671	3,404	11,039	8,212	5,582	2,827
NDMFG[d]	8,435	4,942	3,287	3,493	7,741	4,578	3,045	3,163
TPU[e]	7,087	5,334	3,869	1,753	5,082	3,743	2,715	1,339
WTRADE[f]	4,217	3,083	2,028	1,134	5,278	3,863	2,541	1,415
RTRADE[g]	15,716	7,712	3,822	8,004	15,179	7,515	3,724	7,664
FIRE[h]	5,898	2,476	1,685	3,422	5,341	2,142	1,458	3,199
Services	27,976	10,879	7,056	17,097	19,036	7,697	4,992	11,339
Total					73,729	42,272	27,064	31,457

a. Constructed estimate based on 1980 Decennial Census data.
b. Construction.
c. Durable manufacturing.

Table 7: Private Nonfarm Employment Changes in the 1960s and 1980s (Panel 2)

Industry Division	1982 demographic employment distribution by industry				Employment by industry			
	Total	Men	M2554	Women	1963	1969	1982	1988
Mining	1.53	2.35	2.52	0.43	635	619	1,128	721
CON	5.30	8.34	8.59	1.20	3,010	3,575	3,905	5,125
DMFG	14.97	19.43	20.63	8.99	9,616	11,895	11,039	11,437
NDMFG	10.50	10.83	11.25	10.05	7,380	8,272	7,741	7,967
TPU	6.89	8.85	10.03	4.26	3,903	4,442	5,082	5,548
WTRADE	7.16	9.14	9.39	4.50	3,248	3,907	5,278	6,029
RTRADE	20.50	17.78	13.76	24.36	8,530	10,798	15,179	19,110
FIRE	7.24	5.07	5.39	10.17	2,830	3,512	5,341	6,676
Services	25.82	18.21	18.45	36.05	8,277	11,169	19,036	25,600
Total	100.00	100.00	100.00	100.00	47,429	58,189	73,729	88,213

d. Nondurable manufacturing.
e. Transportation, public utilities.
f. Wholesale trade.

(continued on next page)

Table 7: Private Nonfarm Employment Changes in the 1960s and 1980s (Panel 3)

	Industry employment growth (percent)		Demographic weighting of industry employment growth			
	1963 to 1969	1982 to 1988	Total	Men	M2554	Women
Mining	-2.5	-36.1		1963 to 1969	1963 to 1969 [i]	
Con[b]	18.8	31.2	24.4	22.8	22.5	26.6
DMFG[c]	23.7	3.6				
NDMFG[d]	12.1	2.9		1982 to 1988	1982 to 1988 [i]	
TPU[e]	13.8	9.2				
WTRADE[f]	20.3	14.21	19.6	17.0	16.4	23.2
RTRADE[g]	26.6	25.9				
FIRE[h]	24.1	25.0	1982 to 1988	1982 to 1988	1963 to 1969	
Services	34.9	34.5				
Total	22.7	19.6	0.805	0.747	0.728	0.871

g. Retail trade
h. Finance, Insurance, and Real Estate.
i. Industry employment growth times 1982 industry employment percentages for each demographic group.
SOURCES: Decennial Census of 1980 and U.S. Department of Labor Establishment Survey. Employment measured in thousands.

Table 8:   Displaced Workers in the Labor Force and Unemployment, 1984, 1986, and 1988

	Civilian labor force			Unemployment		
	Total	Exp. displaced workers	Displaced worker %	Total	Exp. displaced workers	Displaced worker %
January 1984, unemployment rate—8.8%						
All persons 16 and older	111.0	5.1	4.6	9.8	1.3	13.1
Men 25 to 54	41.7	2.6	6.2	3.2	0.7	21.8
Male 25 to 54 share	0.375	0.505		0.323	0.531	
January 1986, unemployment rate—7.3%						
All persons 16 and older	115.4	5.1	4.4	8.5	0.9	10.8
Men 25 to 54	43.9	2.6	5.9	2.7	0.5	18.8
Male 25 to 54 share	0.380	0.508		0.321	0.560	
January 1988, unemployment rate—6.3%						
All persons 16 and older	119.7	4.9	4.1	7.6	0.7	8.7
Men 25 to 54	45.8	2.4	5.3	2.4	0.4	15.2
Male 25 to 54 share	0.382	0.490		0.321	0.561	

SOURCE: U.S. Department of Labor, Bureau of Labor Statistics (BLS). Total labor force and unemployment from Employment and Earnings. Displaced worker counts from BLS Special Reports on displaced workers. Worker counts in thousands.

counterparts from the 1960s. For women, the ratio was 0.871, higher than the overall ratio of 0.805 and considerably higher than the ratio of 0.747 for all men. For men aged 25 to 54, the ratio was lowest at 0.728. Thus, the industries employing prime-age men have had especially low rates of employment growth in the present decade. Lower employment growth in male industries may have slowed the declines in male unemployment in the 1980s.

A second and closely related labor-market development of the present decade has been the ongoing phenomenon of senior workers being displaced from employment. Three displaced worker surveys were conducted with the Current Population Survey in January of 1984, 1986, and 1988. Each yielded an estimate of about 5 million workers aged 20 and older with three or more years of seniority, who suffered permanent job losses over the five years preceding the survey—losses from actions such as plant closings, assembly line shutdowns, or elimination of individual jobs. Although we do not have comparable data from earlier periods, it seems probable that the flow of displacements has been unusually large in the present decade.

Demographic data from the three surveys show that men aged 25 to 54 constitute a major fraction of the displaced worker population. Table 8 helps to illustrate this with data for all workers and prime-age men. The table shows displaced workers

Table 9:   Means and Standard Deviations of the Variables Used in the Microanalysis

Variable	Mean (1)	Std. deviation (2)
% Nominal wage change (annual rate)	5.96	3.37
U rate (Men 25 to 54)	3.93	1.65
Key settlements (% nominal wage change) (Most recent steel or auto settlement)	6.15	4.33
Expected inflation (Livingston Index)	3.89	2.72
Inflation surprise:		
uncapped contracts	0.21	1.35
capped contracts	0.12	0.80
Lagged inflation surprise:		
unescalated contracts	0.92	1.75
Uncapped contracts	0.31	1.23
Capped contracts	0.14	0.75
% Δ industry prices (annual rate)	3.93	7.35
wtd. % Δ App Dom Cons.	6.10	7.75
wtd. % Δ exports	0.68	1.91
wtd. Δ import pen	0.33	1.23
Lagged wage change	5.83	3.37
Δ log (employment)	−0.02	0.15

SOURCE: Listings in *Current Wage Developments,* U.S. Department of Labor.

relative to the labor force and unemployed displaced workers relative to unemployment in January of the three years. In relation to the entire labor force, experienced displaced workers ranged from 4.6 percent to 4.1 percent of the total. The corresponding percentages for men aged 25 to 54 ranged from 6.2 percent to 5.3 percent. In each of the three surveys, prime-age men constituted slightly more than half of all experienced displaced workers.

The representation of displaced workers among the unemployed is even more substantial. They constituted 13.3 percent of the total in January 1984, 10.8 percent in January 1986, and 8.7 percent in January 1988. The corresponding percentages among men aged 25 to 54 were 21.8, 18.8 and 15.2, respectively. Thus, while prime-age men constituted less than one-third of the unemployed, they accounted for over half of the unemployed displaced workers. Although we have not tried to quantify the size of the effect, continuing displacements from employment have undoubtedly been a factor in the failure of the adult male unemployment rate to decline in the 1980s. Concerns for job security raised by displacements have probably tempered wage demands in general and, perhaps to a greater extent, have tempered the demands from this demographic group with high average earnings.

Issues of job security are unusually important to many union workers in the present decade. Unionization rates have declined continuously reaching 14.2 percent among private nonfarm wage and salary workers in 1988.[10] Absolute numbers as well as unionization rates are declining. Major agreements in the private sector covered only 6.0 million workers in 1988, down from 7.7 million in 1983.[11] Since the conference paper by Bell and Neumark (chapter 3) deals extensively with unions and union compensation, we will not pursue this topic further except to note two things. First, men aged 25 to 54 have above-average unionization rates, 25.3 percent in 1988 versus an overall average of 19.0 percent. Second, union wages have grown more slowly than the average since 1983. Wage-growth data from the ECI show annual averages from 1983 to 1988 of 3.0 percent and 4.3 percent for union and nonunion workers, respectively.

To conclude, several factors besides the increased openness of the economy have been contributing to the persistence of high relative unemployment among adult men during the current recovery. We have not attempted to assign separate weights to: (1) the reduced growth in employment opportunities within industries where adult men traditionally work, (2) increased numbers of job displacements, (3) continuing declines in unionization, and (4) increased international competition. The preceding list is not offered as being exhaustive, and the four elements are not statistically independent. From the earlier empirical work of this paper, however, we conclude that increased international competition is probably not the most important element in the preceding list.

VIII. Summary

Growth in the internationalization of the U.S. economy in the 1980s roughly coincides with a major slowdown in the rate of money-wage inflation. Money wages in 1989 are growing about 5 percentage points more slowly than in 1980 to 1981. In both time series and microdata, however, we do not find that developments in international trade provide the main explanation for the wage-growth slowdown. A major reduction in inflationary expectations has been a much larger factor, accounting for at least half of the slowdown. We also find that unusually high unemployment among prime-age men in the 1980s has exerted a restraining effect on money-wage growth, accounting for about 15 percent of the slowdown. Our estimates suggest that international trade accounted for, at most, 18 percent of the slowdown in selected years, and that most of the estimated effects were much smaller.

Notes

1. Table 1 in Mitchell (1989) shows annual wage-growth rates from 1983 to 1988 for the HEI, the ECI, and for a constructed ECI having the same occupational mix as the HEI. The latter series more closely tracks the HEI than the ECI.

2. One ready source for long-run comparisons of wage growth with fringe-benefit growth is the data on employee compensation in the National Income Accounts (NIA). The NIA data in Tables 6.4B and 6.5 show that fringe benefits have grown more rapidly than wages in almost every year since 1950.

3. The means of the 12-month CPI forecasts from the Livingston survey were 4.7 percent, 5.1 percent, and 5.1 percent, respectively, for June 1988, December 1988, and June 1989. For the University of Michigan's survey mean, 12-month CPI expectations averaged 4.7 percent in the first half of 1988, 5.4 percent in the second half of 1988, and 5.2 percent in the first half of 1989.

4. A larger effect of imports than exports on wage adjustments was found by Freeman and Katz (1987) and by Vroman and Abowd (1988).

5. Table 3 in Vroman and Abowd (1988) shows input-output-based estimates of the effects of international trade on industry employment in 1984. For the overall economy, imports reduced employment by 7.8 percent in that year. The corresponding estimates for durables and nondurables were 25.4 percent and 25.1 percent, respectively.

6. This decomposition is discussed in Freeman and Katz (1987).

7. Out of 695 agreements in this sector, only 32 had capped escalators.

8. The effect of expected price inflation was calculated by multiplying the coefficient in column (1) of Table 4, 0.44, by the change in the value of the variable between 1980 and 1984, –4.6. Similarly, the effect of the key-settlements variable was found by multiplying its coefficient, 0.18, by the change between 1980 and 1984, –8.1. The maximum effect of increased import penetration was calculated by multiplying its coefficient, –0.1, times an estimate of the maximum change in wdr of 7 percent per year.

9. See Blau and Beller (1988) for an analysis of the relative earnings of women. Analyses of rates of return to schooling have been conducted by Bound and Johnson (1989) and Murphy and Welch (1987). Katz and Murphy are currently examining rates of return with attention to high school–college differentials. One analysis of union wage differentials that has a time-series perspective is the paper by Wachter and Carter (1989).

10. The 14.2 percent refers to workers represented by unions. Only 12.9 percent of the private nonfarm workers actually were unionized in 1988.

11. Major agreements affect at least 1,000 workers. Mitchell (1989) has argued that employment covered by major agreements has declined more rapidly in recent years than overall unionized employment.

Comments

Louis Jacobson

This excellent paper begins by using "standard" nationwide, aggregate, time-series data to measure the importance of factors that affect wage inflation. Next a unique microdata set covering 2,767 collective bargaining agreements is used to test the same basic hypotheses and to test additional hypotheses that cannot be addressed using aggregate data. Fortunately, the results of these two sections reinforce each other.

The author's basic conclusion is that of the 5.9 percentage point reduction in the annual rate of wage inflation that occurred between 1980 and 1984:

2.0 percentage points were due to a reduction in inflation;

1.4 percentage points were due to a reduction in key settlements in autos and steel; and

0.7 percentage points were due to an increase in import penetration.

Thus, the relative importance of the three major factors is roughly in the ratio of 1:2:3—a rather elegant finding!

In contrast, unemployment increases had only a small effect on stemming wage growth. Prime-age male (PAM) unemployment increased slightly between 1980 and 1984, reducing wage inflation by 0.3 percentage points.

Table 1 in the Vroman paper shows that PAM-unemployment fell from 8.2 percent in the trough of the 1982 to 1983 recession to 5.9 percent in 1984, but has fallen less than two percentage points since 1984. The authors point out that the failure of PAM unemployment to fall to levels observed in the 1960s and even mid-1970s could be the major factor preventing current wage inflation from falling. They thus devote the final section of the paper to discussing some of the reasons that PAM unemployment has remained high by historical standards.

The authors were in the enviable position of extending their earlier work to examine the role of international trade on wage inflation. Their basic results are carefully honed, leaving me little to say. I was particularly impressed by the fact that they took the trouble to exclude the key-agreement variable to check its collinearity with other variables.

I do have a few comments on the new work attempting to capture the effect of the dramatic "internationalization" of the United States economy, which occurred in the early 1980s.

The authors made a number of intelligent choices. Foremost of these is testing the effect of import penetration, not only import prices. Second, they look separately at the effects of imports and exports. Not surprisingly, they found that import penetration has the most importance.

However, they missed some opportunities. They omitted any discussion of the role of trade barriers. Most likely the existence of those barriers is what made the quantity of imports, not their price, the key factor. Perhaps, the authors even could have measured the influence of import-protection provided to the auto, steel, and apparel industries by introducing variables describing those restrictions into their equations.

Although the overall findings discussed above are quite plausible, the net effect of "internationalization" could be considerably underestimated. Arguably, by the mid-1980s, the threats to unionized, domestic companies from foreign competitors were as much due to direct foreign investment as to shipment from abroad.

This was particularly true in autos, and true to a lesser extent in steel. But the authors show that those two industries play a pivotal role in reducing inflationary expectations. Thus, the effect of "foreign" competition could be much greater than indicated simply by the volume of imports (and other trade measures). Testing the effect of domestic production by foreign companies would be a most valuable extension. The necessary data should be readily available, at least for autos.

The effect of direct foreign investment by U.S. companies (as opposed to exports of goods services) was similarly untested. Although probably less potent than U.S. production by foreign competitors, it still would be valuable to try to measure that effect.

Another issue that could have been explored more thoroughly is how wage inflation varied across areas. My thinking of this was stimulated by the authors' finding about the importance of settlements in autos and steel, as well as knowledge that those industries are concentrated geographically. Thus, it could be that the effects of trade were much greater in Pittsburgh, in Cleveland, and in other major labor markets in what is often called the "Rust Belt."

In fact, my own work on Pennsylvania clearly shows that there were substantial earnings reductions resulting from the changes in industry mix. I estimated that, on average, earnings (not the wage rate) paid in Pittsburgh declined by 3.1 percent between 1979 and 1985. But earnings would have increased by 3.0 percent if the employment distribution across industries had not changed over this period. Thus, even ignoring the effects of slower growth of wages, the changes in industrial mix "caused" earnings to decline by 6.1 percent.

Clearly, it is feasible to use the microdata to examine differences across areas (and industries). This could be done by introducing variables reflecting the local concentration of autos and steel, the concentration of trade-sensitive industries in general, or simply by using regional dummies. Perhaps the best method would be to estimate separate equations by region, and to use Chow tests to determine if there are significant cross-region differences.

These equations would tell us if the coefficients of the model varied substantially across areas. At the same time, we could multiply the coefficient times the values of the key parameters to measure how the effects of trade varied in areas with different rates of penetration. In particular, the analysis might show a strong effect of exports in areas such as Seattle, which benefited from expanding trade.

Breaking down the data by region would also help determine whether the coefficients are primarily influenced by time-series or cross-section variation. This is often ambiguous in pooled analysis, but here the appropriateness of interpreting the results as reflecting time-series variation is greatly strengthened because the pooled results and the "standard" time-series analysis using nationwide data are reasonably similar.

More troubling is the inconsistency of the equations over time. The wage-settlement equations differed substantially when estimated for 1959 to 1973 versus 1973 to 1985. Although the import-penetration coefficient differed little, there were massive differences in coefficients on unemployment, key settlements, and expected inflation. If we want to use the equations to try to predict the future pattern of wage settlement, it might be better to use the post-1973 results. The ideal solution, however, would be to introduce variables that would help explain why the structure of the model differed strongly over time.

In summary, the paper provided an excellent analysis of the key factors shaping wage inflation. It made very good use of a valuable new microdata set, even if it left at least a little room for additional useful work in this area.

3

Lump-Sum Payments and Wage Moderation in the Union Sector

Linda Bell and David Neumark

I. Introduction

Wage inflation in the unionized sector of the United States economy was considerably more moderate in the latter half of the 1980s than was anticipated, given prevailing unemployment rates and price inflation (Bell [1989]; Gordon [1988]; Mitchell [1985 and 1986]; and Neumark [1989]). Part of this moderation in wage inflation was undoubtedly related to the well-publicized retrenchment of union wage settlements, entailing outright givebacks or reduced wage growth. At the same time, there was a rapid expansion of alternative pay schemes, such as lump-sum payments and profit sharing (Bell [1989]). While the relationship between union settlements with wage givebacks or freezes and aggregate wage moderation is clear, this chapter explores the more difficult question of whether the shift away from base wage adjustments to lump-sum payments also contributed to wage moderation.

Three alternative but complementary hypotheses regarding the effects of lump sums on wage inflation are considered in this chapter. First, lump sums may simply change the structure of pay, shifting some labor costs out of wages and salaries. The apparent moderation in wage inflation might then be illusory, with lump-sum payments representing nothing more than a change in the structure of union compensation. Second, lump-sum payments may increase labor-market flexibility by introducing a profitsharing component into compensation. At first blush, a profitsharing system would tend to create more labor-cost inflation at low unemployment rates, and less labor-cost inflation at high unemployment rates. This seems to contradict the experience of the latter part of the 1980s, in which seemingly low unemployment rates were accompanied by moderate wage inflation. However, the introduction of a profitsharing component into compensation may lead to employment growth that drives down the natural rate of unemployment (Weitzman [1984 and 1985]). Thus, unemployment rates in the latter half of the 1980s may have actually been high, relative to a new "adjusted" natural rate of unemployment. Finally, lump-sum payments may provide firms with a means to hold down labor costs. In an unchanged bargaining environment, the shift to lump sums could have arisen from either changed preferences on the part of workers in favor of lump-sum payments, relative to base-wage settlements, or alternatively, from a strengthened management stance in collective bargaining. The chapter examines evidence—at the aggregate and firm level—on whether the spread of lump-sum payment plans can explain the decline in wage inflation, or more precisely the apparent downward shift of the aggregate union sector Phillips curve.

Section II presents evidence on the growth in the use of lump-sum payments in major collective bargaining agreements during the 1980s. It also reviews evidence on the tendency for standard Phillips curves to overpredict wage inflation in this period. Section III explores the association between the moderation in aggregate union wage inflation and the growth in lump-sum payments, considering evidence on each of the three hypotheses discussed above. In Section IV, this relationship is examined at the firm level, using employment and labor-cost data from the Compustat data base, combined with Bureau of Labor Statistics (BLS) contract data.

II. Wage Moderation and the Growth of Lump-Sum Payments

The use of lump-sum payments expanded rapidly in the 1980s. Evidence on the growth of lump-sum payments was compiled from Bureau of Labor Statistics contract reports, published monthly in *Current Wage Developments*. This source lists all major collective bargaining settlements covered by the Labor Department involving more than 1,000 workers, and includes data on the bargaining union and establishment, the industry, the number of workers covered, and settlement terms. Furthermore, the contract reports indicate settlements that included a lump-sum or profitsharing provision.[1] The data set used in this chapter compiles information from 5,443 contracts negotiated in 1,241 establishments between 1975 and May 1988, in private industry, excluding construction.[2]

The first column of Table 1 (Lump-Sum Payments) reports workers signing contracts with lump-sum payments as a percentage of all workers signing contracts in a year, for the years 1975 to 1988, for manufacturing and nonmanufacturing industries separately. The figures in this column reveal the strong growth of lump-sum payments in the latter half of the 1980s. In 1986 and 1987, in particular, more than half of all union workers were covered by contracts with lump-sum provisions. For purposes of comparison, the last two columns of the table document the overlap of lump-sum payments with contracts entailing wage givebacks. A comparison of the columns reveals three findings. First, except for 1982 and 1983, lump sums have been considerably more prevalent in the union sector than wage givebacks. Second, at least in the manufacturing sector, while wage givebacks have tapered off (especially when account is taken of large wage increases negotiated in the steel industry in 1989), lump sums have remained prevalent. Finally, lump sums have often been implemented independently of wage givebacks. This last finding suggests that any effects of lump-sum payments on wages or labor costs are unlikely to reflect a direct pass-through from wage givebacks, although this possibility is explored in more detail with the firm-level data.

Table 1:   Workers Affected by Lump-Sum Payments, Profitsharing Plans, and Wage Concessions

(Percentage of all workers negotiating contracts in year)

	Lump-sum payments	Wage concessions	Lump-sum and wage concessions
Manufacturing			
1975	1.4	0.9	0.0
1976	0.0	0.2	0.0
1977	0.0	0.2	0.0
1978	0.0	0.4	0.0
1979	6.4	0.1	0.0
1980	0.1	0.2	0.0
1981	16.6	2.6	1.4
1982	1.7	44.8	1.7
1983	5.9	40.1	5.5
1984	69.5	14.8	9.5
1985	56.5	70.0	44.0
1986	34.1	67.2	29.1
1987	75.4	20.5	13.4
1988	67.1	19.6	9.0
Nonmanufacturing			
1975	1.4	0.7	0.0
1976	0.3	5.1	0.0
1977	0.0	0.2	0.0
1978	6.7	1.1	0.0
1979	0.8	0.0	0.0
1980	0.0	0.0	0.0
1981	1.8	6.5	0.0
1982	0.0	35.9	0.0
1983	0.7	12.9	0.4
1984	15.1	14.1	4.5
1985	22.7	17.2	10.4
1986	57.7	13.6	6.8
1987	49.8	24.4	17.4
1988	25.8	31.3	20.5

NOTE: Wage concession is defined as a nominal wage freeze or reduction in the first year of the contract.
SOURCE: Authors. Matched collective bargaining/Compustat data set.

Table 2:   Aggregate Union Wage Equations[1]

	(1)	(2)	(3)	(4)	(5)	(6)	(7)	(8)
Constant	1.72	0.81	2.27	2.69	2.45	3.05	2.48	3.09
	(0.80)	(0.94)	(0.70)	(0.86)	(0.69)	(0.86)	(0.70)	(0.88)
Prime-age UR[2]	−0.35	—	−0.36	—	−0.38	—	−0.38	—
	(0.14)		(0.12)		(0.12)		(0.12)	
Union UR[3]	—	−0.14	—	−0.33	—	−0.37	—	−0.37
		(0.13)		(0.12)		(0.11)		(0.11)
Lump-sum share[4]	—	—	—	—	−0.03	−0.04	−0.04	−0.05
					(0.007)	(0.007)	(0.03)	(0.03)
Post-1983	—	—	−1.41	−1.73	—	—	0.38	0.35
			(0.33)	(0.35)			(1.28)	(1.28)
$\bar{R}^2$	0.85	0.84	0.87	0.87	0.88	0.88	0.88	0.88
D.W.	1.34	1.19	2.00	1.95	2.14	2.14	2.16	2.15

1. Dependent variable is quarterly change in Employment Cost Index for union wages and salaries, at an annual rate. All specifications include a 12-quarter polynomial distributed lag of inflation in the personal consumption expenditures deflator, with the coefficient constrained to unity. Because the ECI is not seasonally adjusted, quarterly dummy variables are also included. The sample period is 1975:Q4 to 1988:Q4. Standard errors are shown in parentheses.
2. Prime-age male unemployment rate.
3. Unemployment rate for major sector weighted by sectoral unionization rates in each year.
4. Percentage of workers signing contracts with lump-sum payments.
SOURCE: Authors.

It is well known that aggregate wage equations have tended to overpredict wage inflation in the 1980s, for the economy as a whole (Gordon [1988]; and Neumark [1989]), and in the union sector (Bell [1989]; Mitchell [1986]; and Neumark [1989]). Table 2 documents this tendency for the union sector, using the Employment Cost Index (ECI) for wages and salaries for union workers. The sample period covers the Employment Cost Index for union workers, from its inception in 1975 through 1988. The first two columns report estimates from standard wage equations for the union sector, using quarterly data. In the first column, the unemployment rate for prime-age males is used as the measure of aggregate cyclical activity, while in the second column a union unemployment rate estimated from unemployment rates for major industrial sectors, weighted by union coverage in those sectors, is used. Both specifications also include (as do the remaining specifications in this table), a 12-quarter polynomial distributed lag of inflation in the personal consumption expenditures deflator, with coefficient constrained to unity, and quarterly seasonal dummy variables. Columns (3) and (4) include a dummy variable set to one for the 1984 to 1988 period. The estimated coefficients of this variable indicate that wage inflation was about one-and-one-half percentage points per year lower than would have been predicted by a stable Phillips curve estimated over the entire sample period.

Columns (5) to (8) show that the moderation of wage inflation in the 1984 to 1988 period can be attributed, at least statistically, to the growth of lump sums over this same period. Given that there is little variation in the share of workers covered by lump sums prior to 1984, this result is hardly surprising; the lump-sum-share variable entered in columns (5) to (8) is not much different from the post-1983 dummy variable. The point estimates of the lump-sum-share coefficient in columns (5) and (6) imply that a 10 percentage point increase in the share of workers covered by lump-sum contracts reduces the annual rate of wage inflation by 0.3 or 0.4 percentage points. The estimates in columns (7) and (8) show that the 1984 to 1988 shift in the Phillips curve disappears entirely once account is taken of the changes in workers covered by lump sums. In the following two sections, aggregate and firm-level data are used to explore the reasons for this association between lump-sum payments and wage moderation.

III. The Relation between Lump-Sum Payments and Wage Moderation: Evidence from Aggregate Data

A literal "behavioral" interpretation of the Phillips-curve estimates in Table 2 is that lump sums caused the Phillips curve to shift downward in the latter half of the 1980s by reducing the level of wage inflation associated with any rates of unemployment and price inflation, or, equivalently, by reducing the natural rate of unemployment. As a result, the Phillips-curve specification that excludes the percentage of contracts with lump-sum payments leads to overprediction of wage inflation in this period.

There are, however, two alternative explanations for the observed relationship. First, the spread of lump-sum payments could lead wage inflation measures to increasingly understate true labor-cost inflation in the economy. Indeed the ECI for wages and salaries, which was used in the Phillips-curve estimates in Table 2, explicitly excludes lump-sum payments. One way to gather partial evidence on this mismeasurement hypothesis is to consider the ECI for total compensation for union workers, which has been compiled since the beginning of 1980. This latter index includes lump-sum payments, as well as other components of compensation costs, such as fringe benefits. Although this provides only a very short time series for comparison, it is nonetheless instructive to compare Phillips curves estimated with the wages-and-salaries ECI to Phillips curves estimated with the compensation ECI.

Admittedly, the mismeasurement hypothesis is unlikely to account for large differences between wage and salary growth and compensation growth, because lump-sum payments represent a very small component of nonwage and salary employment costs. Beginning in 1988, the BLS has published the components of nonwage and salary compensation in the ECI for union and nonunion workers. In

Table 3: Supplemental Pay as Proportion of Total Employment Costs in the Employment Cost Index

	1988		1989	
	Union	Nonunion	Union	Nonunion
Supplemental pay	3.5	2.0	3.8	2.0
Premium pay	2.5	0.9	2.6	0.9
Shift pay	0.6	0.2	0.7	0.2
Nonproduction bonuses (includes lump-sum payments)	0.4	1.0	0.5	0.9

NOTES: Supplemental pay includes premium pay for overtime, shift pay, nonproduction bonuses, and lump-sum payments provided in lieu of wage payments. In the published data, lump-sum payments are included in the "nonproduction bonuses" category. Prior to 1988, data on the components of supplemental pay were not published; they are available from BLS, but only with a weighting scheme that is not consistent with the published ECI data.
SOURCE: Bureau of Labor Statistics.

both years, nonwage and salary costs accounted for 27.3 percent of total compensation costs. But as Table 3 shows, the component of compensation costs that could be accounted for by lump-sum payments is very small, particularly in the union sector. The table reports all supplemental pay as a fraction of compensation costs, and the breakdown of supplemental pay. The share going to nonproduction bonuses (which is not exclusively lump-sum pay) is reported to be about one-half of one percent for union workers.[3]

Table 4 reports estimates of Phillips curves for the compensation ECI. For purposes of comparison, the first two columns report estimates of the same Phillips curves estimated in columns (3) and (4) of Table 2 (with the wages-and-salaries ECI) for the shorter period during which both ECI measures are available. Despite the shorter sample period, a considerable degree of overprediction persists in 1984 to 1988. In columns (3) and (4), these equations are reestimated using the compensation ECI. In contrast to the prediction of the mismeasurement hypothesis, there is no evidence that the extent of overprediction is lower in the compensation series than in the wages-and-salaries series. Furthermore, when the share of workers covered by lump-sum payments is added to these equations in columns (5) to (8), it enters with a statistically significant coefficient that is nearly as large as the coefficients in the wages-and-salaries ECI regressions in Table 2. In sum, the mismeasurement explanation of the shift in the Phillips curve estimated for wages and salaries receives no support from the aggregate data.

An alternative to the view that lump sums have led to a downward shift in the Phillips curve is that the introduction of lump-sum payments has increased labor-

Table 4:   Aggregate Union Wage Equations: Wages and Salaries and Compensation[1]

	ECI wages and salaries		ECI compensation					
	(1)	(2)	(3)	(4)	(5)	(6)	(7)	(8)
Constant	0.75	0.83	0.81	0.93	1.06	1.39	1.05	1.39
	(1.27)	(1.52)	(1.22)	(1.45)	(1.24)	(1.51)	(1.26)	(1.54)
Prime-age UR[2]	−0.21	—	−0.14	—	−0.17	—	−0.17	—
	(0.19)		(0.18)		(0.18)		(0.18)	
Union UR[3]	—	−0.17	—	−0.13	—	−0.18	—	−0.18
		(0.18)		(0.17)		(0.18)		(0.18)
Lump-sum share[4]	—	—	—	—	−0.03	−0.03	−0.02	−0.03
					(0.01)	(0.01)	(0.03)	(0.03)
Post-1983	−0.97	−1.09	−1.24	−1.34	—	—	−0.20	−0.22
	(0.47)	(0.57)	(0.45)	(0.54)			(1.33)	(1.33)
$\bar{R}^2$	0.87	0.87	0.89	0.89	0.89	0.89	0.89	0.89
D.W.	1.95	1.92	1.86	1.86	1.92	1.94	1.92	1.94

1. Dependent variable is quarterly change in Employment Cost Index for union wages and salaries (in columns [1] and [2]), and for union compensation (in columns [3] to [8]), at an annual rate. All specifications include a 12-quarter polynomial distributed lag of inflation in the personal consumption expenditures deflator, with the coefficient constrained to unity. Because the ECI is not seasonally adjusted, quarterly dummy variables are also included. The sample period is 1975:Q4 to 1988:Q4. Standard errors are shown in parentheses.
2. Prime-age male unemployment rate.
3. Unemployment rate for major sector weighted by sectoral unionization rates in each year.
4. Percentage of workers signing contracts with lump-sum payments.
SOURCE: Authors.

market flexibility by introducing a performance-related component into compensation. Although the evidence on the impact of lump-sum plans on the overall value of worker compensation is mixed (Bell [1989]; and Erickson and Ichino [1989]), some of the differences between lump-sum payments and standard wage adjustments suggest that labor-market flexibility may increase at the firm level—and, by extension, in the aggregate—when lump sums are introduced. Unlike base wages, lump-sum payments do not enter into the calculation of worker overtime, fringe benefits, or pensions. If benefits are more rigid downwards than are wages, then lump-sum payments may be less rigid downwards, since base wages affect the level of benefits while lump sums do not. For the same reason, firms may be more willing to increase the size of the lump-sum payment when profits rise, since this increase would not factor into base wages and hence benefits, and would therefore be easier to reduce if firm performance falters. It might therefore be expected that the spread of lump-sum plans acts to make labor costs more sensitive to demand conditions, by effectively building a profitsharing component into the compensation plan.

If this is the case, then the growth of lump-sum plans may have led to a clockwise rotation of the Phillips curve, making it more vertical as wage flexibility is substituted for employment fluctuations. This steepening of the Phillips curve can be reconciled with the overprediction of wage inflation in the latter half of the 1980s if, during this period, the economy was functioning at a rate of unemployment consistently above the natural rate. This seems unlikely given the low aggregate unemployment rate observed over this period, unless lump-sum payments, as a profitsharing system, reduced the natural rate considerably in the latter half of the 1980s.[4]

To explore the possibility that the true Phillips curve may have rotated clockwise, while simultaneously allowing for a more standard vertical shift, a specification of the Phillips curve in which lump sums can affect both the natural rate of unemployment, as well as the slope of the Phillips curve (independently of the natural rate) was estimated.[5] The specification is

$$\dot{w}_t = \sum_i \alpha \dot{p}_{t-i} + \beta_1 (UR_t - (\delta_0 + \delta_1 \, Lump\text{-}Sum_t))$$
$$+ \beta_2 (UR_t - (\delta_0 + \delta_1 \, Lump\text{-}Sum_t)) \cdot Lump\text{-}Sum_t + \varepsilon_t,$$

where $\dot{w}_t$ and $\dot{p}_t$ are, respectively, the rates of wage and price inflation, UR_t is the unemployment rate, and $Lump\text{-}Sum_t$ is the share of workers covered by lump-sum provisions. As in Table 2, the price-inflation term is a distributed lag of past price inflation, with coefficient constrained to unity.

The prediction that lump sums increase labor-market flexibility implies that $\hat{\beta}_2$ should be negative, so that the spread of lump sums steepens the Phillips curve. If δ_1 is constrained to zero, then lump sums affect the slope of the Phillips curve without affecting the natural rate of unemployment, which is given, as before, by δ_0. Alternatively, if δ_0 is not constrained to zero, lump sums may also influence the natural rate.

Nonlinear least squares estimates of this specification are reported in Table 5. Columns (1) and (1') report estimates with β_2 constrained to zero, for each of the two unemployment rate series. These specifications are observationally equivalent to those in columns (7) and (8) of Table 1. The difference is that now the effect of lump sums that is estimated is the effect on the natural rate, not the direct effect on the rate of wage inflation. To recover the estimated effect on wage inflation (in Table 2), $\hat{\delta}_1$ must be multiplied by $\hat{\beta}_1$. As before, lump sums appear to have a statistically significant effect in lowering wage inflation.

Columns (2) and (2'), in contrast, estimate the impact of lump sums on the slope of the Phillips curve, constraining δ_1 to zero, thereby leaving the natural rate

Table 5:   Aggregate Union Wage Equations:
Intercept Shift vs. Slope Shift

	(1)	(1')	(2)	(2')	(3)	(3')
β_1	−0.38	−0.37	−0.51	−0.46	−0.43	−0.43
	(0.12)	(0.11)	(0.12)	(0.12)	(0.12)	(0.12)
β_2	—	—	0.02	0.01	0.005	0.005
			(0.008)	(0.003)	(0.003)	(0.003)
δ_0	6.45	8.30	6.24	7.91	6.55	8.42
	(0.95)	(0.98)	(0.49)	(0.70)	(0.86)	(0.87)
δ_1	−0.08	−0.11	—	—	−0.14	−0.15
	(0.03)	(0.03)			(0.07)	(0.07)
$\bar{R}^2$	0.88	0.88	0.89	0.89	0.88	0.88
D.W.	2.14	2.14	2.29	2.27	2.15	2.14

NOTES: Dependent variable is quarterly change in Employment Cost Index for union wages and salaries, at an annual rate. The equation estimated is:

$$\dot{w}_t = \sum_i \alpha_i \dot{p}_{t-i} + \beta_1 (UR_t - (\delta_0 + \delta_1\ Lump\text{-}Sum_t))$$
$$+ \beta_2 (UR_t - (\delta_0 + \delta_1\ Lump\text{-}Sum_t)) \cdot Lump\text{-}Sum_t + \varepsilon_t.$$

The distributed lag of price inflation is described in the footnotes to Table 2. Also, as in Table 2, quarterly dummy variables are included. The sample period is 1975:Q4 to 1988:Q4. Standard errors are shown in parentheses. β's and δ's not reported in any column are constrained to zero. Columns without primes use the prime-age male unemployment rate, while columns with primes use the union unemployment rate.
SOURCE: Authors.

unaffected by lump sums. In contrast to the prediction of the flexibility hypothesis, the estimate of β_2 is positive, not negative, and is statistically significant. This suggests that, if anything, the spread of lump sums is associated with a slight flattening of the Phillips curve. To attempt to distinguish between the two potential effects of lump sums, columns (3) and (3') report estimates of the unrestricted model. The positive effect of lump sums on the slope of the Phillips curve, and the negative effect on the natural rate, persist, although the slope shift parameter (β_2) becomes statistically insignificant.

These results do not support the hypothesis that lump sums have led to increased labor-market flexibility. Instead, the results support the view that lump sums have shifted down the Phillips curve in a manner that is consistent with the pattern of wage inflation captured by a "vertical" structural shift.

IV. The Relation between Lump-Sum Payments and Wage Moderation: Evidence from Firm-Level Data

A. *Evidence on Effects of Lump Sums on Labor Costs*

To explore the relationship between lump-sum payments and labor costs at the firm level, data from the collective bargaining data set were matched to firm data from Standard and Poor's Compustat database. The Compustat database contains detailed financial information on all publicly held firms. Not every firm in the bargaining data set is included in Compustat. The matching between the two databases reduced the number of establishments from 1,241 to 304. In terms of location, length of contract, and payment terms, the matched subsample is quite similar to the full collective-bargaining data set. By industry, the subsampled matched data set is more heavily weighted toward manufacturing industries.[6] The observations retained are the contract-firm pairs for the years in which the contracts were negotiated. Intermediate years were not retained because contract-firm pairs could not be matched consistently for noncontract years.[7]

In this subsection, the matched collective bargaining/Compustat data set is used to ask questions similar to those studied with the aggregate data. First, the relationship between labor-cost growth and the presence of a lump-sum payment in the contract is explored at the firm level, in order to examine the basic empirical finding of an association between lump sums and lower wage or compensation growth. Second, an attempt is made to ask whether this association originates from lower wage growth per se, or instead from greater labor-cost flexibility. Because there is a single labor-cost measure in Compustat, which includes all components of compensation, the mismeasurement hypothesis cannot be explored directly. However, because this labor-cost measure is not restricted to wages and salaries, the pure measurement error hypothesis would be contradicted by lower labor-cost growth in lump-sum firms.

It must be emphasized that the data are far from ideal. Although the Compustat database contains measures of employment and labor costs at the firm level, these data cover all employees of the firm, not exclusively the unionized workers to whom the contract data refer. In addition, data on labor costs and employment are missing frequently in the Compustat database.

Table 6 reports descriptive statistics for the sample of matched firm-union pairs. The columns report means and standard deviations of labor-cost growth over a one-, two-, and three-year period, for lump-sum and non-lump-sum firms. The point estimates indicate that labor costs grew more slowly in lump-sum firms, although the differences are not statistically significant. The next three rows report these statistics for employment growth. Lump-sum firms exhibit faster employment growth, although again the differences are not statistically significant. The combined results for labor cost and employment growth are broadly consistent with

Table 6:   Firm-Level Wage and Employment Growth by Lump-Sum Groups

	Lump-sum provision		No lump-sum provision	
	Mean[1]	Std. Dev.	Mean[1]	Std. Dev.
Δ Labor costs (-1)[2]	0.015 (0.011)	0.063	0.039 (0.009)	0.072
Δ Labor costs (-2)	0.028 (0.007)	0.036	0.039 (0.007)	0.057
Δ Labor costs (-3)	0.037 (0.006)	0.030	0.046 (0.006)	0.049
Δ Employment (-1)	0.003 (0.024)	0.222	−0.019 (0.014)	0.184
Δ Employment (-2)	0.029 (0.030)	0.275	−0.016 (0.010)	0.129
Δ Employment (-3)	0.003 (0.013)	0.115	−0.019 (0.009)	0.115
Δ Sales (-1)	0.106 (0.022)	0.205	0.050 (0.012)	0.161
MAXIMUM N[3]	371		1,062	

1. Data cover the period 1984 to 1987. Standard errors of means are reported in parentheses.
2. Changes represent one-, two-, and three-year average annual changes from current period values, as indicated.
3. Missing data for labor costs, employment, and sales imply less than the maximum number of observations in most cells.
SOURCE: Authors.

the aggregate results, since together they suggest that lump-sum firms exhibit slower labor-cost growth for any given level of employment growth.

Similarly, the standard deviations reported in the second and fourth columns of Table 6 are also consistent with the aggregate evidence, contradicting the view that lump sums have increased labor-cost flexibility at the firm level. Firms that had a lump sum included in the contract in the period 1984 to 1987 had less labor-cost variability, and more employment variability, than did firms without lump sums. The next step is to ask whether these differences between lump-sum and non-lump-sum firms remain once appropriate controls are added, and to explore the labor-market flexibility hypothesis more directly.

Table 7 reports estimates that evaluate the extent to which lower labor-cost growth in lump-sum firms persists when various controls are added. Many observations are missing data for some of the variables in this table; regression results for the consistent but smaller sample are reported. Column (1) gives the mean differential in labor-cost growth between lump-sum and non-lump-sum firms, for the period 1980 to 1987. Lump-sum firms, on average, had labor cost growth that was lower by 3.9 percentage points. Columns (2) and (3) show that this differential persists when controls are added for sales and industry. In column (4), single-year dummy variables are added. The point estimate on the lump-sum variable remains negative, but becomes statistically insignificant. However, including year dummy variables may overcontrol for the influence of lump sums, since much of the variation in lump sums occurs across time, and the inclusion of year dummy variables removes this variation. In columns (5) and (6) the change in employment is added to the specifications, with and without single-year dummy variables. The coefficient of the change in employment is negative, as expected, since this is now a labor-demand relationship. But the results for the lump-sum dummy variable are largely unchanged. In columns (7) and (8) the change in profits is added. It enters with a statistically insignificant coefficient, and does not affect the coefficient of the lump-sum dummy variable. Thus, lump-sum firms do appear to exhibit lower labor-cost growth, even after controlling for factors that affect firm performance, although this relationship is statistically significant only when the single-year dummy variables are excluded.

Finally, columns (9) and (10) of Table 7 report estimates using the same specification in columns (1) and (2), but adding a dummy variable indicating whether the firm negotiated a contract entailing a wage giveback. The purpose of this specification is to test whether lower labor-cost growth in lump-sum firms is attributable to lower wage growth in firms that negotiated both wage givebacks and lump-sum payments. While the wage concession dummy variable has a relatively large negative coefficient (as expected) of around five percent, its inclusion has virtually no effect on the estimated negative association between lump-sum payments and labor-cost growth.

The flexibility explanation of lower labor-cost growth in lump-sum firms suggests that these firms exhibit relatively more labor-cost responsiveness, and relatively less employment responsiveness, to changes in demand. To explore this explanation, the responsiveness of labor costs and employment to changes in sales (as a proxy for changes in demand) is estimated, and compared across lump-sum and non-lump-sum firms.

Table 8 reports regression results for specifications in which the dependent variable is the percentage change in labor costs per employee. These specifications can be interpreted as reduced-form, labor-demand functions for output-constrained firms, in which sales is a proxy for demand. Because the equations are estimated in first-difference form, the prices of other inputs drop out to the extent that they are constant. The coefficient estimate in column (1), in which the independent variable is the percentage change in sales, indicates that labor costs rise one percentage point for every 10 percentage point increase in sales. In column (2), the change in sales variable is interacted with a dummy variable indicating whether the firm had a

Table 7: Labor Cost Regressions
Dependent Variable: *ln* Change in Labor Costs

	(1)	(2)	(3)	(4)	(5)	(6)	(7)	(8)	(9)	(10)
Δ *ln* Sales		0.111 (0.045)	0.151 (0.054)	0.140 (0.053)	0.341 (0.047)	0.328 (0.044)	0.348 (0.048)	0.325 (0.045)		0.095 (0.046)
Lump-sum dummy variable	−0.039 (0.014)	−0.040 (0.014)	−0.036 (0.015)	−0.012 (0.015)	−0.029 (0.012)	−0.010 (0.011)	−0.030 (0.012)	−0.010 (0.012)	−0.037 (0.014)	−0.039 (0.014)
Δ *ln* Employment					−0.514 (0.053)	−0.505 (0.048)	−0.537 (0.060)	−0.498 (0.055)		
Year dummy variables				X		X		X		
Δ *ln* Profit							0.003 (0.003)	−0.001 (0.002)		
Industry dummy variables			X	X	X	X	X	X		
Wage concession dummy variable[1]									−0.052 (0.021)	−0.045 (0.021)
R̄²	0.037	0.063	0.104	0.235	0.433	0.557	0.432	0.554	0.065	0.082

NOTES: There are 180 observations. The sample period is 1980 to 1987. The mean of the dependent variable is 0.055.
1. The wage concession dummy variable equals one if there is a nominal wage freeze or reduction in the first year of the contract.
SOURCE: Authors.

Table 8:   Labor Cost Regressions
Dependent Variable: *ln* Change in Labor Costs

	(1)	(2)	(3)	(4)	(5)	(6)	(7)	(8)
Δ *ln* Sales	0.106	0.144	0.181	0.165				
	(0.049)	(0.049)	(0.057)	(0.272)				
Lump sum∗ Δ *ln* sales		−0.239	−0.180	−0.148				
		(0.115)	(0.118)	(0.124)				
Industry dummy variables			X				X	
Industry- Δ *ln* sales interaction				X				X
Δ *ln* Productivity					0.368	0.420	0.454	0.097
					(0.042)	(0.044)	(0.044)	(0.129)
Lump sum∗ Δ *ln* productivity						−0.318	−0.360	−0.311
						(0.092)	(0.098)	(0.104)
$\overline{R}^2$	0.023	0.041	0.084	0.128	0.297	0.338	0.411	0.406

NOTES: There are 180 observations. The sample period is 1980 to 1987. The mean of the dependent variable is 0.055.
SOURCE: Authors.

lump-sum contract. These estimates imply that non-lump-sum firms have a 1.44 percentage point increase in labor costs for every 10 percent increase in sales. In lump-sum firms, however, the response is the sum of the two coefficients. The point estimate of the response coefficient is negative (0.144 − 0.239). But the hypothesis that the sum of these coefficients is zero cannot be rejected, while the constraint that the response coefficients are equal in lump-sum and non-lump-sum firms is rejected. In column (3), industry dummy variables are added. The difference between the response coefficients in lump-sum and non-lump-sum firms is virtually unchanged. In column (4), interactions between industry dummy variables and the change in sales variable are added. This allows the response coefficients to differ across industries, removing the influence on the estimates of any systematic differences across industries in the response coefficients. The coefficient of the change in sales variable now refers to the omitted industry (stone, clay, and glass products). But the coefficient on the interaction variable remains negative, and is considerably less than an average of the industry-change in sales interactions.

In columns (5) to (8), this analysis is repeated, defining the right-hand-side variables on a "per unit of labor" basis, using sales per employee as a proxy for

Table 9: Employment Regressions
Dependent Variable: _In_ Change in Employment

	(1)	(2)	(3)	(4)	(5)	(6)
Δ _In_ Sales	0.098	0.089	0.759	0.490	0.516	0.516
	(0.024)	(0.024)	(0.421)	(0.046)	(0.054)	(0.054)
Lump sum∗	0.318	0.287	−0.201		−0.245	−0.245
Δ _In_ sales	(0.092)	(0.091)	(0.096)		(0.110)	(0.110)
Industry dummy variables		X			X	
Industry- ΔIn sales interaction			X			X
Δ _In_ Labor cost				−0.681	−0.710	−0.727
				(0.073)	(0.073)	(0.073)
N	499	499	499	180	180	180
Mean of dep. variable	−0.012	−0.012	−0.012	−0.017	−0.017	−0.017
$\bar{R}^2$	0.067	0.108	0.414	0.486	0.506	0.570

NOTE: The sample period is 1980 to 1987.
SOURCE: Authors.

productivity, and thus controlling explicitly for employment changes. While the point estimates change considerably, the qualitative conclusions are unaffected. If "productivity" shifts measured in this way are better indicators of labor demand, it is still the case that labor costs are less responsive in lump-sum firms.

The results in Table 8 suggest that labor costs are less flexible in lump-sum firms than in non-lump-sum firms. This is consistent with the findings from the aggregate data suggesting that the spread of lump sums does not appear to steepen the Phillips curve. Thus, the flexibility hypothesis receives no support from either the firm-level or aggregate labor-cost data.

The firm-level data can be used in a similar manner to explore the flexibility hypothesis by looking at the variation in employment. The results of these tests appear in Table 9. The specifications are similar to those in Table 8. Once interactions between the industry dummy variables and sales are added, in column (3), lump-sum firms exhibit less employment flexibility in response to changes in sales. This negative relationship holds up when the change in labor costs is added to the regressions. In sum, though, the overall evidence from the firm-level data is inconsistent with the hypothesis that slower labor-cost growth in lump-sum firms is attributable to increased labor-market flexibility.

B. Explanation of the Effects of Lump Sums on Labor Costs

This section turns briefly to consideration of an alternative explanation of the reduction in labor-cost growth associated with lump-sum payments. Simply put, lump-sum payments—and the lower labor costs that they entail—may have been negotiated as union concessions in firms with flagging economic performance. To examine this question, the relationship between firm performance and the probability of negotiating a contract with a lump-sum provision is estimated. The measures of firm performance in the Compustat database that are considered are percentage changes in labor cost per employee, percentage changes in employment, a measure of profits (net income divided by total assets), percentage changes in sales, and percentage changes in stock price.

Table 10 reports results from probit specifications of the effects of firm performance on the probability that a firm negotiated a lump-sum contract. The table provides no evidence that firm-union pairs settling on lump-sum payments were responding to environments that differed significantly from non-lump-sum firms, in directions likely to have forced unions to agree to lump sums as concessions. In fact, the data suggest that no single measure of firm performance for either one- or three-year periods can explain the probability of a lump sum in the contract.[8]

V. Conclusion

To summarize the findings of this chapter, the use of lump-sum payments in the union sector expanded dramatically in the latter half of the 1980s. The spread of lump-sum payments appears to explain a portion of the moderation in wage growth in the union sector in this period. Including measures of the prevalence of lump-sum payments in standard Phillips curves reduces the overprediction exhibited by Phillips-curve equations in the latter half of the 1980s. This pattern does not appear to be illusory; the moderation of the growth of wages and salaries is also echoed in overall compensation. Furthermore, the association between lump sums and lower labor-cost growth also exists at the firm level, which makes it less likely that the aggregate findings reflect a spurious time-series correlation.

An appealing theoretical explanation for the moderation in labor-cost growth associated with lump-sum payments is that lump sums increase labor-market flexibility, by increasing the responsiveness of labor costs and decreasing the responsiveness of employment to changes in demand. Estimates with both the aggregate and firm-level data provided little empirical support for this explanation.

Table 10: Probit Estimates of Lump Sums and Firm Characteristics[1]
Dependent Variable: Lump Sum
(=1 if lump sum; = 0 otherwise)

	(1)	(2)	(3)	(4)	(5)	(6)	(7)	(8)
$\Delta \ln$ Profit[2] (−1)	−0.015 (0.022)	−0.010 (0.018)	−0.015 (0.022)	−0.011 (0.018)				
$\Delta \ln$ Profit (−3)					−0.163 (0.124)	−0.293 (0.173)	−0.159 (0.124)	−0.314 (0.174)
$\Delta \ln$ Sales (−1)			−0.123 (0.167)	0.007 (0.184)				
$\Delta \ln$ Sales (−3)							−0.091 (0.513)	0.076 (0.528)
$\Delta \ln$ Employment (−1)			0.039 (0.363)	0.589 (0.416)				
$\Delta \ln$ Employment (−3)							−0.082 (0.716)	0.840 (0.837)
$\Delta \ln$ Productivity (−1)	−0.113 (0.161)	−0.065 (0.166)						
$\Delta \ln$ Productivity (−3)					−0.043 (0.478)	−0.120 (0.475)		
$\Delta \ln$ Stock price (−1)	−0.072 (0.204)	0.188 (0.223)	0.074 (0.204)	0.190 (0.225)				
$\Delta \ln$ Stock price (−3)					0.144 (0.449)	0.850 (0.549)	0.161 (0.454)	0.808 (0.554)
Industry dummy variables		X		X		X		X
Log L	−202.1	−177.4	−202.1	−176.4	−168.8	−146.1	−168.1	−145.5
N	442	442	442	442	340	340	340	340
% Pos. N	17.0	17.0	17.0	17.0	25.0	25.0	25.0	25.0

1. The sample period is 1983 to 1987.
2. Changes are current period minus one- and three-period lagged annual averages, respectively.
SOURCE: Authors.

Finally, the spread of lump-sum payments does not appear to be related to concessionary behavior on the part of unions. This suggests either that workers do not regard contracts with lump-sum payments but lower labor costs as inferior, or that there has been a fundamental change in the overall bargaining environment, independent of individual firms' performance.

The most important policy questions regarding wage inflation center on the Phillips curve. Labor-market developments in the latter half of the 1980s suggested that unemployment rates could be driven to quite low levels, compared to the experience of the last two decades, without igniting serious labor-cost inflation. The evidence in this chapter suggests that the spread of lump-sum payments may be partly responsible for this changed trade-off between unemployment and wage inflation, although the exact role of lump-sum payments remains unexplained. If this conclusion is correct, then compensation innovations such as lump-sum payments may enhance the ability of macroeconomic policymakers to stimulate aggregate demand and lower unemployment rates without generating inflationary pressures in the labor market.

Notes

1. Unfortunately, formulas for lump-sum payments specified in the contract language are often based on levels of pay that are not reported. Consequently, it is not possible to determine the value of lump-sum payments.

2. For more details on the construction of the data set, see Bell (1989).

3. The size of nonproduction bonus payments in these data may, however, be understated. Using actual contract data, Erickson and Ichino (1989) have tabulated characteristics of contracts with lump-sum provisions for manufacturing, over the 1982 to 1988 period, for firms with over 500 workers. Their figures indicate that for these firms, lump-sum payments averaged between 1.6 and 3 percent of the base wage over the life of the contract. Multiplying these estimates by the 72.7 percent share of compensation costs going to wages and salaries, as reported in the ECI, and then halving these estimates to reflect the approximately 50 percent of workers who received lump-sum payments in 1988, yields estimates in the range of 0.6 to 1.1 percent. The differences between these estimates and the ECI estimates may be because lump sums are lower in nonmanufacturing, or in firms with 500 to 999 employees. (Our contract data cover firms with more than 1,000 workers.)

4. Weitzman (1984, 1985) discusses the relationship between profitsharing plans and unemployment.

5. This specification was developed in Neumark (1989).

6. This database was initially developed for use in Bell (1989). Further details on its construction are given in her paper.

7. It is an anomaly of the *Current Wage Development* data that firm-union pairs often "disappear" from the data for certain contract cycles.

8. Bell (1989) provides corroborating evidence on this point for union givebacks more generally.

Comments

Ken Ross

As a practitioner in the field of labor-management relations, I find the results reported by Bell and Neumark to be consistent with many of my impressions of the labor-market changes associated with the widespread adoption of lump-sum payments. In these comments, I will try to place their work in context by describing the economic circumstances under which the prevalence of lump-sum payments has risen.

It is very important to position the impact of lump-sum wage increases in a fundamentally changed economic environment. This suggests that part of the problem with traditional Phillips-curve estimates (such as those reported by Bell and Neumark) of the relationship between the unemployment rate and wages is a narrow focus on domestic companies and the labor market, combined with an overbroad generalization around the wage issues without discussing skill requirements for jobs.

Why has the use of lump-sum payments grown so much? Lump-sum wages are, in general, a response to the emerging world economy, which has low wages, particularly for low-skill jobs. The current wage-cost structures of most unionized United States industries were developed following World War II as a product of one of two conditions. Either the United States held a dominant (if not monopoly) position in these industries, or the industry had a backlog of domestic demand that absorbed the entire output. During this period, the "pattern-bargaining" followed by major unions equalized labor costs across industries, which took the cost of labor out of the competitive process.

Now the globalization of markets is reversing these effects. Capital is easily transferred all over the world electronically, so that the cost of capital is beginning to level internationally. Technology travels the same way and the major multinational enterprises all have great research and development capacity so that no market can be protected for long by technological superiority. Also, companies tend to be specialized either in component production or in assembly and marketing, so that production capacity does not have to be integrated geographically. This puts the wage levels and skill requirements of the work force under intense worldwide competitive pressure because labor costs now have become the major focus of competition.

Lump-sum payments were introduced as a means to close the international wage gaps that was adaptable to both management and labor. This brings into focus why the use of local unemployment rates to explain local wage rates is less appropriate than it once was, as Bell and Neumark demonstrate. The correct measure of labor-market tightness would be a complex formula that factored in skill levels, wage levels, and barriers to product/service movement, such as transportation costs, tariffs, and political constraints. Compounding this problem, unemployment rates are a worse measure of the labor market than they once were because, in the late 1970s, the direct correlation between output and work force was broken by technology. Robotics and other forms of technological innovation have created relentless pressure to downsize the work force and to upgrade the skills of those who remain.

This approach to understanding lump-sum payments also helps to explain why Bell and Neumark find that lump-sum payments have not increased the responsiveness of labor costs to changes in demand. Since lump sums were an adaptation to the pressures listed above, they were used first in the manufacturing sector because manufacturing had the high-wage/low-skill jobs that were most vulnerable to competition from the low wage and skill levels in developing countries. Profit sharing was not an acceptable alternative to workers because, in many cases, there weren't any profits, or they were trending the wrong way. (Companies love to give away profits when there aren't any, but the workers don't find this attractive.) Both Audrey Freedman of the Conference Board and I predicted that lump-sum plans would later evolve into profit sharing, but this has been slow in coming. However, according to a 1989 survey by Hewitt Associates, while lump-sum payments remained constant in about 19 percent of the agreements in 1988 and 1989, profit sharing is growing. In this survey of over 700 firms, 16 percent of the employers surveyed had some form of profit sharing and 19 percent of those plans were implemented in the past year.

The reason that lump-sum payments have worked is that most were introduced at the trough of the business cycle, following work force downsizing in response to loss of market demand. As firms increased production without increasing their work force, employees found lump sums acceptable because of the existing low inflation rates and opportunities for overtime. The short-term issue was the relative wage rates in a market-driven economy. Firms implemented lump sums because they were one of the few rewards that did not pose a long-term threat to employment security and corporate viability.

Because of the timing of lump-sum payments and the concurrent application of technology and work force upgrading, it is logical that one would see a relationship with improved profits, sales, and stock performance as the cost structure of these companies became more competitive.

I agree with the implication by Bell and Neumark that lump sums may at least partially reflect a shift in workers' desired form of compensation, although this may not be easily distinguished from benefits to the firm. An interesting impact on the bargaining process has been the demand in some industries to continue lump-sum payments, particularly among young workers. In the 1989 Boeing strike, for example, a union circular noted that since 1983, Boeing had paid bonuses equal to 32 percent of each worker's gross pay. For a worker earning twelve dollars an hour, that means six pre-Christmas bonuses totaling $7,738. If those same bonuses had been delivered as a 31 percent raise in base pay, the compounding would have produced more than three times as much new income, or $25,938 over the same six years. This example also makes it clear that the lump-sum strategy has effectively moderated wage increases in the recent past.

In conclusion, I can accept the Bell and Neumark finding that the Phillips curve overestimates wage inflation because it does not reflect the fundamental changes in the economy. My explanation for this result is that local unemployment rates are a poor proxy for labor availability in a world economy where the application of technology can reduce the number of jobs. As alternatives to hiring become evident, there has been a dramatic expansion in worker acceptance of lump-sum wage payments. Continuing acceptance will be based upon inflation rates, timing of the bonus, availability of overtime, and potential to eliminate jobs through technology. The most critical is inflation. A sharp rise in inflation that eroded wage values would create pressure for the increases in base wages.

Finally, although lump sums may not directly increase compensation flexibility, they are apparently increasingly being transformed into group incentive plans, such as gain sharing and profit sharing. In my view, these plans will increase labor-market flexibility, increase responsiveness of labor costs, and decrease the responsiveness of employment to changes in demand.

4

Profit Sharing in the 1980s: Disguised Wages or a Fundamentally Different Form of Compensation?

Douglas Kruse

I. Introduction

The formal sharing of profits with employees is an old idea—dating back over a century—that has received new attention in the 1980s. The renewed attention can be traced to two sources. First, productivity growth has lagged in the late 1970s and 1980s below its historical levels. Profit sharing is often promoted as a means to spur employee interest in profitability and productivity by tying workers' compensation more directly to the performance of the firm. Second, Martin Weitzman at Harvard has developed and promoted the idea that widespread profit sharing can help to stabilize output and employment at the macroeconomic level, thereby avoiding some of the first-order gross national product (GNP) losses associated with business cycles. Both of these sources of interest are evident in legislation passed in Great Britain in 1986, which established tax incentives to encourage profit sharing; similar legislation was proposed in the United States by Senator Dale Bumpers (D-Ark.) in 1987.[1]

This paper will broadly address the question: Is profit sharing, as currently practiced, a meaningfully different form of compensation, or is it basically conventional wages in disguise? If it is a distinct phenomenon, this raises the question of whether government has a policy interest in seeing it promoted. The primary focus will be on the employment-stabilization hypothesis of Weitzman, which has been addressed in a small but growing number of empirical studies.

Three specific purposes of the paper are (1) to review existing evidence on the prevalence and growth of profit sharing, and to present new evidence on the growth of deferred profitsharing plans in the 1980s; (2) to provide a tour through the empirical work on the employment effects of profit sharing (after briefly discussing the stability theory and propositions); and (3) to present original research on the employment effects of deferred profit sharing in U.S. publicly traded corporations.

One proposition of Weitzman's stability theory is that profitsharing payments are not viewed by the firm as part of the short-run marginal cost of labor. If this is true, the elasticity of employment with respect to profitsharing payments should be close to zero. If, however, profit sharing does not have employment-stabilizing effects (and is basically disguised wages), then the elasticity of employment with respect to profitsharing payments should be close to the wage elasticity. To preview the results, the profitsharing elasticity of employment, unlike the wage elasticity, is consistently close to zero, which is consistent with the stability theory. Profit-sharing payments do not appear to be "disguised wages."

II. Growth and Prevalence of Profit Sharing

Profitsharing plans fall into three categories. One category is cash plans, in which the employer simply pays employees a profit-related bonus at regular intervals (generally, either annually or quarterly). These bonuses are tax-deductible for the employer as a payroll expense, but taxable for the employee as regular income. A second category is deferred plans, in which the employer pays any bonus into a pension trust, where it is allocated to employee accounts and the employees receive the value of the accounts at retirement (subject to vesting requirements). These payments are not taxable for the employee until they are received at retirement. The third category is combination plans, in which the profit-related bonus may be paid as cash or deferred compensation. While there is no complete information on the prevalence of cash plans, it is clear that they are much less common than deferred plans. In the latest survey of members of the Profit Sharing Council of America, cash plans represented only 4.3 percent of the total, with deferred plans representing 78.0 percent and combination plans representing 17.6 percent (Bell [1989]).

Very little systematic data are available on the extent of profit sharing over a long time period. Gilman (1899) reports 23 cases of profit sharing in the United States in 1899, but these are only cases with which he was acquainted. The longest series on the prevalence of all forms of profit sharing comes from the Chamber of Commerce's Survey of Employee Benefits, which dates from 1955. As seen in Table 1, 13 percent of firms responding to the survey had profitsharing plans in 1955, a figure that increased to 21 percent in 1963 and has since remained fairly stable (hovering between 19 percent and 23 percent).[2] The series on percent of payroll accounted for by profitsharing payments shows very little change over this period.

While this series shows little if any growth in profit sharing since the early 1960s, other surveys show growth in the 1980s. The Bureau of Labor Statistics' (BLS's) Survey of Employee Benefits in Medium and Large Firms (which first included profitsharing information in 1981) shows growth from 1981 to 1984 in the percent of employees working in firms with plans. Switching the definition in 1985 to include only employees actually participating in plans, the survey shows growth between 1985 to 1988 in the percent of each employee group in plans (although the growth was uneven for production workers). Hewitt's survey of salaried employee benefits in 250 large companies likewise shows a growth in the percentage of companies with profitsharing plans (from 19 percent in 1979 to 23 percent in 1984). In general, the BLS and Hewitt numbers are more reliable than the Chamber of

Commerce numbers, since the latter do not include profitsharing companies that did not make payments into those plans in a given year.[3]

Although the BLS and Hewitt surveys indicate a gradual increase in profit sharing over the 1980s, it is also interesting to note that the prevalence of profit sharing does not appear to differ greatly by occupational group (according to the BLS numbers and the Mitchell, Lewin, and Lawler comparison of clerical and production employees) or by firm size (the Chelius and Smith survey of small firms indicates a prevalence only slightly higher than do the Hewitt and Chamber of Commerce figures). However, the prevalence does differ according to union status: Mitchell, Lewin, and Lawler's (1990) evidence from 495 business units indicates that nonunion clerical and production workers are more than twice as likely as union workers to be in profitsharing plans.[4]

Even among union workers, though, profitsharing coverage appears to be growing. The data presented by Bell and Neumark (chapter 3) indicate that, unlike in the 1970s, profit sharing has entered many union contracts in the 1980s. Furthermore, this phenomenon was not limited to the recession years of the early 1980s. As the numbers in Table 1 indicate, the percentage of workers affected by contracts containing profitsharing provisions shows no general tendency to decline (the percentage varies greatly between years due to the timing of contracts—the spikes in 1982, 1984, and 1987 are primarily due to autoworker contracts negotiated in those years).

The numbers in Table 1 have the common defect that they are derived from survey samples, which are subject to several biases (most notably nonresponse bias, which can make the final sample unrepresentative of the sample universe). The one source of profitsharing information that is not subject to survey biases is administrative data on deferred profitsharing plans reported to the federal government. Pension plan administrators must fill out Form 5500 reports each year for plans with 100 or more participants (and at least once every three years for plans with fewer than 100 participants).[5] These data, which are available on computer tape from 1980 on, provide a census of large deferred profitsharing plans in the United States, and a reliable means of estimating the number and characteristics of small deferred profitsharing plans.

Table 2 contains calculations for 1980 to 1986 of the number of employees in plans, and the percent of economywide employment represented by different types of pension plans. The top three rows give statistics for all profitsharing plans. It can be seen that the number of participants in deferred profitsharing plans (using the "low estimate") has grown from roughly 9.9 million (representing 13.3 percent of the private wage and salary work force) to 15.4 million (representing 18.4 percent of the private wage and salary work force). In other words, the percentage of the private wage and salary work force covered by profit sharing has been growing by about 0.8 percentage points per year in the 1980s.

A potential problem with counting all pension plans legally designated as "profit sharing" is that the contributions in many of these plans may have a very weak link

Table 1: Survey Evidence on Growth and Prevalence of Profit Sharing

	Percent of companies with plans							Percent of all employees who work in companies with plans			Percent of employees in plans			B&W (union contracts negotiated in given year)	Profit share/total payroll in cos. with plans[c]
Source:	CCC (hourly employees)[a]	Hewitt (salaried, large firms)	C&S (small firms)	MLL (bus.units, public cos.)				BLS (medium & large firms)			BLS (medium & large firms)				COC (hourly employees)[a]
Type of plan	Cash and deferred	Deferred	Cash and deferred	Cash and deferred				Cash and deferred			Cash and deferred			Cash and deferred	Cash and deferred
Employee class				Clerical and production											
Year				U	NU	U	NU	P/A	T/C	PR	P/A	T/C	PR		
1988											23	24	18	8.2	
1987	23[a]		28	15	42	18	46							30.1	3.3[a]
1986											22	22	22	7.2	
1985	22	17[b]									19	22	16	6.4	5.1
1984	21	23						28	31	23				27.6	5.1
1983	20	22						27	31	23				9.4	5.2
1982	23	20						25	28	18				10.5	4.8
1981		19						25	26	17				4.8	
1980		19												0.4	
1979	21	19													6.7
1978	21														6.6
1977	20														5.5
1976															
1975	20													0.0	5.5
1974															
1973	20														5.7

(continued on next page)

Table 1: Survey Evidence on Growth and Prevalence of Profit Sharing (continued)

	Percent of companies with plans							Percent of all employees who work in companies with plans			Percent of employees in plans			B&W (union contracts negotiated in given year)	Profit share/total payroll in cos. with plans[c]
	CCC (hourly employees)[a]	Hewitt (salaried, large firms)	C&S (small firms)	MLL (bus.units, public cos.)				BLS (medium & large firms)			BLS (medium & large firms)				COC (hourly employees)[a]
Source:	Cash and deferred	Deferred	Cash and deferred	Cash and deferred				Cash and deferred			Cash and deferred			Cash and deferred	Cash and deferred
Type of plan				Clerical and production											
Employee class				U	NU	U	NU	P/A	T/C	PR	P/A	T/C	PR		
1972	19														
1971															5.5
1970															
1969	22														5.2
1967	21														5.7
1965	19														5.5
1964															
1963	21														3.9
1961	17														4.7
1959	15														5.6
1957	14														5.4
1955	13														5.5

a. 1987 Chamber of Commerce survey excludes cash profit sharing and includes salaried employees.

b. 1979-84 Hewitt numbers from constant sample of 250 large employers; 1985 number reflects larger sample of 812 employers.

c. Total payroll includes payroll of nonparticipants.

SOURCES: CO = Chamber of Commerce of the United States (various years); Hewitt = Hewitt Associates (1985, 1986); C&S = Chelius and Smith (1990); MLL = Mitchell, Lewin, and Lawler (1990); U = Union; NU = Nonunion; BLS = Bureau of Labor Statistics (various years); P/A = Professional and administrative employees; T/C = Technical and clerical employees; PR = Production employees.

72

Table 2: Growth of Deferred Profit Sharing Relative to Defined Benefit Plans and ESOPs, 1980 to 1986

Numbers in 1000s		1980	1981	1982	1983	1984	1985	1986
All profit-sharing	Participant estimates: high	10,365	10,773	11,486	12,931	14,418	16,143	17,003
	low	9,856	10,192	10,885	12,135	13,261	14,694	15,403
	Percent of employment (a)	13.3%	13.5%	14.6%	16.1%	16.7%	18.1%	18.4%
Nonthrift profit-sharing	Participant estimates: high	8,772	8,796	9,261	10,469	11,441	12,838	13,752
	low	8,419	8,459	8,903	9,958	10,750	11,917	12,755
	Percent of employment (a)	11.4%	11.2%	12.0%	13.2%	13.6%	14.6%	15.3%
Defined benefit	Participant estimates: high	29,908	29,632	29,236	28,119	28,277	29,395	28,278
	low	25,525	25,419	25,125	24,241	24,310	25,245	24,456
	Percent of employment (a)	34.5%	33.8%	33.8%	32.1%	30.6%	31.0%	29.3%
ESOPs	Participant estimates: high	4,940	5,141	6,236	9,041	10,307	10,849	10,426
	low	4,621	4,895	5,896	8,496	9,438	9,669	9,292
	Percent of employment (a)	6.2%	6.5%	7.9%	11.2%	11.9%	11.9%	11.1%
Private wage and salary workers in economy (1000s)		74,013	75,289	74,430	75,522	79,327	81,356	83,488

NOTES: "High" participant estimate represents total participants in plans and contains some double-counting of workers in multiple plans. "Low" participant estimate represents total of participants in largest plan in company. (a) represents the low estimate of employees in plans divided by total private wage and salary workers.

SOURCE: U.S. Department of Labor. Calculated from Form 5500 tapes, adjusted for small plans with information from Daniel Beller. See Appendix B for details.

to profits. This is especially the case with 401(k) and other thrift plans, which allow employee contributions that may be matched by employer contributions. The existence of a 401(k) option does not mean that the plan is not a true profitsharing plan, since the employer match to employee contributions may be based on profits;[6] however, it is clear that many firms adopt 401(k) plans in which the employer contribution is tied only to employee contributions, and not to profits (even though they are legally designated "profitsharing" plans).[7] What this means is that it is useful to examine profitsharing plans without 401(k) or other thrift features. The rows for "nonthrift profit sharing" in Table 2 show that most plans did not have thrift features, and the growth of this subset was slightly less than the growth for all profitsharing plans.

One could object that the growth of deferred profitsharing plans may simply reflect the growth of pension plans in general over this period. However, the number of employees in defined-benefit pension plans (in which employees are guaranteed a particular amount of income upon retirement) is stable over this period. As shown in Table 2, the percent of private wage and salary workers covered by defined-benefit plans actually declined from 34.5 percent to 29.3 percent over this period. This is consistent with numerous press accounts about firms terminating defined-benefit plans and replacing them with profitsharing plans, because of the increased flexibility allowed by the latter.

Finally, Table 2 shows the growth of plans with ESOP (Employee Stock Ownership Plan) features over this period, covering 6.2 percent of the private wage and salary work force in 1980, and growing to 11.1 percent in 1986.[8] Profitsharing plans are similar to ESOPs in that ESOPs are a form of flexible compensation in which employee rewards are tied to company profitability (through the stock price and dividends of the company).[9] While ESOPs will not be further analyzed here, their growth is consistent with the idea that the economy is slowly moving toward more flexible compensation arrangements (see Blasi [1988] and Conte and Svejnar [1990] for a review of evidence on ESOPs).

Table 3 provides an industry breakdown of profitsharing, defined-benefit, and ESOPs plans for 1986. Two points are worth noting about this table. First is that the distribution of each type of plan varies substantially across industry—participants as a percentage of the private wage and salary work force range from 8 percent to 43 percent for profitsharing plans, and 14 percent to 47 percent for defined-benefit plans. Second, if profit sharing were adopted only for purposes of enhancing firm stability, one would expect it to be most prevalent in the historically unstable industries (agriculture, construction, and manufacturing). As can be seen in Table 3, this simple expectation is not neatly confirmed. Column 3 shows that the greatest prevalence of profit sharing is in manufacturing (28 percent of private wage and salary workers) and finance, insurance, and real estate (30 percent covered). The prevalence is especially low in construction (8 percent) and services (10 percent). In no industry are there more workers covered by profit sharing than by defined-benefit plans.

Table 3: Industry Breakdown of Number of Employees in Profitsharing, Defined-Benefit, and ESOP Plans, 1986

| | All profitsharing | | | Nonthrift profitsharing | | | Defined-benefit pensions | | | ESOPs | | | Private wage and salary workers |
| | Estimate | | % of empl.[a] | Estimate | | % of empl.[a] | Estimate | | % of empl.[a] | Estimate | | % of empl.[a] | |
All numbers in 1000s	High (1)	Low (2)	(3)	High (4)	Low (5)	(6)	High (7)	Low (8)	(9)	High (10)	Low (11)	(12)	(13)
Total	17,003	15,403	18	13,772	12,755	15	28,278	24,456	29	10,426	9,292	11	83,488
Agriculture	697	660	43	647	613	40	757	685	45	158	131	9	1,531
Mining	186	172	20	111	101	12	276	246	29	79	75	9	852
Construction	469	454	8	428	415	8	1,114	1,094	20	94	84	2	5,373
Manufacturing	6,670	5,664	28	5,327	4,682	23	11,478	8,843	43	4,905	4,372	21	20,423
Dur. mfg.	4,251	3,459	28	3,418	2,935	24	7,099	5,329	43	3,282	2,921	24	12,254
Nondur. mfg.	2,418	2,205	27	1,909	1,747	21	4,379	3,514	43	1,623	1,451	18	8,169
TCU	1,197	1,016	17	614	570	10	3,283	2,762	47	1,995	1,756	30	5,842
Transportation	497	472		339	322		1,529	1,349		428	336		
Communication	402	272		88	78		996	723		876	871		
Utilities	304	272		188	170		758	690		691	550		
Wholesale trade	842	817	20	805	781	19	692	649	16	133	122	3	4,098
Retail trade	2,464	2,395	14	2,163	2,106	13	2,281	2,112	13	1,400	1,352	8	16,715
FIRE[b]	2,098	1,977	30	1,483	1,396	21	2,955	2,806	42	1,018	884	13	6,668
All services	2,288	2,156	10	2,097	1,995	9	3,202	3,053	14	642	505	2	21,986
Business serv.	427	410		396	383		408	388		168	164		
Health serv.	753	710		729	687		1,664	1,607		262	140		
Other serv.	1,108	1,036		972	925		1,130	1,058		213	201		
Tax-exempt	93	91		76	76		2,219	2,184		2	2		

NOTES: "High estimate" of employees in plans counts total participants in all plans, and some double-counting is likely. "Low estimate" of employees in plans counts only the participants in the largest plan in the company.
a. Represents low estimate of employee participants divided by total private wage and salary workers (Bureau of Labor Statistics, 1988).
b. Finance, insurance, and real estate.
SOURCE: U.S. Department of Labor. Calculated from Form 5500 and 5500C series tapes. See Appendix B for details.

In summary of this section, estimates based on existing surveys are that between 20 percent and 25 percent of employees are in profitsharing plans, and between 20 percent and 28 percent of U.S. companies have profitsharing plans (although the percentage appears higher in nonunion business units). Administrative data on deferred profitsharing plans, which constitute the large majority of all profitsharing plans, indicate a steady growth throughout the 1980s—covering 13.3 percent of the private wage and salary work force in 1980 and 18.4 percent in 1986. There is no firm evidence to explain this growth. One possibility is that it at least partly represents a movement toward more flexible compensation on the part of firms in order to adjust to severe demand shocks (as represented by the early 1980s recession, and increasing import penetration in many industries). Another possibility, also lacking in hard evidence, is that there is a growing perception by managers that profit sharing can complement other company policies designed to increase employee motivation and innovation and to decrease turnover.[10]

III. Theory and Empirical Propositions

The primary sources of interest in profit sharing, as noted, concern its potential to enhance productivity by motivating workers, and its potential to stabilize employment and output. A fundamental difference between these two sources of interest lies in the implications for public policy. If profit sharing increases productivity, there is no clear-cut argument on this basis alone for public policy intervention, since the productivity gains will accrue to the firm and workers (although there may still be an argument, in the presence of imperfect information and institutional rigidities, that government should act as a catalyst to shorten the learning curve on the use of profit sharing). If profit sharing helps to stabilize employment and output, however, Weitzman argues that public policy encouraging profit sharing is justified, since the gains from stabilized output and employment accrue to the economy as a whole (as will be explained below). Because the employment stability theory has more clear-cut policy implications, and because the potential productivity-enhancing aspects of profit sharing have been recently covered in Weitzman and Kruse (1990),[11] the remainder of this paper focuses on the stability theory.

The theory of how profit sharing may promote employment stability has been developed by Martin Weitzman (1983, 1984, 1985, and 1986). The essence of the theory is that under a demand shock, a profitsharing firm will find it less costly to maintain employment than would a fixed-wage firm. The theory relies on the idea that the fixed wage will be lower in a profitsharing firm than in a firm without profit sharing; however, when the profit share is added, average compensation will be comparable between the two types of firms.[12] The differences in form of compensation cause different incentives for managers in the two firms. Stated informally, managers in both firms must pay each worker the fixed wage, and will lay off workers if the workers' product does not equal or exceed that fixed level. Since the fixed wage is lower in a profitsharing firm, the product of the worker is more likely to exceed the fixed wage level, and the manager will be less likely to lay off workers.The profit share, acting as a tax on profits, will not enter the calculation of how many workers to employ.

Stated more formally, a profitsharing firm will have a short-run marginal cost of labor that is less than the marginal revenue product of labor, causing the firm to want to hire more workers. This motivation will exist even in a market equilibrium, where labor supply constrains the firm from hiring more workers. The equilibrium compensation and employment levels will be the same in profitsharing and fixed-wage firms, but different incentives will cause them to behave differently out of equilibrium. Following is a brief discussion of the logic of this theory.

Within equilibrium, both profitsharing and fixed-wage firms must pay the market compensation level in order to attract workers, and both will equate the total compensation level with the marginal revenue product of labor (MRPL) so that employment levels will be the same (factors other than form of compensation are assumed to be the same, so that the MRPL schedules will be identical). If the profitsharing firm does not meet the market compensation level, it must increase either its base wage or the share of profits paid to workers. While behaving similarly in equilibrium, the nature of the compensation will cause different incentives between the two types of firms if the labor market is thrown out of equilibrium (due to, e.g., product market shocks or new labor market entrants). If profit shares are distributed equally among workers, each worker's compensation in a profitsharing firm is:

$$c = w + s[(R(L)-wL)/L] = w(1-s) + sR(L)/L,$$

where $R(L)$ = one-input revenue function;
s = share of profits going to workers collectively;
L = number of workers;
w = base wage.

With w and s fixed in the short run, the firm's short-run profit-maximization decision leads to the first-order condition that $R'(L) = w$ (i.e., workers are hired up to the point where MRP_L equals the base wage). This implies that the profitsharing firm in a labor market disequilibrium will hire (or retain) more workers than would a fixed-wage firm, which sets MRP_L equal to total compensation c to determine employment levels. In the labor-market equilibrium, profitsharing firms are prevented from reaching their desired level of employment because of a labor supply constraint (since the market compensation level must be paid in equilibrium), but they will still be eager to hire workers at the current compensation parameters.

The intuition of the theory can be seen most clearly by considering what would happen if new entrants suddenly appeared in a full-employment economy, creating unemployment. Employing the new workers would cause the MRP_L to drop slightly below the old equilibrium value of c, so there is no incentive for fixed-wage firms (whose wage equals c) to immediately hire these workers. In an economy of fixed-wage firms, there would be a possibly lengthy process by which the new workers would bid down wage levels to the point where firms would hire the new workers. In an economy with profitsharing firms, however, the firms should be eager to hire the new workers without delay (assuming the new MRP_L exceeds the base wage w), and the readjustment of compensation levels would take place without any involuntary unemployment.[13]

An important part of the theory concerns how a profitsharing economy would respond to negative demand shocks. A fixed-wage firm that is subject to an inward shift of the product-demand curve would lay off workers in the short run, since the new MRP_L is less than the fixed wage c. A profitsharing firm, however, views the base wage as the marginal cost of labor and will therefore retain workers as long as $MRP_L > w$. With all profitsharing firms acting upon this motive, the economy as a whole should experience less unemployment and decrease in real purchasing power than would a comparable fixed-wage economy in the face of external recessionary pressures.[14] This provides the justification for public policy interventions to encourage profit sharing: the full effects of employment instability are not internalized by individual firms and workers making compensation decisions, but extend throughout the economy through the economic and social costs of unemployment.

Therefore two key empirical propositions of Weitzman's theory are:

(1) Profitsharing payments are not viewed by the firm as part of the short-run marginal cost of labor that determines employment levels.

(2) Firms that pay a higher proportion of average compensation as profit shares will have a lower likelihood, and severity, of employment cutbacks in the face of demand shocks.

This theory has been criticized on numerous grounds. Among these criticisms are: 1) Employed workers may resist the hiring of new workers, since the pay of existing workers would be decreased (Summers [1986]); 2) Employers may invest less in new capital since some of the resulting profits would have to be shared with workers (Summers [1986], and Estrin, Grout, and Wadhwani [1987]); 3) If labor productivity depends on worker compensation, as predicted by efficiency-wage theories, firms would not have an excess demand for labor, since hiring new workers would lower the productivity of all workers (Levine [1987]); 4) If tax incentives are granted for profit sharing, "cosmetic" schemes may be designed to gain the incentives without having the desirable properties of true profit sharing (Estrin, Grout, and Wadhwani [1987]); 5) In full-employment equilibrium, firms may regard average compensation as the marginal cost of labor (due to the labor-supply constraint), which would eliminate the stabilization properties of profit sharing (Nordhaus [1988]).

The task of this paper is not so much to review the theoretical arguments as it is to review the empirical work on the employment behavior of profitsharing firms. Ideally one would study an economy that has switched from a fixed-wage system to a profitsharing system, since Weitzman focuses on macroeconomic stability in economies that are pure profitsharing or pure fixed-wage systems. Lacking such a natural experiment, however, most empirical studies have focused on firm-level behavior of profitsharing and fixed-wage firms, since Weitzman's macroeconomic results are driven by microeconomic incentives at the level of the firm. It should be kept in mind, however, that there is a potential fallacy of composition: even if profit sharing causes greater employment stability for individual firms, this does not necessarily imply that an entire economy of profitsharing firms would be more stable than a fixed-wage economy.[15]

The empirical work can be broadly classified according to which one of the two empirical propositions is addressed. Studies addressing Proposition 1 use information on dollar amounts of profit sharing to test whether profit sharing acts as part of the marginal cost of labor, while studies addressing Proposition 2 directly measure employment stability using profitsharing status as an explanatory variable.

The first type of study uses some variant of a basic labor-demand equation:

(1) $Ln(L) = \beta_0 + \beta_1 ln(w) + \beta_2 ln(b/w) + \beta_3 X,$

where L = employment;
w = base wage;
b = size of profitsharing bonus;
X = other explanatory variables (demand measures, lagged employment, time trend).

The coefficient β_1 measures the elasticity of the conventional labor-demand curve; its expected negative sign indicates that exogenous wage increases result in employment decreases by firms. The coefficient β_2 indicates the responsiveness of employment to changes in bonus payments, holding wages constant. If β_2 is negative and equal to or greater than β_1 in magnitude, compensation increases in the form of profit sharing would appear to have employment consequences just as severe as wage increases.[16] If, however, β_2 is positive or smaller than β_1 in magnitude, there would appear to be merit to the idea that profit sharing behaves differently than wages, and that it may not be considered by the firm as part of the short-run marginal cost of labor, which determines employment decisions. (A key problem in these specifications is to account for the potential endogeneity of profitsharing payments: factors that influence labor demand are very likely to influence profitability and therefore the profitsharing payments made to workers. Researchers using this approach have consequently instrumented profitsharing payments on presumably exogenous variables.)

The second type of study does not focus on whether profitsharing payments are part of the marginal cost of labor, but attempts to directly measure whether profitsharing firms have greater stability of employment. The key problem in this type of study is to sort out causality: if profitsharing firms have more stable employment than other firms, this may be because profit sharing causes greater stability, or because more stable firms are more likely to adopt profit sharing. The econometric specifications are again based on an employment equation; demand-shock measures appear as independent variables, and profitsharing status is entered either alone or interacted with the demand-shock measure in order to determine whether profitsharing firms respond differently to the demand shocks. An example is the following first-difference specification:

(2) $\Delta ln(L) = \Theta_0 + \Theta_1 *(\Delta D) + \Theta_2 *(PS*\Delta D) + \Theta_3 *\Delta X$,

where D = measure of demand for firm's products;
PS = measure of profit sharing within firm (dummy variable, percent of employees covered, or size of typical profitsharing payment / payroll);
X = other control variables (time trend, wage changes, capital stock changes, etc.).

In this specification, the coefficient Θ_1 is expected to be strongly positive, indicating a close connection between demand and the labor required by the firm to meet that demand. The coefficient Θ_2 will be zero if profitsharing firms have the same employment response to demand changes as do nonprofitsharing firms. A negative sign for Θ_2, however, would indicate that employment is less sensitive in profitsharing firms to short-run changes in demand (the responsiveness is $\Theta_1 + \Theta_2$). A refinement used by the authors of studies employing equation (2) has been to separate negative and positive demand shocks, and their interactions with profit sharing, to determine whether the profitsharing effect on employment stability may be asymmetrical (e.g., profitsharing firms may have smaller employment responses to negative demand shocks, but similar employment responses to positive shocks).

IV. Review of Evidence

Ten econometric studies on profit sharing and employment stability are briefly summarized in Table 4.[17] A clear division in level of data exists between studies 1 to 8, which use firm-level (or, in one case, individual-level) data, and studies 9 to 10, which use aggregate data on the Japanese economy. The last column contains a quick reference to the principal findings.[18]

The two aggregate studies use data over 1959 to 1983 on the Japanese bonus system. Freeman and Weitzman (1986) found that bonuses are more responsive to business conditions than are base wages, suggesting a larger profitsharing component in bonuses than in base wages. Using a modification of equation (1) above (replacing $ln(b/w)$ with $ln(w+b)$, and with lagged employment, time trend, and ln[net domestic product] as control variables), they find that the wage coefficient has the expected negative sign, while the coefficients on wages, plus bonuses, are consistently positive. This modification, referred to as equation (1b), suggests that bonuses are not seen as part of the marginal cost of labor, and the authors conclude that "they contribute somewhat to the success of the Japanese economy by automatically helping to stabilize unemployment at relatively low levels" (1986: 26).

This finding is disputed by Estrin, Grout, and Wadhwani (1987), who use the same data. Instead of an output measure, they use ln (capital stock) and change in

Table 4: Empirical Studies of Profit Sharing and Employment Stability

Study	Data source	Unit of analysis	n	Time period	Profitsharing measures	Main results relating to theory that profit sharing is positively linked to employment stability
Disaggregated data:						
1. Chelius and Smith (1990)	1) U.S. small businesses	Firm	2,997	1987	PS dummy and B/W (cash and deferred plans)	Generally favorable: PS firms have smaller employment decreases when sales decline; result is stronger for PS dummy than for B/W.
	2) Quality of employment survey	Persons	404	1977	PS dummy	Favorable: Workers in PS plans were less likely to be laid off in previous year.
2. Bradley and Estrin (1987)	Large British retail chains (one with PS)	Firm	5	1971-1985 (balanced)	PS dummy and B/W	Mixed: PS firm had higher employment than others, and B/W positively related to employment changes, but similar employment changes over the business cycle.
3. Estrin and Wilson (1989)	British metal-working and engineering firms	Firm	52	1978-1982 (balanced)	PS dummy and B/W	Generally favorable: Authors reject hypothesis that PS payments are part of the marginal cost of labor.
4. Finseth (1988)	U.S. publicly traded mfg. firms	Firm	132	1971-1985 (balanced)	PS dummy and B/W (both cash and deferred plans)	Mixed: B/W more responsive than W to changes in profits, mixed results on stability (PS increases employment when profits/L is used as demand measure).
5. Fitzroy and Vaughan-Whitehead (1989)	French mfg. firms	Firm	116	1983-1985 (balanced)	PS dummy and profit share per worker	Mixed: Profit share per worker negatively related to employment, but cash PS firms maintain higher employment in downturn.

(continued on next page)

Table 4: Empirical Studies of Profit Sharing and Employment Stability (continued)

Study	Data source	Unit of analysis	n	Time period	Profitsharing measures	Main results relating to theory that profit sharing is positively linked to employment stability
6. Jones and Pliskin (1989)	British printing, footwear, and clothing firms	Firm	127	1890-1975 (unbalanced)	PS dummy and B/W	Mixed: PS dummy associated with lower employment, but B/W coefficient sensitive to whether measures of worker participation are included.
7. Kruse (forthcoming)	U.S. publicly traded firms	Firm	1,383	1971-1985 (balanced)	PS dummy, and % of workers covered (deferred plans)	Generally favorable: PS associated with more stability in the face of negative demand shocks in manufacturing, but not in nonmanufacturing.
8. Wadhwani and Wall (1988)	British publicly traded firms	Firm	101	1972-1982 (balanced)	PS dummy and B/W	Unfavorable: Both PS measures statistically insignificant, but magnitudes indicate B/W depresses employment more than wages do.
Aggregate data:						
9. Estrin, Grout, and Wadhwani (1987)	Japanese aggregate data	Aggregate economy		1959-1983	B/W	Unfavorable: Wages and bonuses have slightly positive, insignificant coefficients when controlling for capital and not output (in contrast to Freeman and Weitzman).
10. Freeman and Weitzman (1986)	Japanese aggregate and industry-level data	Aggregate economy and mfg.		1959-1983	B/W	Favorable: Bonus appears to have profit-sharing component, and unlike wages, relates positively to employment (controlling for output changes).

PS = profit sharing; B/W = profitsharing bonus/wage; W = wage.
NOTES: The dependent variable is *ln*(employment) in all studies. Studies (2), (3), (4), (5), and (6) use firm intercepts or first differences.
SOURCE: Author.

ln (capital stock), and use *b*/*w* as the bonus measure (as in equation 1b above). With this specification, the coefficients on the wage and the bonus/wage ratio are positive, but very small and insignificant. This is taken as evidence against the proposition that bonuses behave differently than the base wage.[19]

Among studies 1 through 8, which use disaggregated data, studies 3, 6, and 8 concentrate on Proposition 1, which concerns whether profitsharing payments are part of the marginal cost of labor. Wadhwani and Wall (1988) provide unfavorable evidence on this proposition, using panel data over 1972 to 1982 on 101 British firms (of which 21 had a profitsharing plan at some point in the period). The empirical specification is equation (1b), above, with lagged instead of current *b*/*w* (with numerous explanatory variables). The coefficient on lagged *b*/*w* was large and negative but statistically insignificant ($t = 1.01$), while the coefficients on the wage variables were smaller, negative, and significant.[20] Estrin and Wilson (1989) test Proposition 1 and provide evidence that is more favorable. They use a sample of 52 firms in the British engineering and metalworking sectors over 1978 to 1982. Of these 52 firms, 21 operated a profitsharing plan (or value-added based bonus plan). Using just the profitsharing firms, the authors' preferred specification is equation (1b), above, but in first-difference form (with controls for change in *ln*(*assets*), lagged *ln*(*L*), time trend, and firm fixed effects). The authors' conclusion based on the results is that profitsharing payments are not seen as part of the marginal cost of labor.

Jones and Pliskin (1989) use a sample of 127 British firms in the printing, footwear, and clothing industries, with up to 77 years of data for individual firms. They were able to control for several measures of worker participation, including worker representation on the board of directors and membership in a producers' cooperative. In their fixed-effects specifications, the authors include *b*/*w* and *b*/*w* interacted with these two worker participation measures. The *b*/*w* coefficient is positive with weak significance, while the interaction coefficients are negative with weak significance—indicating that Proposition 1 is supported only in the absence of these forms of participation. The authors note that, "For firms with average levels of participation, the net effect of profit sharing on employment is positive but modest" (1988: 294).

Proposition 2—that profitsharing firms will have more stable employment—is directly addressed in the remaining studies shown in Table 4 (1, 2, 4, 5, and 6). Chelius and Smith (1990) report results from two samples—one comprising individuals and the other comprising a large survey of U.S. small businesses. Findings from the first sample indicated that, controlling for industry employment changes and for personal characteristics, workers in profitsharing plans were less likely to be laid off in 1976 than workers who were not in profitsharing plans. Analysis of the second sample measured employment stability at the firm level, separating the effects of positive and negative demand shocks for a sample of 2,997 small businesses. The results indicated that, among all firms with sales declines in 1987, profitsharing firms had smaller employment cutbacks (controlling for quits), while among firms with sales increases, there were no significant differences by profitsharing status.

Finseth (1988) used a data set of 132 large U.S. manufacturing firms over 1971 to 1985 with information on both cash and deferred plans. Controlling for changes in profits per employee (as a demand measure), he found that profit sharing was associated with higher employment both when profits/employee were declining and when they were increasing (although with weak statistical significance in most cases). Using changes in gross sales as a demand measure, the employment effects were generally insignificant.[21]

Bradley and Estrin (1987) study the performance of one large British retail chain (the John Lewis Partnership, or JLP) with both profit sharing and employee stock ownership, and compare its performance to that of four rivals. Comparing the change in employment among the five firms, after controlling for changes in sales and remuneration, they find that JLP had more positive changes over the 1970 to 1986 period than three of its rivals, but the differences were not significant. Part of their study addresses Proposition 1; using a specification based on equation (1), they find that profitsharing payments do not appear to be part of the short-run marginal cost of labor. Combined with the finding that employment levels were higher in JLP relative to its rivals, the authors conclude that this "suggests that Weitzman-type effects as well as purely motivational factors might explain the JLP's employment record" (1987: 20).

A sample of 116 French firms was analyzed by Fitzroy and Vaughan-Whitehead (1989). Comparing employment changes from 1984 to 1985, they find that average employment declined in nonprofitsharing firms, but increased in profitsharing firms (while the size of the profit share decreased). They also find, in testing whether profit shares act as part of the marginal cost of labor, that the profitsharing coefficients are negative, but smaller in magnitude than the wage coefficients; whether this supports or contradicts the stability theory is unclear.

Finally, in Kruse (forthcoming), I matched administrative data on deferred profit-sharing plans (from the federal Form 5500 series) with Standard & Poor's Compustat data set, producing a final sample of 1,383 firms with full employment information over the 1971 to 1985 period. Information on the starting date of the profitsharing plan was included, so that panel comparisons with fixed effects were feasible. Demand shocks were measured alternatively as changes in industry-level unemployment rates, shipments, prices, and gross domestic product. In the manufacturing sample, profitsharing firms were less likely to decrease employment in response to a negative demand shock, but were equally likely to increase employment in response to a positive shock. In the nonmanufacturing sample, however, there were no differences in responsiveness between profitsharing and other firms. Restriction of the sample to consistently profitable firms and to firms with pension plans made little difference in the results, as did the inclusion of changes in the capital stock and wages. A question raised by this study is why the results differ between manufacturing and nonmanufacturing firms; one possibility is that there may be differences in the function of profitsharing plans, with profit sharing playing more of a stabilizing role in the generally more unstable manufacturing sector.

There is no clear conclusion from the research to date on the relationship between profit sharing and employment stability. As summarized in Table 4, Proposition 1 is generally supported in studies 2, 3, and 10, with negative evidence in studies 8 and 9, and mixed evidence in studies 5 and 6. Proposition 2 receives mixed, but generally favorable, support from studies 1, 4, and 7, and little support from study 2. Overall, there is somewhat more favorable than unfavorable evidence for the stability theory; at the least, these studies indicate that there is a good possibility that there are important differences between wages and profitsharing payments, and between the behavior of profitsharing firms and nonprofitsharing firms.

V. Data and Regression Results

This study provides additional evidence on the question of whether firms view profitsharing payments as part of the marginal cost of labor. The data set is related to the data set used in Kruse (forthcoming), both of which combine Standard & Poor's Industrial Compustat data with the federal Form 5500 pension-plan data. The previous data set used 15 years' worth of Compustat data (1971 to 1985) matched to one years' worth of deferred profitsharing-plan data (1984), which included the year of plan adoption so that longitudinal and panel comparisons of employment behavior could be made. In contrast, the current data set uses financial information from seven years' worth (1980 to 1986) of administrative pension-plan data, includes defined-benefit pension plans as well as profitsharing plans, and is limited to firms that report payroll data within the 1980 to 1986 period, so that labor-demand elasticities can be calculated. A detailed description of the data set is in Appendix A.

Under the assumption of Cobb-Douglas technology with two inputs (labor and capital), with input prices taken as given, the labor-demand function is specified as:

(3) $ln(L) = b/\Theta + (1/\Theta)ln(Q) - (\alpha/\Theta)ln(w) + (\alpha/\Theta)ln(r)$

where $ln(L) = ln(employment)$;
$ln(Q) = ln(output)$;
$ln(w) = ln(wage)$;
$ln(r) = ln(cost\ of\ capital)$;
Θ = measure of returns to scale ($= \alpha + \beta$);
b = constant;
α = elasticity of output with respect to capital;
β = elasticity of output with respect to labor;
α/Θ = elasticity of employment with respect to wages (substitution effect only).

This implies that the coefficients on $ln(w)$ and $ln(r)$ should be of equal magnitudes but opposite in sign; Clark and Freeman (1980) showed how this constraint is inappropriate in the presence of measurement error (particularly for capital cost) and differences in adjustment lags. Consequently, this constraint is not imposed in the empirical work reported here.

The point of the empirical work presented here is to test whether profitsharing payments behave as part of the short-run marginal cost of labor—i.e., whether they have the same elasticity as do base wages. Since the type of profit sharing analyzed here is deferred profit sharing (put into a pension trust), and since pension payments in themselves may behave differently than wages in the short run, profitsharing and defined-benefit payments will be analyzed separately. In this case, the total monetary labor cost is approximately $w(1+DB+PS)$, where DB (PS) is the ratio of the firm's defined benefit payments (profitsharing payments) to wages. Substituting this into equation (3), and using a Taylor's series expansion, leads to the equation to be estimated:[22]

$$(4) \quad ln(L) = \beta_0 + \beta_1 ln(Q) + \beta_2 ln(w) + \beta_3 DB + \beta_4 PS + \beta_5 ln(r).$$

If deferred profitsharing and defined-benefit payments are part of the short-run marginal cost of labor, then $\beta_2 = \beta_3 = \beta_4$; however, if defined-benefit payments are part of the short-run marginal cost of labor but profitsharing payments are not, then $\beta_2 = \beta_3$, but β_4 is closer to zero. Due to the possibility of endogeneity, the wage and pension variables have been instrumented.[23]

Descriptive statistics for the sample are presented in Table 5. The number of firms represented is 568, with 3,399 observations across the 1980 to 1986 period. As can be seen in the lower right corner, there were contributions to defined-benefit plans in 59 percent of these firm-years, and contributions to deferred profitsharing plans in 32 percent (as described in Appendix A, this does not include contributions to plans with thrift features). It is worth noting that utilities and banks constitute more than one-third of the sample; this heavy representation is due to their higher propensity to report payroll figures (the results, however, are not dependent on these two industries, since as will be seen, separate regressions for the manufacturing subsample give equivalent results). Within the profitsharing companies, the average ratio of profitsharing payments to total payroll (including the payroll of nonparticipants) is 0.022 over this period, while the average ratio of defined-benefit-plan payments to total payroll within companies with defined-benefit plans is 0.041.[24]

The regression results, presented in Table 6, are broadly consistent with the proposition that while wages and defined-benefit payments are viewed as part of the short-run marginal cost of labor, profitsharing payments are not. A rise in wages or defined-benefit payments is consistently associated with lower employment, while a rise in profitsharing payments does not have a consistent association with employment. As will be seen, however, it is not possible in most estimates to formally reject the hypothesis that defined-benefit and profitsharing payments have the same relationship to employment.

Table 5: Variable Definitions and Descriptive Statistics

Variable	Brief definition
Ln(emp)	Ln(company employment)
Ln(emp)(−1)	Ln(emp) lagged once
Ln(wage)	Ln(deflated company payroll/employment); Instrumented to remove effects of measurement error in Ln(emp); Instruments: ln(industry wage) with two lags (from Survey of Current Business), plus time trend
Ln(wage)(−1)	Ln(wage) lagged once
Ln(R)	Ln(cost of capital)—see Appendix A for construction
Ln(R)(−1)	Ln(R) lagged once
Ln(output)	Ln(company sales plus change in inventory of finished goods)
Ln(output)(−1)	Ln(output) lagged once
DB	Employer contribution to defined-benefit pension plans, as percent of payroll. Instrumented to correct for potential endogeneity of contributions Instruments: participant ratios (plan participants/employment) and vested ratios (fully vested/participants) for both defined-benefit and profitsharing plans, industry benefits as percent of industry payroll (lagged twice) (from Survey of Current Business), and time trend
DB(−1)	DB lagged once
PS	Employer contribution to profitsharing pension plans, as percent of payroll; Instrumented with the same instruments as for DB
PS(−1)	PS lagged once

Table 5: Variable Definitions and Descriptive Statistics (continued)

Descriptive statistics:

	Full sample Mean	(s.d.)	Manufacturing Mean	(s.d.)	Nonmanufacturing Mean	(s.d.)
Ln(emp)	1.580	(1.619)	2.639	(1.577)	1.161	(1.433)
Ln(wage)	10.091	(0.488)	10.140	(0.352)	10.072	(0.532)
Ln(R)	−1.944	(0.237)	−1.934	(0.217)	−1.947	(0.244)
Ln(output)	6.449	(1.602)	7.251	(1.738)	6.131	(1.426)
DB	0.024	(0.034)	0.024	(0.033)	0.024	(0.034)
PS	0.007	(0.017)	0.008	(0.018)	0.006	(0.017)
Number of obs.	3,399		965		2,434	
First-differenced						
Ln(emp)	0.034	(0.128)	−0.008	(0.115)	0.051	(0.129)
Ln(wage)	0.030	(0.142)	0.033	(0.104)	0.029	(0.155)
Ln(R)	0.058	(0.182)	0.044	(0.193)	0.064	(0.178)
Ln(output)	0.064	(0.158)	0.024	(0.149)	0.080	(0.159)
DB	−0.003	(0.021)	−0.005	(0.024)	−0.003	(0.020)
PS	0.000	(0.009)	0.001	(0.008)	0.000	(0.010)
Number of obs.	2,797		786		2,011	
Number of firms	568		166		402	

Industry breakdown:	Number of firms	Proportion of firm-years with contributions	
		ned benefit	Profit sharing
Mining	6	0.56	0.13
Construction	1	0.00	0.20
Food processing	12	0.87	0.51
Paper	14	0.94	0.21
Publishing	12	0.45	0.63
Chemicals	21	0.66	0.41
Petroleum	12	0.56	0.37
Steel/metals	17	0.90	0.35
Machinery	38	0.77	0.47
Trans. equip.	13	0.91	0.70
Other manuf.	27	0.71	0.58
Transportation	32	0.29	0.25
Communications	11	0.82	0.29
Utilities	128	0.80	0.18
Wholesale/retail	31	0.39	0.34
Banking	113	0.49	0.30
Ins./real estate	55	0.34	0.25
Services	25	0.14	0.48
Total	568	0.59	0.32

SOURCE: Data set constructed as described in Appendix A.

Table 6: Employment Equations

	Firm-intercept specifications (dep. var. = ln(emp))									First-difference specifications (dep. var. = change in ln(emp))[b]		
	All firms			Manufacturing			Nonmanufacturing			All	Mfg.	Non-mfg.
Regression:	(1)	(2)	(3)	(4)	(5)	(6)	(7)	(8)	(9)	(10)	(11)	(12)
Ln(emp)(−1)		0.221 (0.023)			0.222 (0.039)			0.138 0.027				
Ln(wage)[a]	−0.527 (0.020)	−0.526 (0.023)	−0.519 (0.030)	−0.357 (0.055)	−0.377 (0.058)	−0.397 (0.062)	−0.555 (0.023)	−0.604 (0.026)	−0.667 (0.039)	−0.483 (0.025)	−0.261 (0.058)	−0.541 (0.029)
Ln(wage)(−1)[a]			−0.142 (0.045)			−0.007 (0.083)			0.043 (0.059)			
Ln(R)	0.060 (0.012)	0.009 (0.014)	0.004 (0.014)	0.006 (0.021)	0.032 (0.023)	0.046 (0.024)	0.064 (0.017)	−0.016 (0.017)	−0.016 (0.017)	0.059 (0.011)	0.015 (0.017)	0.082 (0.013)
Ln(R)(−1)			0.057 (0.017)			0.016 (0.024)			−0.004 (0.022)			
Ln(Output)	0.608 (0.012)	0.546 (0.017)	0.542 (0.017)	0.598 (0.021)	0.572 (0.025)	0.565 (0.026)	0.590 (0.014)	0.553 (0.020)	0.551 (0.020)	0.493 (0.013)	0.496 (0.022)	0.489 (0.015)
Ln(Output)(−1)			0.147 (0.015)			0.149 (0.028)			0.094 (0.020)			
DB[a]	−0.345 (0.254)	−0.408 (0.280)	−0.472 (0.281)	−0.328 (0.372)	−0.143 (0.400)	−0.148 (0.401)	−0.334 (0.330)	−0.581 (0.360)	−0.603 (0.363)	−0.510 (0.223)	−0.154 (0.319)	−0.846 (0.292)
DB(−1)[a]			−0.437 (0.328)			−0.892 (0.449)			−0.044 (0.387)			
PS[a]	0.083 (0.297)	−0.105 (0.327)	−0.082 (0.328)	0.279 (0.426)	0.119 (0.474)	0.139 (0.474)	0.020 (0.386)	−0.191 (0.415)	−0.214 (0.415)	0.065 (0.260)	0.050 (0.374)	0.062 (0.336)

Table 6: Employment Equations (continued)

	Firm-intercept specifications (dep. var. = ln(emp))									First-difference specifications (dep. var. = change in ln(emp))[b]		
	All firms			Manufacturing			Nonmanufacturing			All	Mfg.	Non-mfg.
Regression:	(1)	(2)	(3)	(4)	(5)	(6)	(7)	(8)	(9)	(10)	(11)	(12)
PS(−1)[a]			0.127 (0.355)			−0.052 (0.528)			0.303 (0.444)			
Trend	0.013 (0.002)	0.019 (0.002)	0.016 (0.003)	−0.011 (0.003)	−0.009 (0.004)	−0.018 (0.006)	0.024 (0.002)	0.038 (0.003)	0.043 (0.004)	0.012 (0.001)	0.001 (0.002)	0.016 (0.002)
Firm intercepts	yes	yes	yes	yes	yes	yes	yes	yes	yes			
AR1 correction	yes	yes	yes	yes	yes	yes	yes	yes	yes			
R^2	0.993	0.995	0.995	0.996	0.998	0.998	0.992	0.994	0.993	0.381	0.424	0.360
n	3,399	2,797	2,797	965	786	786	2,434	2,011	2,011	2,797	786	2,011
Implied elasticities												
Wage	−0.527	−0.675	−0.661	−0.357	−0.485	−0.404	−0.555	−0.701	−0.624	−0.483	−0.261	−0.541
DB	−0.345	−0.524	−0.909	−0.328	−0.184	−1.040	−0.334	−0.674	−0.647	−0.510	−0.154	−0.846
PS	0.083	−0.135	0.045	0.279	0.153	0.087	0.020	−0.222	0.089	0.065	0.050	0.062
P-value for equality of wage and PS elasticities:	0.024	0.148	0.110	0.101	0.242	0.446	0.101	0.269	0.198	0.034	0.417	0.071

a. Instrumented as described in Table 5.

b. In first-difference regressions, independent variables (except for trend) are changes from $t − 1$ to t of variables listed at left.

Standard errors in parentheses. See Table 5 for variable definitions and descriptive statistics.

SOURCE: Data set constructed as described in Appendix A.

All regressions presented in Table 6 use firm-specific intercepts or first-differences, so that coefficients can be interpreted as within-firm employment responses. Four regressions are presented for each sample: the first using equation (4) without any lags; the second using a partial adjustment model with lags constrained to be equal (implemented by including the lagged dependent variable); the third using unconstrained single lags for each of the independent variables;[25] and the fourth using first-differences of all variables. The regressions using firm-specific intercepts have been corrected for first-order autocorrelation of disturbances.[26] At the bottom of the table are estimates of employment elasticities based on the equation coefficients.

Regression 1 indicates a highly significant wage elasticity of 0.527 (within the range of estimated elasticities summarized in Hamermesh [1986]), indicating that a 10 percent increase in wages is associated with a 5.3 percent decline in employment. The coefficients of primary interest are those on the DB and PS variables. The DB coefficient is -0.345, indicating that a compensation increase of 10 percent in the form of defined-benefit pension payments is associated with 3.5 percent lower employment. The PS coefficient is 0.083, indicating close to no relationship between employment and compensation increases in the form of profit sharing. F-tests reveal that constraining the coefficient of DB to be equal to the coefficient of $ln(w)$ cannot be rejected, while constraining the PS coefficient to be equal to the $ln(w)$ coefficient can be rejected at the 5 percent level ($p = 0.024$). This is consistent with Proposition 1—that profitsharing payments (unlike defined-benefit payments) are not seen as part of the short-run marginal cost of labor.

The same pattern emerges in the specifications reported in regressions 2 and 3 presented in Table 6. The estimated wage elasticities increase somewhat in magnitude (to -0.675 and -0.661) along with the DB elasticities (to -0.524 and -0.909), while the PS elasticities stay close to zero (-0.135 and 0.045). The statistical-significance levels for the constraint of equality between the wage elasticity and PS elasticity decline; the null hypothesis of equality can be rejected at a 15 percent level (p-values = 0.148 and 0.110). In the first-differenced equation for the full sample (regression 10), the wage and DB elasticities are close to equal (-0.483 and -0.510), while the PS elasticity is 0.065 and is significantly different from the wage elasticity at $p = 0.034$.

While the DB and PS coefficients are not estimated as precisely as the wage coefficient, the results in regressions 1 to 3 and 10 are consistent with the idea that defined-benefit payments are viewed as part of the short-run marginal cost of labor, while profitsharing payments are not (or at least to a much lesser extent). The results are not substantially different in the manufacturing and nonmanufacturing sub-samples. The estimated wage elasticities are roughly 20 log points lower for manufacturing firms than for nonmanufacturing firms. In none of these eight regressions can one reject the hypothesis that the coefficients on $ln(w)$ and DB are equal, which is consistent with the idea that defined-benefit pension payments are equivalent to wages in affecting the firm's labor demand. The equality of the wage and PS elasticities is rejected at the 10 percent level in regression 12, nearly rejected at the 10 percent level in regressions 4 and 6, and rejected at the 25 percent level in regressions 5 and 9. The smaller sample sizes in these subsamples clearly decrease the precision of estimates relative to those in the full sample, making it more difficult to reject constraints. Nonetheless, the pattern consistently shows that employment is less responsive to changes in profitsharing payments than to changes in wages and defined-benefit payments, which is consistent with Proposition 1.

VI. Conclusion

Profit sharing has recently been of interest for its potential both in enhancing productivity and in stabilizing employment and output. Evidence on profit sharing in the U.S. generally indicates that it has become more prevalent in the 1980s. The one source of data not based on surveys pertains to deferred profitsharing plans. This data source indicates that deferred profit sharing has grown steadily in the 1980s—from 13.3 percent of the private wage and salary work force in 1980 to 18.4 percent in 1986. The prevalence of these plans differs substantially by industry, with the greatest prevalence in manufacturing and finance, and the least prevalence in trade and construction.

Such growth makes research into the effects of profit sharing very topical. This paper focuses on the theorized effect of profit sharing on employment stability. Previous studies have addressed one of two general propositions derived from this theory: 1) firms do not view profitsharing payments as part of the short-run marginal cost of labor, which determines employment decisions; and 2) firms that pay a greater share of compensation as profit shares should have more stable employment. A review of nine studies on these propositions does not provide any clear answers: four studies provide results generally favorable to one of these propositions; two studies provide unfavorable results; and three studies provide mixed results.

A data set comprising 586 U.S. publicly traded companies over the years 1980 to 1986 was analyzed in order to test the first empirical proposition. If profitsharing payments are really "disguised wages," increases in those payments should have roughly the same employment consequences as increases in wages. The evidence indicates that this was not the case: while the employment elasticities with respect to wages were estimated in the 0.36 to 0.70 range, the elasticities with respect to profitsharing payments were consistently close to zero. The precision of the latter estimates, however, was not high: in only five of the twelve regressions could the hypothesis that the wage elasticities equal the profitsharing elasticities be rejected at or near a 10 percent level. Therefore, this should be regarded as weak evidence in support of the first proposition.

The conclusions from this paper can be summarized rather simply: Profit sharing appears to have been growing in the United States, and does not appear to act like wages in affecting employment. If true, what are the policy implications of the finding that profitsharing payments are not treated as part of the short-run marginal cost of labor? Weitzman's theory suggests that there may be a role for public policy encouragement of profit sharing, on the grounds that many of the benefits of employment and output stability are not internalized by those who set compensation packages. His suggestion is that tax incentives be given to firms and workers who adopt the appropriate form of profit sharing, which is the approach embodied in the Bumpers bill. Employees would be allowed to exclude from taxable income up to $3,000 in cash profitsharing benefits, if these benefits exceed 5 percent of the wages received during the year (and if other provisions regarding profit allocation and nondiscrimination are met). While the accumulated evidence is not sufficient to fully justify a large tax-incentive program, it is sufficient to warrant further research on the employment effects of profit sharing.[27]

More generally, apart from the stability theory, the growth of profit sharing is an intriguing development. Given that existing studies on productivity and employment suggest behavioral differences between profit sharing and conventional wage firms, further research is needed on whether these differences are real, and on whether profit sharing is a cause or symptom of different kinds of economic behavior.

Acknowledgments

This work was supported by a Henry Rutgers Fellowship. Useful comments have been made by Steve Director, Dan Hamermesh, Larry Katz, Jeffrey Keefe, Mark Killingsworth, Sanders Korenman, Alan Krueger, Olivia Mitchell, David Levine, and Martin Weitzman—although none bear responsibility for the final product. Useful research assistance was provided by Paul Hempel.

Appendix A: Description of Dataset

The data set was constructed by matching the Form 5500 datasets for 1980 to 1986 with Industrial Compustat firms reporting payroll information for at least two years in the 1980 to 1986 period (1978 and 1979 values of variables were included to allow for lags). The match was done with the IRS Employer Identification Number, which is common to both data sets.

Form 5500C data, covering plans with fewer than 100 participants, were not included, since the data are not reported each year: changes in reported profitsharing payments would largely reflect changes in reporting rather than actual payments, and efforts to interpolate would be biased toward average values, understating annual changes. Furthermore, the contribution sums for small pension plans are very small relative to the sums for large plans, so that excluding the small plans may be seen as a small increase in measurement error. Compustat companies with fewer than 100 employees, which could only have plans covering fewer than 100 employees, were excluded from the sample.

Approximately 20 percent of the Form 5500 plans had fiscal years (FY) that differed from the Compustat fiscal years. In these cases, the Form 5500 financial information was divided up to match the Compustat fiscal years. For example, for a firm with a Compustat 1983 fiscal year ending on December 31, 1983, and a pension plan 1983 fiscal year ending on June 31, 1984, half of the pension plan contributions reported for FY 1983 were allocated to 1983 and half to 1984. While this is unlikely to be literally the case, it is also unlikely to present any serious bias.

Monetary data were deflated by two-digit industry price deflators. The deflators employed are as follows. Manufacturing: value of shipments price index from the National Bureau of Economic Research Trade and Immigration Dataset. Mining: Producer Price Index for crude materials. Construction: GNP implicit price deflator for fixed investment (residential and nonresidential). Transportation: Consumer Price Index for transportation services. Communications: Consumer Price Index for telephone services. Utilities: Producer Price Index for finished energy goods. Wholesale/retail: Producer Price Index for finished consumer goods. Banking and services: GNP implicit price deflator for personal consumption expenditures on services.

Definitions of each variable follow.

Defined-benefit contributions : This represents the sum of all employer cash contributions to defined-benefit pension plans within a given year (adjusted as described above if the fiscal year did not match the Compustat fiscal year).

Profitsharing contributions : This represents the sum of all employer cash contributions to profitsharing pension plans that were not thrift-savings plans (i.e., there was no option for employees to make contributions). This understates the true amount of profitsharing contributions, since many true profitsharing plans have thrift-savings options; however, the exclusion was justified on the basis that many thrift-savings plans, while legally designated as "profit sharing," simply have employers match employee contributions in a fixed ratio (subject to the legal requirement, dropped immediately after this sample period, that total contributions in a year cannot exceed profits). Other defined-contribution plans (e.g., stock bonus, target benefit, money purchase) were excluded.

Employment : total employment as reported in Compustat, including full-time and part-time employees. No information on hours worked is available.

Wage : average annual wage in the company calculated as (labor and related expenses)/(total employment). The value of pension benefits, including all defined-benefit and defined-contribution plan payments, was subtracted from labor and related expenses if it was included in the original variable.

Output : company sales plus the change in inventory of finished goods.

Capital cost : This measure was computed as an average of the cost of equipment and structures, weighted by their shares in total investment as reported in the National Income and Product Accounts (NIPA). The cost for equipment (structures) was calculated as:

$$C = Q[r + \delta - \pi][(l - k - uz)/(1 - u)] \, ,$$

> where Q = implicit deflator for investment in nonresidential durable equipment (structures) (NIPA);
> $r = s(1/PE) + (1 - s)B$;
> s = equity/(equity plus long-term debt) for the firm;
> PE = median value of (company earnings/closing price) among the entire sample of Compustat companies;
> B = interest rate on long-term corporate bonds (Survey of Current Business);
> δ = annual depreciation rate, assumed as 0.135 for equipment, 0.0675 for structures;
> π = expected rate of inflation in equipment (structures), computed using a first-order autoregression on the fifteen years prior to the period being forecasted, with the forecast representing an average of forecasted values for the following five periods;
> k = rate of investment tax credit (= 0 for structures);
> u = corporate tax rate;
> z = present value of depreciation using the straight-line method: $(T/r)(1 - exp(-rT))$, where $T = 5$ for equipment and 15 for structures (other values were substituted with negligible differences in results).

Industry wage level : This variable, used as an instrument for company wages, was calculated as (total wages and salaries)/(total employment) from NIPA data as reported in the Survey of Current Business.

Industry benefit ratio : Calculated as [(total compensation) − (total wages and salaries)]/(total wages and salaries), using NIPA data as reported in the Survey of Current Business.

Participant ratio : Calculated as total number of participants in all defined-benefit (profitsharing) plans, divided by total employment as reported on the Form 5500.

Vested ratio : Calculated as the total number of fully vested participants in all defined-benefit (profitsharing) plans, divided by the total number of participants.

Several observations with extreme outliers in changes in the dependent variable were trimmed. In many of these cases, it is likely that the extreme employment change was due to a merger or divestiture with strong effects on the wage bill, making it less likely that wage changes are exogenous events. Including the outliers does not change the magnitude or pattern of results, but makes the estimates less stable. Separately for manufacturing and nonmanufacturing, companies were deleted if they had a *ln(L)* change in one year that was in the upper or lower 0.5 percent of the distribution. In manufacturing, companies with *ln(L)* changes of less than –0.5 or more than 0.5 were deleted (eight companies), and in nonmanufacturing, companies with *ln(L)* changes of less than –0.5 or more than 1 were deleted (nine companies).

Appendix B: Construction of Tables 2 and 3

Estimates of the number of participants in the different types of plans in Tables 2 and 3 were done in a two-step process. First, a count of participants for all plans with 100+ participants ("large plans") was made (from the Form 5500 tapes). Second, to obtain estimates of the number of participants in plans with fewer than 100 participants ("small plans"), a 10 percent sample of companies was taken from the Form 5500C for each year (using a selection procedure that would produce data for the same companies across the entire period).

Since small plans may report as seldom as once every three years, the small-plan estimate had to account for the plans that did not report in any given year. This was done by creating a three-year panel for each year being analyzed, during which time any plans existing in the given year would have had to report. The given year's extract was merged with the extracts for the two closest available years (e.g., 1984 was merged with 1983 and 1985, while 1986 was merged with 1984 and 1985). If a plan did not report in the given year, the number of participants for that plan was estimated as the reported participants from one of the other years in the three-year panel (if reports were made in both of the other years, the estimate was taken from the following year, or in the case of 1986, from the 1985 reports). Each of the seven years had their own three-year panel from which estimates for a given year were constructed.

The limitation of this method for estimating small-plan participants is that the data substituted from other years in the panel will not be exact, although a systematic bias is unlikely. A second estimation method was used for comparison purposes, in which participant data were not substituted from other years; instead, the participant totals for a given year were weighted to reflect the number of plans that did not report in that year. The limitation of this latter method is that the estimates are more sensitive to the average size of plans that report in a given year. Results were roughly comparable from the two methods.

For both the Form 5500 and Form 5500C data, quality checks were made to ensure reasonableness of reported data. For the Form 5500 (5500C) data, reported values of participants or employment greater than 200,000 (200) were individually checked; in a number of cases, the data were recoded to rectify obvious errors (using other reported data, including vested employees, excluded employees, and ineligible employees). The details of this unpleasant process can be further described to anyone who wishes to know.

Notes

1. See Florkowski (forthcoming) for a survey of profitsharing policies in 52 countries.

2. It should be noted that this only includes firms that made profitsharing payments in the given year. A firm that had a profitsharing plan, but did not make payments because there were no profits, would not be included.

3. This could easily depress the estimates of profitsharing companies in the early 1980s, because the recession presumably left many firms without profits to share. The 1987 number is also depressed because, unlike earlier years, payments into cash plans were not included.

4. This finding also has some support from longitudinal evidence: Freeman and Kleiner (1987) find that firms tend to drop profit sharing after a union election win. For evidence on union attitudes toward profit sharing, see Cardinal and Helburn (1987). For a general discussion of the relationship between unions and profit sharing, see Mitchell (1987).

5. The Form 5500C, filed by administrators of small pension plans, must also be filed whenever a plan is begun, terminated, or amended. In the years in which a Form 5500C is not filed for a small pension plan, the administrator must file a one-page report (Form 5500R). While the form 5500R contains very little information on the plan, the number of these findings can be used to weight the information gained from the Form 5500C filings. In this sense, the Form 5500 series is not a full census in any given year.

6. For example, 36 percent of the plans reported by members of the Profit Sharing Council of America in 1988 had 401(k) options (Bell [1989]).

7. Prior to 1987, while contributions to profitsharing pension plans were supposed to have some link to profits, the only specific constraint was that the contributions could not exceed profits in a given year. Starting in 1987, even this constraint was dropped.

8. This almost certainly overstates the number of true ESOPs in the economy; the U.S. General Accounting Office (1986) found in a survey that many plans listed as having "ESOP features" were not true ESOPs.

9. Another similarity between deferred profitsharing plans and ESOPs is that profitsharing plans may invest more than 10 percent of their assets in company stock (unlike defined-benefit plans). The main dissimilarity is that the initial contributions of company stock to an ESOP (or cash to buy stock) need have no relation to profits. In addition, ESOPs may be leveraged, allowing companies to deduct principal payments on loans made to ESOPs.

10. See, for example, Schroeder (1988).

11. Weitzman and Kruse (1990) review a wide variety of evidence on the relationship between profit sharing and company performance, and conclude that it generally points toward a positive link. The strongest evidence comes from 16 econometric studies, which strongly tend to show positive relationships between productivity and profitsharing measures.

12. The average compensation in a profitsharing firm would include a compensating differential for income risk, which may be positive (since income for employed persons will vary more in the profitsharing firm) or negative (since there would be a lower probability of losing income through layoffs, if Weitzman's theory is valid).

13. Although there may be some voluntary unemployment as workers in the disequilibrium situation search for jobs with higher levels of average compensation.

14. While nominal purchasing power would decrease in a profitsharing economy from the lower compensation per worker due to recessionary pressures, Weitzman argues that prices will also be more downwardly flexible in a profitsharing economy, causing a smaller decrease in real purchasing power.

15. This depends in part on how aggregate purchasing power is affected by compensation flexibility versus employment cutbacks; Summers and Wadhwani (1987) present evidence suggesting that compensation flexibility does not enhance employment and output stability.

16. Note that changes in $ln(w)$ and changes in b/w both represent approximate percentage changes in total compensation. The magnitudes of their coefficients should be equal if the form of compensation increases does not matter. This equation will be derived in the discussion of equations (3) and (4).

17. Excluded from this review are studies of the employment effects of employee ownership plans (e.g., Blanchflower and Oswald [1987]) and noneconometric evidence on employment growth in profitsharing firms (e.g., Blanchflower and Oswald [1988]).

18. This column denotes the findings as "favorable," "generally favorable," "mixed," or "unfavorable" with respect to the theory that profitsharing stabilizes employment. Obviously these designations are highly simplified and subject to dispute; they are intended to reflect the tone of the authors' conclusions based on their results.

19. The estimated wage coefficient is very close to zero, implying that the scale effect of wage increases is zero (while the capital-substitution effect is controlled through the inclusion of the captial stock).

20. Partially offsetting the apparent negative effect of lagged bonuses was a positive coefficient on the profitsharing dummy, indicating 2 percent higher employment associated with the presence of profit sharing, although the t-statistic was only 1.59.

21. Weitzman predicts greater output stability as well as employment stability with profit sharing. To the extent that Finseth's sales variable is measuring output changes rather than price changes, it is not an appropriate control (since the theory does not predict greater employment stability holding output fixed).

22. Under the assumption that total compensation is regarded as the marginal cost of labor, the fourth term of equation (3) becomes $-(\alpha/\Theta) \ ln \ [w \ (1+DB+PS) \ ]$, which can be expanded to $-(\alpha/\Theta)ln(w \ ) \ - (\alpha/\Theta) \ /ln(1+DB+PS)$ and approximated under a Taylor's series expansion as $- (\alpha \ /\Theta)ln \ (w) - (\alpha/\Theta)DB - (\alpha \ /\Theta \ )PS$ (assuming DB and PS are close to zero).

23. It is very unlikely that pension-plan payments are truly exogenous variables—they are likely to be influenced by the same things that influence product demand and therefore labor demand. This is especially clear in the case of profitsharing plans: payments will be high in profitable years when it is likely that the firm is expanding and low in unprofitable years when the firm is stable or contracting. It is also probably the case with deferred-benefits plans: although the firm must meet actuarial standards under ERISA for meeting the defined benefit, the firm may exceed the required payment in profitable years to insure against future unprofitable years, may not meet actuarial standards in unprofitable years, and/or may not need to make payment for years in which the pension portfolio has risen sufficiently to meet the standards. To correct for this potential endogeneity, the pension contribution variables have been instrumented on the participant ratios (participants/employment) and vested ratios (fully vested participant/total participants) for both profitsharing and defined-benefit plans, plus a time trend and industry benefit ratio (industry benefits/industry payroll) for two years prior.

The wage variable is defined as company wages and salaries divided by total employment; any measurement error in total employment will lead to a spurious negative correlation between $ln(L)$ and $ln(w)$. To correct for this, $ln(w)$ was instrumented on the current and two lagged values of ln (average industry wages), plus a time trend.

24. While profitsharing payments as a percentage of payroll are not high, it should be remembered that company behavior is driven by changes at the margin.If average profitsharing payments/payroll equal 0.02 in a labor market equilibrium, a profitsharing firm would view the short-run marginal cost of labor as being 2 percent lower than would a fixed-wage firm; also, it will maintain its work force in a recession, which would cause a fixed-wage firm to lay off 1 percent of its work force. Therefore, the employment behavior of profitsharing firms should be noticeably different from that of fixed-wage firms, even when such a small amount of compensation is paid as profit sharing.

25. In the presence of autocorrelation, the lagged dependent variable will be correlated with the error term. To remove this correlation, the lagged dependent variable was instrumented on the lags of the independent variables prior to an autocorrelation correction.

26. The autocorrelation coefficients prior to correction for regressions 1 to 9 were respectively 0.41, 0.29, 0.28, 0.35, 0.20, 0.20, 0.39, 0.28, and 0.28. In the presence of short time series on panel data, Solon (1984) shows that the autocorrelation coefficients were adjusted according to the AR(1) formula that he presents, without substantive changes in the results (not reported here).

27. Florkowski (forthcoming) suggests a research institute, similar to the National Institute of Occupational Safety and Health, which would support data collection and research of profit sharing.

Comments

Sharon P. Smith

The 1980s have seen a striking increase in profitsharing and shareholding schemes in many nations. The growth has been worldwide, though uneven—being most advanced in such countries as Australia, Denmark, France, Japan, Norway, Spain, the United Kingdom, and the United States; much less so in such countries as Ireland, Italy, and Switzerland; and quite uncommon in such developing areas as Hong Kong and Malaysia (Poole [1989], pp. 1-24).

James Meade (1986) has suggested in his paper "Different Forms of the Share Economy" that such schemes respond to a widespread perceived need to change the way in which labor is compensated and, as such, serve three purposes. The first is that profitsharing and employee-shareholding schemes maintain the advantages of market competition while putting greater emphasis on the common interests of labor and management and thereby increase productivity as workers perceive that their fortunes are directly linked to the firm's profitability. Indeed, John Purcell (Vice President of Weyerhaeuser Forest Product Company's Oregon division and chairman of the company's labor relations committee) has observed "With no incentive, you're only buying someone's time. With productivity pay, you're getting their brains, too" (Bureau of National Affairs, Inc. [1988], p. 175).

The second purpose that Meade has submitted for profitsharing and employee-shareholding schemes comes from a broader macroeconomic perspective. Meade has argued that these share arrangements set the rewards of both labor and capital so that expansionary monetary and fiscal policies stimulate increases in output and employment instead of inflation in wage rates, prices, and profit margins. This is the heart of Martin Weitzman's case for a "share economy" and the point of greater interest at this conference, namely that :

> The lasting solution to stagflation requires going inside the workings of a modern capitalist economy and correcting the underlying structural flaw directly at the level of the individual firm by changing the nature of labor remuneration. An alternative payment system where it is considered perfectly normal for a worker's pay to be tied to an appropriate index of the firm's performance, say a share of its revenues or profits, puts in place exactly the right incentives automatically to resist unemployment and inflation. (Weitzman [1984], p. 3)

101

The third purpose which Meade has suggested that share arrangements serve is that they change the distribution of income, wealth, and power to be more equal and fair which, in turn, will reinforce the sense of a "shared fate" of labor and capital.

Mr. Kruse's paper considers this recent heightened attention to profit sharing, focusing on the question of its ability to enhance employment stability. By way of introduction, he provides a concise exposition of the theoretical foundation for this role for profit sharing and an excellent summary of the empirical support. As Mr. Kruse clearly indicates, the evidence is mixed, at best, with no powerful data to support Weitzman's contention that this form of a "share economy" offers a "lasting solution to stagflation."

Mr. Kruse makes his contribution to this literature by offering an additional test of Weitzman's hypothesis, based on company-level profitsharing contribution data from the federal Form 5500 series and wage and employment data from Compustat. He provides a careful and most impressive analysis. Nevertheless, I have several comments to make.

In his review of the spread of profit sharing, Mr. Kruse noted that the data on profit sharing from a number of sources are incomplete, as they do not include companies that do not make contributions into the plan in the year. Moreover, no source provides a lengthy history of data. These problems are especially severe for cash profitsharing plans, which are, in fact, the smallest portion of all plans (as Mr. Kruse reports, 4.3 percent—deferred plans comprise 78.0 percent, and combination plans 17.6 percent). Better data are available through the Form 5500 reports that pension-plan administrators must file. These data enable Mr. Kruse to consider whether firms view profitsharing payments as part of the marginal cost of labor. He acknowledges that pension payments in general may behave differently than wages in the short run. Therefore, in his analysis, he tests separately whether profit sharing (that is, deferred profit sharing put into a pension trust) and defined-benefit pension payments have the same elasticity as wages.

There are two points to be noted here. The first is that although the deferred profit sharing is linked to the firm's performance, I would argue that the deferred aspect weakens the link. Indeed Weitzman (1984) has clearly indicated that "In a share system a worker's compensation is directly and automatically adjusted by some index of the firm's well-being, such as profits per worker or product price" (p. 82). It is this direct and automatic connection that is thought to motivate the worker and to be translated into increased productivity. To suggest that a deferred profitsharing/defined-contribution pension plan, which is not available until a later age for most workers without incurring a tax penalty, satisfies this definition requires some very special assumptions about workers' intertemporal substitutions and rates of discount.

The second point to be made here is that while Mr. Kruse acknowledges that there is an endogeneity problem because the same factors that influence product demand and labor demanded would influence pension-plan payments, he implies the problem applies equally to profitsharing and defined-benefit plans.

Mr. Kruse also suggests that contributions to defined-benefit plans, like those to a deferred profitsharing, defined-contribution pension plan, will probably be varied with firm performance—that the firm may exceed the required payment during profitable years to insure against unprofitable years when it may not be able to meet actuarial standards. However, given recent changes in Financial Accounting Standards Board (FASB) requirements with respect to pension accounting (which limit the acceptable methods and time periods for amortizing prior service costs), I find this proposition *highly* unlikely. Defined-benefit pension plan payments will be changed in response to changing assumptions on the performance of the plan fund, but these changes will not be made lightly or often.

Within this data set, the average profitsharing payments as a proportion of total payroll equal 0.022, while the average defined-benefit allocation as a proportion of total payroll amounts to 0.041. Mr. Kruse concedes that these numbers are small, but argues that because firm behavior is driven by changes at the margin, the difference in behavior between the profitsharing firm and the fixed-wage firm will be noticeably different. His illustration indicates that with a labor-demand elasticity of 0.5 and a recession in which a fixed-wage firm laid off 1 percent of its work force, the profitsharing firm would maintain its work force intact. In contrast, the Lincoln Electric Company, which Weitzman and others have cited as one of the few true immediate cash distribution profitsharing plans in the United States, pays year-end bonuses that have ranged from 70 percent to 130 percent over the postwar years, and have averaged about 105 percent (Weitzman [1984], p. 81). Using Mr. Kruse's same figures for labor-demand elasticity, in a severe downturn, where the fixed-wage firm would lay off one-half of its force, Lincoln Electric would retain its force intact—a difference that is surely noticeable.

The estimates that Mr. Kruse does obtain are weak. In only five of the regressions can the hypothesis that wage elasticity is equal to profitsharing elasticity be rejected at or near a 10 percent level. Mr. Kruse interprets these results as weak confirmation that the firm does not view profit sharing as part of the short-run marginal cost of labor and, consequently, that profit sharing can contribute to employment stability.

I, too, am convinced that profit sharing can contribute to employment stability. But, I would suggest that the weakness of the results obtained by Mr. Kruse is due to the analysis of profit sharing in the form of deferred-pension plans. If sufficient data on immediate cash distribution plans were available, I suspect that the results would be very strong indeed.

5

The Decline of Fringe-Benefit Coverage in the 1980s

Stephen A. Woodbury and Douglas R. Bettinger

Introduction

Fringe benefits that are voluntarily provided by employers have been a significant part of total compensation in the United States for over 30 years. Comprising mainly pensions and health insurance, voluntary benefits are broad in their coverage and significant as a percentage of total compensation. In 1988, 55 percent of wage and salary workers over age 24 were included in an employer-provided pension plan, and 72 percent were covered by employer-provided health insurance (see Table 1 below). In 1986, voluntary benefit expenditures accounted for nearly 8 percent of total compensation, or $158 billion out of total compensation costs of over $2 trillion.[1]

The voluntary provision of fringe benefits (hereafter simply "benefits") may be important to macroeconomic fluctuations and policy for at least two reasons. First, some benefits, such as employer-provided health insurance, represent a cost to the employer that is fixed—that is, independent of hours per worker—and this has special implications for firms' demand for labor (Ehrenberg [1971]). Second, as discussed by Hart and Woodbury (1990), benefits such as pensions are likely to be associated with a high degree of firm-specific human capital because they represent a form of deferred compensation. Acceptance of significant elements of deferred compensation may be interpreted as a signal by both the firm and its work force of their long-term employment intentions. Firms gain because they amortize specific investments over a longer period while workers obtain better job and income security. Further, there may be agency gains from pension provision in that deferred compensation may stimulate higher productivity (Lazear [1990]).

It follows that both wage and employment adjustments are likely to be different in the presence of benefits than would otherwise be the case. The fixed nature of some benefits and the deferred aspect of others imply less fluctuation in total compensation over the cycle than would otherwise occur. Also, the correlation between benefits and firm-specific human capital implies that employment fluctuations over the cycle will be less than would otherwise be the case (Oi [1962]; Becker [1975]; and Hashimoto [1981]).

The links between provision of benefits and labor-market adjustments suggest the importance of examining the extent of benefit coverage, the determinants of benefit coverage, and changes in that coverage over the past decade. In this paper, we use the

1979 and 1988 May Benefits Supplements to the Current Population Survey (CPS) to examine the pattern of benefit provision over the last 10 years. The first goal of the paper is to describe and explain the pattern of provision of benefits in each of the years considered. This is accomplished both by means of simple coverage proportions tabulated from the CPS (Section I), and by means of probit models of pension and health-insurance coverage (Section II). The second goal of the paper is to examine the degree to which changes in observable characteristics (including demographic characteristics, wages, and marginal tax rates faced by workers) can explain the drop in benefit provision that occurred during the last decade. This is accomplished by using the estimated probit models to simulate the impacts of various factors that have tended to increase and decrease benefit coverage (Section III).

I. Patterns of Benefit Coverage

How are pension and health-insurance benefits distributed among individual workers? What are the characteristics of those workers who are and are not covered? What changes have occurred over the past 10 years?

Supplements to the May CPS in 1979 and 1988 included questions about the inclusion of workers in employer-provided pension and health-insurance plans, and allow us to address these questions.[2] Regarding pensions, the survey questions of main interest are, "... does your employer or union have a pension plan or retirement plan for any of its employees (please do not include Social Security or Railroad Retirement)?" and "Are you included in such a plan?" Regarding private health insurance, the questions of interest concern whether a worker was included in an employer-provided group health insurance plan.[3] Note that our main concern is whether a worker is included in an employer-provided pension or health-insurance plan. Whether a plan covers others in the worker's household and whether a member of a household is covered by someone else's plan are distinct issues. Also, workers who are eligible for coverage but who choose not to be included in their employer's pension or health-insurance plan are counted as excluded from the plan.[4]

A limitation of the pension and health-insurance coverage questions asked in the May CPS Supplements is that they yield no information about the generosity or cost to the employer of either benefit. Increased health-insurance costs have led many employers to require covered workers to contribute to their health-insurance premiums, to pay higher deductibles and copayments, or to face restricted choice of health-care providers. A response to a simple question about inclusion in a plan fails to capture such changes. Hence, coverage is a rough measure of benefit provision that may mask important aspects of a benefit. Nevertheless, coverage data can offer important insights into the provision of benefits, and are the only data available at the level of the individual worker.[5]

A. Coverage Patterns

Table 1 displays data on the distribution of employer-provided pensions and health insurance among wage and salary workers over age 24 in 1979 and 1988. (The two annual samples exclude workers who were self-employed, in the military, who did not have positive earnings in the previous year, or who did not respond to the May Benefits Supplement.) The first row of the table shows that the percentage of workers who were included in an employer-provided pension plan dropped from 60 percent in 1979 to about 55 percent in 1988. Also, the first row shows that inclusion of workers in employer-provided group health-insurance plans fell from about 74 percent in 1979 to 72 percent in 1988. These changes, although they may perhaps seem small in percentage terms, are significant in absolute terms: a 1 percentage point change in coverage represents a change in coverage status of roughly 1 million workers. Also, the changes are statistically significantly different from zero at a high confidence level.

Additional figures in Table 1 show that there is much variation among different groups of workers in pension and health-insurance coverage. Women are less likely to be covered than men; younger and older workers are less likely to be covered than prime-age workers; Hispanics are less likely to be covered than other workers; workers with lower educational attainment are less likely to be covered; part-time workers, workers with less job tenure, workers in small establishments, and non-unionized workers all are less likely to be covered. These unadjusted coverage patterns (which do not control for other explanators of benefit coverage) hold for both pension and health-insurance provision in both 1979 and 1988.

There is much variation in benefit coverage by household status. Married household heads are most heavily covered. Spouses, relatives of the head, and other members of the household are much less likely to be covered.

There are also sharp differences in pension and health-insurance coverage among industries. Four industries (public administration; transportation, communications, and utilities; and manufacturing [both durable and nondurable goods]) all have relatively high percentages of workers covered by both pension and group health plans. Three other industries (wholesale trade; finance, insurance, and real estate; and professional and health services) follow closely. Agriculture, services (other than professional and health), and retail trade have relatively low percentages of covered workers. Industries that have relatively high pension coverage also tend to have relatively high health-insurance coverage: the Spearman rank correlation coefficient between industry pension and group health coverage is very high, 0.96.

The variation in benefit coverage across occupations is somewhat less striking than the variation across industries. Managers, professional/technical workers, and craft workers have had consistently high coverage by both pension and health-insurance plans. Farm workers, service workers, sales workers, and laborers have had relatively low coverage. But if we exclude agricultural industries and farm workers, it becomes clear that there is greater variation in coverage among industries than among occupations.

(text continued on p. 114)

Table 1:   Proportion of Workers Included in Employer-Provided Pension and Group Health Insurance Plans, 1979 and 1988

(Total number of workers in each category in parentheses)

Worker characteristics	Proportion included in pension plan		Proportion included in group health insurance plan	
	1979	1988	1979	1988
All workers	0.599	0.550	0.737	0.720
	(15,088)	(16,961)	(15,088)	(16,961)
Hourly wage and salary rate:				
(1982 dollars)				
Less than $4.51	0.209	0.193	0.356	0.360
	(1,905)	(2,771)	(1,905)	(2,771)
$4.51 to $6.50	0.428	0.436	0.608	0.652
	(3,015)	(3,564)	(3,015)	(3,564)
$6.51 to $10.00	0.641	0.607	0.792	0.791
	(4,584)	(5,175)	(4,584)	(5,175)
$10.01 to $14.00	0.778	0.743	0.886	0.868
	(3,523)	(3,250)	(3,523)	(3,250)
Greater than $14.00	0.812	0.768	0.903	0.896
	(2,061)	(2,201)	(2,061)	(2,201)
Gender:				
Female	0.495	0.496	0.613	0.630
	(6,401)	(8,025)	(6,401)	(8,025)
Male	0.676	0.598	0.829	0.800
	(8,687)	(8,936)	(8,687)	(8,936)
Age:				
25 to 34	0.566	0.474	0.743	0.715
	(5,485)	(6,018)	(5,485)	(6,018)
35 to 54	0.640	0.605	0.755	0.738
	(6,910)	(8,682)	(6,910)	(8,682)
55 to 64	0.626	0.601	0.740	0.714
	(2,262)	(1,846)	(2,262)	(1,846)
Greater than 64	0.220	0.284	0.350	0.436
	(431)	(415)	(431)	(415)
Ethnicity:				
White non-Hispanic	0.611	0.555	0.746	0.725
	(12,911)	(14,405)	(12,911)	(14,405)
Black	0.554	0.551	0.681	0.708
	(1,205)	(1,354)	(1,205)	(1,354)

**Table 1 (continued): Proportion of Workers Included in Employer-
Provided Pension and Group Health Insurance
Plans, 1979 and 1988**

(Total number of workers in each category in parentheses)

Worker characteristics	Proportion included in pension plan		Proportion included in group health insurance plan	
	1979	1988	1979	1988
Hispanic	0.472 (634)	0.429 (701)	0.677 (634)	0.649 (701)
Other	0.544 (338)	0.569 (501)	0.692 (338)	0.699 (501)
Education:				
0 to 8 years	0.426 (1,360)	0.342 (751)	0.622 (1,360)	0.579 (751)
9 to 11 years	0.509 (1,645)	0.411 (1,428)	0.685 (1,645)	0.615 (1,428)
12 years	0.592 (6,020)	0.525 (6,905)	0.725 (6,020)	0.692 (6,905)
13 to 15 years	0.606 (2,668)	0.558 (3,437)	0.754 (2,668)	0.722 (3,437)
16 years	0.678 (1,907)	0.627 (2,501)	0.793 (1,907)	0.799 (2,501)
Greater than 16 years	0.769 (1,488)	0.710 (1,939)	0.847 (1,488)	0.845 (1,939)
Household status:				
Married head	0.694 (7,105)	0.632 (6,784)	0.839 (7,105)	0.817 (6,784)
Married head with spouse covered	0.786 (1,617)	0.730 (2,073)	0.831 (1,858)	0.801 (2,269)
Not married head with family	0.565 (1,129)	0.487 (1,294)	0.758 (1,129)	0.736 (1,294)
Single head	0.563 (1,780)	0.544 (2,328)	0.766 (1,780)	0.771 (2,328)
Spouse	0.483 (4,131)	0.499 (5,193)	0.552 (4,131)	0.576 (5,193)
Spouse with head covered	0.539 (2,212)	0.594 (2,561)	0.537 (2,620)	0.567 (3,193)
Relative of head	0.525 (663)	0.417 (918)	0.706 (663)	0.672 (918)

(continued on next page)

Table 1 (continued): Proportion of Workers Included in Employer-Provided Pension and Group Health Insurance Plans, 1979 and 1988

(Total number of workers in each category in parentheses)

Worker characteristics	Proportion included in pension plan		Proportion included in group health insurance plan	
	1979	1988	1979	1988
Other	0.425 (280)	0.383 (444)	0.679 (280)	0.705 (444)
Employment status:				
Part time	0.232 (1,871)	0.247 (2,191)	0.299 (1,871)	0.287 (2,191)
Full time	0.651 (13,217)	0.595 (14,770)	0.799 (13,217)	0.784 (14,770)
Job tenure:				
Less than 1 year	0.271 (2,104)	0.195 (2,361)	0.511 (2,104)	0.456 (2,361)
1 to 2 years	0.411 (2,537)	0.331 (2,822)	0.643 (2,537)	0.608 (2,822)
3 to 5 years	0.555 (2,932)	0.503 (3,427)	0.703 (2,932)	0.709 (3,427)
6 to 10 years	0.709 (3,138)	0.660 (3,429)	0.803 (3,138)	0.788 (3,429)
11 to 15 years	0.789 (1,815)	0.763 (1,979)	0.857 (1,815)	0.855 (1,979)
Greater than 15 years	0.836 (2,562)	0.829 (2,943)	0.889 (2,562)	0.880 (2,943)
Employer size:				
Fewer than 25 workers	0.358 (5,201)	0.303 (5,409)	0.531 (5,201)	0.513 (5,409)
25 to 99 workers	0.622 (3,642)	0.553 (4,212)	0.765 (3,642)	0.744 (4,212)
More than 99 workers	0.786 (6,245)	0.731 (7,340)	0.892 (6,245)	0.858 (7,340)
Union membership:				
Covered	0.859 (4,507)	0.836 (3,848)	0.911 (4,507)	0.885 (3,848)
Not covered	0.488 (10,581)	0.466 (13,113)	0.663 (10,581)	0.671 (13,113)

Table 1 (continued): Proportion of Workers Included in Employer-Provided Pension and Group Health Insurance Plans, 1979 and 1988

(Total number of workers in each category in parentheses)

Worker characteristics	Proportion included in pension plan		Proportion included in group health insurance plan	
	1979	1988	1979	1988
Industry:				
Agriculture	0.263 (247)	0.188 (239)	0.368 (247)	0.360 (239)
Mining/Construction	0.576 (970)	0.459 (1,054)	0.733 (970)	0.633 (1,054)
Durable goods	0.740 (2,354)	0.671 (2,113)	0.908 (2,354)	0.874 (2,113)
Nondurable goods	0.669 (1,507)	0.619 (1,598)	0.851 (1,507)	0.841 (1,598)
Transportation, communication, and public utilities	0.715 (1,096)	0.682 (1,377)	0.857 (1,096)	0.857 (1,377)
Wholesale trade	0.580 (628)	0.476 (680)	0.815 (628)	0.760 (680)
Retail trade	0.333 (1,846)	0.303 (2,075)	0.570 (1,846)	0.531 (2,075)
Finance, insurance, and real estate	0.578 (900)	0.570 (1,236)	0.740 (900)	0.736 (1,236)
Business services	0.336 (423)	0.333 (714)	0.617 (423)	0.605 (714)
Personal services	0.168 (453)	0.149 (422)	0.318 (453)	0.379 (422)
Entertainment services	0.216 (111)	0.312 (138)	0.522 (111)	0.587 (138)
Professional and health services	0.632 (3,489)	0.595 (4,188)	0.676 (3,489)	0.691 (4,188)
Public administration	0.879 (1,064)	0.858 (1,127)	0.854 (1,064)	0.850 (1,127)

(continued on next page)

Table 1 (continued): Proportion of Workers Included in Employer-Provided Pension and Group Health Insurance Plans, 1979 and 1988

(Total number of workers in each category in parentheses)

Worker characteristics	Proportion included in pension plan		Proportion included in group health insurance plan	
	1979	1988	1979	1988
Occupation:				
Managerial	0.626 (1,719)	0.627 (2,333)	0.823 (1,719)	0.808 (2,333)
Professional/technical	0.736 (2,940)	0.675 (3,228)	0.798 (2,940)	0.796 (3,228)
Sales	0.410 (804)	0.387 (1,613)	0.618 (804)	0.643 (1,613)
Clerical	0.589 (2,959)	0.575 (2,983)	0.708 (2,959)	0.694 (2,983)
Craft	0.667 (2,169)	0.596 (2,075)	0.824 (2,169)	0.776 (2,075)
Operatives, except transport	0.606 (1,677)	0.558 (1,352)	0.824 (1,677)	0.803 (1,352)
Transport operatives	0.596 (554)	0.504 (815)	0.747 (554)	0.746 (815)
Laborers	0.574 (479)	0.477 (509)	0.724 (479)	0.682 (509)
Service	0.386 (1,626)	0.365 (1,827)	0.489 (1,626)	0.505 (1,827)
Farm	0.168 (161)	0.164 (226)	0.267 (161)	0.323 (226)
Region				
New England	0.569 (1,224)	0.516 (1,538)	0.727 (1,224)	0.714 (1,538)
Middle Atlantic	0.678 (2,206)	0.603 (2,298)	0.792 (2,206)	0.765 (2,298)
East North Central	0.659 (2,554)	0.598 (2,707)	0.786 (2,554)	0.729 (2,707)

Table 1 (continued): Proportion of Workers Included in Employer-Provided Pension and Group Health Insurance Plans, 1979 and 1988

(Total number of workers in each category in parentheses)

Worker characteristics	Proportion included in pension plan		Proportion included in group health insurance plan	
	1979	1988	1979	1988
West North Central	0.513 (1,441)	0.545 (1,761)	0.672 (1,441)	0.676 (1,761)
South Atlantic	0.584 (2,313)	0.533 (3,235)	0.736 (2,313)	0.720 (3,235)
East South Central	0.556 (859)	0.514 (870)	0.710 (859)	0.715 (870)
West South Central	0.526 (1,190)	0.503 (1,408)	0.670 (1,190)	0.704 (1,408)
Mountain	0.589 (1,341)	0.521 (1,582)	0.713 (1,341)	0.702 (1,582)
Pacific	0.601 (1,960)	0.557 (1,562)	0.736 (1,960)	0.707 (1,562)
Urban residence:				
SMSA	0.631 (8,707)	0.565 (9,079)	0.761 (8,707)	0.749 (9,079)
Non-SMSA	0.555 (6,381)	0.533 (7,882)	0.704 (6,381)	0.686 (7,882)

SOURCE: Authors' tabulations of wage and salary workers who responded to the May 1979 or May 1988 Employee Benefits Supplements to the Current Population Survey, who were 25 years old or older, who had earnings in the previous year, and who were not self-employed

Regional variations in both pension and health-insurance coverage are relatively minor. The Middle Atlantic and East North Central states consistently have relatively high coverage, but regional differences are minor compared with those that occur among certain other groupings of workers.

B. Changes in Coverage, 1979 to 1988

Further examination of the data reveals interesting changes over time in the pattern of benefit coverage within each subgroup. Most notable are changes by gender and ethnicity. Men have become less likely to be covered by a pension plan, whereas women have had no change in their probability of coverage. Also, women have become increasingly likely to be covered by health insurance, whereas men have become less likely to be covered. We will return to these changes in the pattern of coverage by gender below. Regarding ethnicity, the unadjusted coverage differential between white and black workers declined during the 1980s. But Hispanics appear to have fallen behind in benefit coverage.

Several other changes over time in benefit coverage are apparent. Variations in benefit coverage by age, education, and job tenure have become more pronounced. This suggests that the declines in pension and health-insurance coverage during the 1980s tended to fall most heavily on younger, less educated, lower seniority workers. In contrast, the unadjusted union-nonunion coverage differential has narrowed— especially in health-insurance coverage—suggesting that union members bore a disproportionately large share of the reduction in health insurance that occurred during the 1980s.

The figures on employer size deserve special consideration. The prevailing belief seems to be that small employers have been dropping workers from benefit coverage— especially health-insurance coverage—whereas larger employers have not. But the evidence suggests otherwise. Among employers with fewer than 25 workers, pension coverage dropped by about 5.5 percentage points between 1979 and 1988, and health-insurance coverage dropped by less than 2 percentage points. During the same period, both pension and health-insurance coverage among larger employers dropped by at least as much. In other words, the decline in benefit coverage during the 1980s did *not* fall most heavily on workers in smaller firms.

Regarding changes in coverage by industry, the decline in pension coverage seems to have been concentrated in agriculture, mining and construction, manufacturing, and wholesale trade, while the decline in health-insurance coverage was concentrated in mining and construction, and in wholesale and retail trade. (Some service industries actually experienced increased health-insurance coverage.) Regarding occupations, some of the more heavily covered groups experienced large declines in pension coverage—professional/technical workers, craft workers, operatives, and laborers— although health-insurance coverage declined only among craft workers and operatives. Finally, both pension and health-insurance coverage increased among spouses, but declined among household heads with a family. These latter changes would suggest a trend toward more equal treatment of workers in benefit provision, some of which could be a response to actual or anticipated regulation of pensions and health insurance.[6]

II. Models of Benefit Coverage

The coverage proportions displayed in Table 1 offer a picture of the distributional pattern of benefits, but provide little insight into the reasons for that pattern. For example, it is clear that female workers remain less likely than male workers to be included in employer-provided pension or health-insurance plans, but it is unclear whether this differential should be attributed to gender per se, or whether it is partly due to the part-time/full-time status, job tenure, industry of employment, or occupation of women. In order to address such issues, we specify and estimate models of pension and health-insurance coverage.

A. Model Specification

We assume that, in making decisions about how much labor to supply, workers respond not just to the wage, but to the total package of benefits. Similarly, we assume that employers consider total compensation costs—not just wage and salary costs— when they make employment decisions. It follows that interaction between labor supply and demand generates an equilibrium level of total compensation (not just an equilibrium wage) for a given group of workers.

The principle of equalizing differences offers an explanation of the division of total compensation into its components. Other components of compensation held constant, an increase in one form of benefit evokes a decrease in another benefit, or equilibrium is upset. That is, an increase in one benefit unaccompanied by a decrease in another draws more workers into the labor market, but employers demand fewer workers because they are paying greater total compensation to each. An excess supply of labor results, and some benefit or combination of benefits must fall to reestablish equilibrium. Together, supply and demand interactions and the principle of equalizing differences imply that all aspects of labor compensation are determined within a single system (Rosen [1974, 1983]; and Antos and Rosen [1975]). This line of reasoning leads to a reduced-form econometric specification of the components of compensation, in which each endogenous component is a function of the same exogenous variables (Woodbury [1983]; and Hamermesh and Woodbury [1990]). Focusing on a worker's probability of pension coverage (pension = 1 if covered, 0 otherwise) and health-insurance coverage (health insurance = 1 if covered, 0 otherwise), one could write a reduced form for each:

(1) Pr [pension = 1] = p (τ, c, z)

(2) Pr [health insurance = 1] = h (τ, c, z),

where τ represents the marginal tax-price of benefits facing the worker, c denotes a vector of individual worker characteristics that influence the probability of inclusion in a pension or health-insurance plan, and z represents a vector of characteristics of the labor market in which the worker is employed.[7]

Numerous hypotheses are testable within the framework set out in equations (1) and (2). Our model specifies the probability of benefit coverage to be conditional on the tax-price of benefits facing each worker (τ) because much existing work (Long and Scott [1982]; Alpert [1983]; Woodbury [1983]; and Sloan and Adamache [1986]) has suggested strongly that the exclusion of benefit contributions from income and payroll taxes has created an effective incentive for workers to demand compensation as benefits. That is, wage and salary earnings are taxed under federal and state income tax codes, whereas employer contributions to pensions and health insurance are not. Hence, there is a tax incentive to receive benefits—the higher the marginal tax rate on earnings, the lower the effective tax-price of benefits, and the stronger the incentive to receive benefits. Accordingly, we expect the probability of benefit coverage to be inversely related to τ.[8]

We construct the tax-price of benefits for each worker in the sample as:

(3) $\tau = 1 - t_f - t_s$,

where t_f is the federal marginal personal income tax rate faced by the worker, and t_s is the state marginal personal income tax rate.[9] In computing t_f and t_s for each worker in the sample, we have used the information available in the CPS to determine whether a worker would file a single or joint return, and have applied the appropriate (individual or household) income to the statutory tax structure in effect in each year at the federal level and in each state to impute t_f and t_s or each worker in the sample.[10]

The individual characteristics (c) controlled for in our specification of equations (1) and (2) are suggested by well-known theoretical considerations. Work by Dorsey (1982) suggests that it is important to use a lifetime measure of the wage in estimating income effects on the probability of benefit coverage. We follow his practice of constructing an estimate of each worker's lifetime wage rate, using available data on each worker in the sample.[11] We expect this constructed variable, which we refer to as the "lifetime wage," to be positively related to the probability of benefit coverage.

Controlling for other individual characteristics is suggested by human capital theory, which points to gender, age, ethnicity, education, household status, part-time/full-time status, and job tenure as important determinants of compensation. The theoretical relationship between age and benefit coverage has been explored extensively by Cymrot (1980), and leads us to expect that, because the value of benefits increases with age, the probability of benefit coverage should increase with age.

Dorsey (1982) has developed the relationship between job tenure and the probability of benefit coverage, and predicts that relationship to be positive as well.

Finally, our specification includes dummy variables (or sets of dummy variables) for employer size, union membership, industry, occupation, region, and urban residence in order to control for characteristics of the labor market in which the worker is employed [z in equations (1) and (2)]. In particular, we include these variables in order to gauge the impact of various structural changes in labor markets and the economy during the 1980s on benefit coverage.

We specify the dependent variable of the pension-coverage equation to equal one if a worker is included in an employer-provided pension plan, zero otherwise. Similarly, the dependent variable of the health-insurance equation is one if a worker is included in an employer-provided health insurance plan, zero otherwise. Because ordinary least squares (OLS) has undesirable properties when the dependent variable is zero-one, we estimate both the pension and health-insurance models by maximum likelihood probit (Goldberger [1964]; and Maddala [1983]).

B. Results of Estimation

Table 2 displays the results of estimating four probit models of benefit coverage: two modeling the worker's inclusion in a pension plan (one each for 1979 and 1988), and two modeling inclusion in a group health insurance plan (one each for 1979 and 1988). The table displays each probit coefficient along with its asymptotic standard error in parentheses, and with a "linear response" shown in square brackets. The linear response gives the change in the probability of being included in a benefit plan associated with a unit increase in the independent variable, holding constant all other variables.[12]

1. *Tax-Price and Lifetime Wage Effects.* Consider the response of benefit coverage to changes in the tax-price of benefits (τ). All four probit coefficients are negative, as expected, and the responses are quite large. For example, in 1979, a 100 percent increase in the tax-price of benefits (that is, a unit increase in $ln\ \tau$) would have lowered a worker's probability of pension coverage by 0.210, or by 21 percentage points (see the linear response figure, –0.210). This response was somewhat smaller in 1988, only 18 percentage points. Also, the response of pension coverage to a doubling of the tax-price of benefits is about twice the response of health-insurance coverage—the latter is about 8 or 9 percentage points (see the linear response figures, –0.094 and –0.076).[13] Overall, the results suggest a high degree of responsiveness of benefit coverage to changes in the tax-price of benefits, with increases in the tax-price (induced by decreases in the marginal tax rate on income) leading to lower benefit coverage.

Consider next the positive response of benefit coverage to increases in the lifetime wage. The results show that a 10 percent increase in the lifetime wage induces an increase of 0.7 to 1.7 percentage points in pension coverage, and a nearly 2 percentage point increase in health-insurance coverage.[14] The findings are consistent with the idea that the demand for benefits is income elastic—or that benefits are a "preferred form of compensation" (Lester [1967]).

Our findings on the response of benefit coverage to tax-prices and lifetime wages are generally consistent with existing evidence. For example, earlier research (Woodbury and Huang [1990]) has found that workers are more willing to substitute pensions and wages than they are willing to substitute health insurance and wages. This is corroborated by our finding in Table 2 that pension coverage responds more strongly than does health-insurance coverage to tax-price changes. The same earlier work also suggests, as do our findings in Table 2, that the demand for benefits is highly income elastic, and that income effects (that is, responses to changes in the lifetime wage) are stronger for health insurance than for pensions.

2. *Effects of Individual Characteristics.* The coefficients of the gender variable are particularly interesting because they suggest that, in 1979, gender had no significant impact on the probability of coverage, once other explanators of benefit coverage had been controlled for. In 1988, women actually had a higher probability of coverage than did men, other things equal. This is surprising in view of the large negative benefit differential that still exists between female and male workers (see the unadjusted coverage proportions in Table 1). It appears that variables such as household status, part-time status, job tenure, and union coverage more than explain the difference between female and male workers in benefit coverage.[15]

The relationship between age and pension coverage is not clear-cut. In 1979, the probability of pension coverage did not vary over workers aged 25 to 64, but in 1988 the expected positive relationship appears. We cannot explain this change, but the positive relationship for 1988 is consistent with the idea that the value of pension coverage increases with age (Cymrot [1980]). Age and health-insurance coverage are virtually unrelated over workers aged 25 to 64, suggesting that a worker's lifetime stock of human capital (as proxied in our model by the lifetime wage and education) is more important to health-insurance coverage than is age.

There is consistent evidence that blacks have had a lower probability than whites of being included in a health-insurance plan, even after controlling for other variables. This differential is interpretable as evidence of discrimination in benefit provision, although at roughly 5 percentage points it is somewhat smaller than recently estimated black-white differentials in earnings (Blau and Beller [1988]). There is only weak evidence of a black-white differential in pension coverage, and somewhat sporadic evidence of differentials between whites, on one hand, and Hispanics and other ethnic groups.

Workers with greater education have a higher probability of pension coverage, other things equal, but there is little evidence of a relationship between education and health-insurance coverage. Human capital theory leads one to expect benefit coverage to be, like a higher wage, part of the return to education. But the differential impact of education on pension and health-insurance coverage suggests that higher education either reflects or generates a lower subjective discount rate, and hence a greater

(text continued on p. 123)

Table 2: **Probit Models of Worker Inclusion in Employer-Provided Pension and Group Health Insurance Plans, 1979 and 1988**
(Standard errors in parentheses; linear response in brackets)

	Dependent variable			
	Included in pension plan		Included in group health insurance plan	
Explanatory variable	1979	1988	1979	1988
Intercept	−1.956	−2.774	−1.749	−1.786
	(0.382)	(0.330)	(0.401)	(0.339)
Log of tax price of fringe benefit	−0.543*	−0.451*	−0.290*	−0.226*
	(0.085)	(0.096)	(0.089)	(0.100)
	[−0.210]	[−0.178]	[−0.094]	[−0.076]
Log of lifetime wage	0.186	0.422*	0.604*	0.513*
(1982 dollars)	(0.146)	(0.135)	(0.154)	(0.140)
	[0.072]	[0.167]	[0.197]	[0.172]
Gender:				
Female	−0.107	0.080	0.143*	0.138*
	(0.073)	(0.059)	(0.077)	(0.062)
	[−0.041]	[0.032]	[0.047]	[0.046]
Male	—	—	—	—
Age:				
25 to 34	—	—	—	—
35 to 54	0.003	0.109*	0.055	−0.031
	(0.049)	(0.043)	(0.052)	(0.045)
	[0.001]	[0.043]	[0.018]	[0.010]
55 to 64	−0.038	0.206*	0.108	0.018
	(0.092)	(0.086)	(0.097)	(0.089)
	[−0.015]	[0.082]	[0.035]	[0.006]
Greater than 64	−0.681*	−0.188	−0.376*	−0.287*
	(0.141)	(0.131)	(0.140)	(0.131)
	[−0.263]	[−0.074]	[−0.123]	[−0.096]
Ethnicity:				
White non-Hispanic	—	—	—	—
Black	−0.103*	−0.040	−0.136*	−0.170*
	(0.050)	(0.046)	(0.051)	(0.046)
	[−0.040]	[−0.016]	[−0.044]	[−0.057]
Hispanic	−0.184*	−0.103	−0.036	−0.142*
	(0.064)	(0.060)	(0.066)	(0.060)
	[−0.071]	[−0.041]	[−0.012]	[−0.048]

(continued on next page)

Table 2 (continued): Probit Models of Worker Inclusion in Employer-Provided Pension and Group Health Insurance Plans, 1979 and 1988

(Standard errors in parentheses; linear response in brackets)

Explanatory variable	Included in pension plan		Included in group health insurance plan	
	1979	1988	1979	1988
Other	−0.124	−0.076	−0.111	−0.174*
	(0.084)	(0.071)	(0.086)	(0.072)
	[−0.048]	[−0.030]	[−0.036]	[−0.058]
Education:				
0 to 8 years	−0.252*	−0.250*	−0.034	−0.006
	(0.062)	(0.070)	(0.064)	(0.068)
	[−0.097]	[−0.099]	[−0.011]	[−0.002]
9 to 11 years	−0.156*	−0.174*	−0.030	−0.110*
	(0.046)	(0.049)	(0.048)	(0.048)
	[−0.060]	[−0.069]	[−0.010]	[−0.037]
12 years	—	—	—	—
13 to 15 years	0.044	−0.008	0.033	−0.017
	(0.038)	(0.036)	(0.047)	(0.037)
	[0.017]	[−0.003]	[0.011]	[−0.006]
16 years	0.148*	0.064	0.096	0.077
	(0.051)	(0.050)	(0.055)	(0.053)
	[0.057]	[0.025]	[0.031]	[0.026]
Greater than 16 years	0.184*	0.053	0.094	0.086
	(0.067)	(0.064)	(0.071)	(0.068)
	(0.071)	[0.021]	[0.030]	[−0.029]
Household status:				
Married head	0.126*	0.011	0.072	0.063
	(0.050)	(0.044)	(0.055)	(0.048)
	[0.049]	[0.004]	[0.023]	[0.021]
Married head with spouse covered	0.179*	0.307*	−0.152*	−0.146*
	(0.047)	(0.041)	(0.047)	(0.043)
	[0.069]	[0.121]	[−0.050]	[−0.049]
Not married head with family	0.177*	−0.062	0.058	0.007
	(0.061)	(0.054)	(0.066)	(0.057)
	[0.068]	[−0.025]	[0.019]	[0.002]

Table 2 (continued): Probit Models of Worker Inclusion in Employer-Provided Pension and Group Health Insurance Plans, 1979 and 1988

(Standard errors in parentheses; linear response in brackets)

Explanatory variable	Dependent variable			
	Included in pension plan		Included in group health insurance plan	
	1979	1988	1979	1988
Single head	—	—	—	—
Spouse	−0.142*	−0.213*	−0.429*	−0.423*
	(0.057)	(0.049)	(0.061)	(0.053)
	[−0.055]	[−0.084]	[−0.140]	[−0.142]
Spouse with head covered	0.231*	0.369*	−0.254*	−0.181*
	(0.047)	(0.042)	(0.047)	(0.042)
	[0.089]	[0.146]	[−0.083]	[−0.061]
Relative of head	−0.090	−0.069	−0.270*	−0.165*
	(0.069)	(0.059)	(0.072)	(0.060)
	[−0.035]	[−0.027]	[−0.088]	[−0.055]
Other	−0.124	−0.130	−0.119	−0.043
	(0.096)	(0.077)	(0.098)	(0.079)
	[−0.048]	[−0.051]	[−0.039]	[−0.014]
Employment status:				
Part time	−0.562*	−0.526*	−0.720*	−0.851*
	(0.043)	(0.039)	(0.040)	(0.036)
	[−0.217]	[−0.208]	[−0.235]	[−0.286]
Full time	—	—	—	—
Job tenure:				
Less than 1 year	—	—	—	—
1 to 2 years	0.276*	0.310*	0.278*	0.329*
	(0.043)	(0.042)	(0.042)	(0.039)
	[0.107]	[0.123]	[0.091]	[0.111]
3 to 5 years	0.596*	0.728*	0.381*	0.566*
	(0.042)	(0.040)	(0.042)	(0.038)
	[0.230]	[0.288]	[0.124]	[0.190]
6 to 10 years	0.911*	1.073*	0.590*	0.789*
	(0.044)	(0.041)	(0.044)	(0.040)
	[0.352]	[0.425]	[0.192]	[0.265]
11 to 15 years	1.134*	1.262*	0.772*	0.959*
	(0.053)	(0.049)	(0.056)	(0.050)
	[0.438]	[0.500]	[0.252]	[0.322]

(continued on next page)

Table 2 (continued): Probit Models of Worker Inclusion in Employer-Provided Pension and Group Health Insurance Plans, 1979 and 1988

(Standard errors in parentheses; linear response in brackets)

Explanatory variable	Included in pension plan		Included in group health insurance plan	
	1979	1988	1979	1988
Greater than 15 years	1.322*	1.492*	0.912*	1.032*
	(0.054)	(0.049)	(0.056)	(0.049)
	[0.510]	[0.591]	[0.297]	[0.347]
Employer size:				
Fewer than 25 workers	—	—	—	—
25 to 99 workers	0.472*	0.435*	0.445*	0.452*
	(0.032)	(0.031)	(0.033)	(0.031)
	[0.182]	[0.172]	[0.145]	[0.152]
More than 99 workers	0.799*	0.801*	0.788*	0.700*
	(0.032)	(0.029)	(0.034)	(0.030)
	[0.309]	[0.317]	[0.257]	[0.235]
Union membership:				
Covered	0.802*	0.715*	0.540*	0.375*
	(0.032)	(0.032)	(0.035)	(0.035)
	[0.310]	[0.283]	[0.176]	[0.126]
Not covered	—	—	—	—
Urban residence:				
SMSA	−0.005	−0.044	−0.061*	0.105*
	(0.028)	(0.025)	(0.030)	(0.026)
	[−0.002]	[−0.017]	[−0.020]	[−0.035]
Non-SMSA	—	—	—	—
Industry (13 categories)	Included	Included	Included	Included
Occupation (10 categories)	Included	Included	Included	Included
Region (9 categories)	Included	Included	Included	Included
Log-likelihood	−3,459.6	−3,754.1	−2,722.7	−2,838.0
Sample size	15,088	16,961	15,088	16,961

SOURCE: Probit estimates from samples of wage and salary workers who responded to the May 1979 or May 1988 Employee Benefits Supplements to the Current Population Survey. Coefficients statistically significantly different from zero at the 5-percent level of confidence or better are denoted by an asterisk (*).

demand for future income, in this case in the form of retirement income. The same lower discount rate would not necessarily generate a higher demand for health insurance.

Three striking relationships between household status and benefit coverage appear in these data. First, if a household head is married to a worker who is covered by a pension plan, that head is more likely to be covered by a pension plan; and symmetrically, if a spouse is married to a worker who is covered by a pension plan, the spouse is more likely to be covered by a pension plan. But for health insurance, the relationship is different: If the household head is married to a worker who is covered by health insurance, that head is less likely to be covered by health insurance, and if the spouse is married to a worker who is covered by health insurance, then the spouse is less likely to be covered by health insurance. Together, these findings imply that the pension coverage of one partner complements the pension coverage of the other; the coverage of one does not serve as a substitute for pension coverage of the other.[16] But couples appear to avoid double coverage by health insurance—here, coverage by one partner does substitute for coverage by the other. These relationships are well worth further research.

A second finding on household status is that being a spouse lowers the probability of benefit coverage, with the negative relationship stronger for health insurance than for pension coverage.[17] Third, there is evidence that relatives of the household head are less likely to be covered by health insurance.

The results show clearly that part-time workers are over 20 percentage points less likely than full-timers to be covered by either a pension or health insurance. It would be surprising not to observe such a strong relationship in view of the requirement imposed by many benefit plans that an individual work full time to be eligible.

The relationship between the probability of benefit coverage and job tenure (or seniority) is interesting because it provides evidence on the relationship between benefits and firm-specific human capital. The results show that the probability of benefit coverage rises with years of job tenure. Moreover, the probability of pension coverage rises more sharply with tenure than the probability of health-insurance coverage. These findings are consistent with the hypothesis that workers with larger investments in specific human capital are more likely to receive benefits, both as a return to specific investment, and as part of the firm's effort to retain those workers. In particular, we would expect the relationship between pension coverage and tenure to be stronger than that between health insurance and tenure if pensions, as deferred compensation, serve as an especially effective means of binding workers to a firm.

3. *Characteristics Associated with Labor Markets.* The results show that workers in larger firms are much more likely to receive benefits than workers in small firms. Also, the relationship between firm size and coverage is stronger for pensions than for health insurance. The positive relationship between firm size and compensation has been interpreted variously, although a recent investigation by Brown and Medoff (1989) concludes that higher compensation in large firms results in part from large

firms' recruitment and retention of higher-quality workers. The relationship could also be interpreted as evidence of a return to specific human capital (Oi [1983]).

Union membership dramatically increases the probability of benefit coverage, and the relationship is again stronger for pensions than for health insurance. But the results suggest that the influence of unionism on health-insurance coverage may be diminishing. The 5 percentage point decline between 1979 and 1988 in the response of health coverage to union membership cannot be explained by cyclical factors; both 1979 and 1988 were years of economic growth, four to five years into a recovery.

All of the models shown in Table 2 control for industry (13 categories), occupation (10 categories), and region of residence (9 categories). We do not report these coefficient estimates to economize on space, and because they suggest relatively minor relationships between benefit coverage and (in particular) occupation and region, once other variables have been controlled for. Three relationships that are consistent across the two samples do exist. First, workers in five industries (durable goods manufacturing; wholesale trade; finance, insurance, and real estate; professional and health services; and public administration) are significantly more likely to be covered by pensions than are workers in other industries, even after controlling for other variables. Also, workers in three industries (durable goods manufacturing; nondurable goods manufacturing; and wholesale trade) are significantly more likely to be covered by health insurance. The important point here is that manufacturing industries are not alone in providing relatively high benefit coverage. Second, the only significant occupational differential is for clerical workers, who are 5 to 10 percentage points more likely to have pension and health-insurance coverage than workers in other occupations. Third, workers in New England are less likely to be covered by pensions, whereas workers in the Southern and Mountain states were (in 1988 only) about 5 percentage points more likely than workers elsewhere to be covered by health insurance, other things equal. This last finding suggests that the Sunbelt's increased importance in providing employment is not a likely source of declining benefit coverage. (A table that includes the industry, occupation, and region coefficient estimates is available from the authors on request.)

4. *Equality of the Models and Summary.* A likelihood-ratio test for equality of coefficients in the 1979 and 1988 pension models rejects the hypothesis that the two models are the same. Similarly, a test for equality of coefficients in the 1979 and 1988 health-insurance models is also rejected, although somewhat less strongly.[18] That the 1979 and 1988 models differ suggests that the structure by which benefit coverage is determined has changed over the last decade. This will have implications for the degree to which we can explain changes over time in benefit coverage, a topic we pursue in the next section.

The findings in Table 2 are interesting both for the relationships that are demonstrated and for those that do not turn up. It is clear that the tax-price of benefits and a relatively small number of individual characteristics—the lifetime wage, education (for pensions), household status, part-time/full-time status, and job tenure—are most important to the probability of pension and health-insurance coverage. Employer size and union membership are also very important, but several factors that are widely believed to be important to benefit coverage—gender, age, ethnicity, industry, occupation, region of residence, and urban/nonurban location—are of decidedly lesser importance.

III. Simulating Changes in Coverage during the 1980s

What factors led to the overall declines in pension and health-insurance coverage during the 1980s? We can address this question by means of simulation. One approach is to select the 1979 probit models of pension and health-insurance coverage, and to substitute into each model changes in the explanatory variables that occurred between 1979 and 1988. This process yields predicted (or explained) changes in pension and health-insurance coverage, based on the structure of benefit provision given by the 1979 models and on the observed changes in explanatory variables. Choosing the 1979 models implies making an out-of-sample forecast for the 1980s using the information we had about the structure of benefit coverage prior to the 1980s. An alternative approach is to use the 1988 probit models and to substitute into each of them the changes in the explanatory variables that occurred between 1979 and 1988. We pursue both of these approaches presently. Each approach yields a slightly different picture of how changes in the explanators of benefit coverage have led to realized changes in benefit coverage.

Table 3 displays means for 1979 and 1988 of all explanatory variables in the models. Some of the evident changes over time that can be seen in the table include: a significant increase in the tax-price of benefits (induced by the steady reduction in marginal income tax rates during the 1980s); a modest decline in the lifetime wage (resulting from the relatively low expected lifetime earnings of the baby-boom cohort); an increase in the proportion of workers who are women; shifts in both the age and educational composition of workers; a decline in the importance of married household heads, and an increase in the importance of single heads and spouses; a movement of workers into larger firms; an erosion of union coverage; a decline in the importance of durable goods manufacturing; a shrinking proportion of craft workers and operatives and a growing proportion of sales workers; and some regional and urban/nonurban shifts.

Table 4 illustrates the importance of these changes for pension and health-insurance coverage. Consider first the pension-coverage simulation based on the 1979 model, which is displayed in the first column. The bottom three rows (under "Totals") show that pension coverage actually dropped by 4.9 percentage points between 1979 and 1988, and that our 1979 model and the changes in explanatory variables during 1979 to 1988 predict a drop of 3.25 percentage points. This leaves a residual, or unexplained change, of 1.65 percentage points, which is attributable to changes in the underlying structure of pension coverage (that is, to changes in the coefficients of the pension-

(text continued on p. 131)

Table 3:   Means of Explanatory Variables

Explanatory variable	1979	1988
Log of tax-price of fringe benefits	−0.381	−0.309
Log of lifetime wage (1982 dollars)	2.509	2.473
Gender:		
Female	0.424	0.473
Male	0.576	0.527
Age:		
25 to 34	0.363	0.355
35 to 54	0.458	0.512
55 to 64	0.150	0.109
Greater than 64	0.028	0.024
Ethnicity:		
White non-Hispanic	0.856	0.849
Black	0.080	0.080
Hispanic	0.042	0.041
Other	0.022	0.030
Education:		
0 to 8 years	0.090	0.044
9 to 11 years	0.109	0.084
12 years	0.399	0.408
13 to 15 years	0.177	0.203
16 years	0.126	0.147
Greater than 16 years	0.099	0.114
Household status:		
Married head	0.471	0.400
Married head with spouse covered by pension	0.107	0.122
Married head with spouse covered by health insurance	0.123	0.134

Table 3 (continued):   Means of Explanatory Variables

Explanatory variable	1979	1988
Not married head with family	0.075	0.076
Single head	0.118	0.137
Spouse	0.274	0.306
Spouse with head covered by pension	0.147	0.151
Spouse with head covered by health insurance	0.174	0.188
Relative of head	0.044	0.054
Other	0.018	0.026
Employment status:		
Part time	0.124	0.129
Full time	0.876	0.871
Job tenure:		
Less than 1 year	0.140	0.140
1 to 2 years	0.168	0.166
3 to 5 years	0.194	0.202
6 to 10 years	0.208	0.202
11 to 15 years	0.120	0.117
Greater than 15 years	0.170	0.173
Employer size:		
Fewer than 25 workers	0.345	0.319
25 to 99 workers	0.241	0.248
More than 99 workers	0.414	0.433
Union membership:		
Covered	0.299	0.227
Not covered	0.701	0.773
Industry:		
Agriculture	0.017	0.016
Mining/construction	0.064	0.062
Durable goods	0.156	0.124

(continued on next page)

Table 3 (continued):   Means of Explanatory Variables

Explanatory variable	1979	1988
Nondurable goods	0.100	0.094
Transportation, communications, and public utilities	0.073	0.081
Wholesale trade	0.042	0.040
Retail trade	0.122	0.122
Finance, insurance, and real estate	0.060	0.073
Business services	0.028	0.042
Personal services	0.030	0.025
Entertainment services	0.007	0.008
Professional and health services	0.231	0.247
Public administration	0.070	0.066
Occupation:		
Managerial	0.114	0.137
Professional/technical	0.195	0.190
Sales	0.053	0.095
Clerical	0.196	0.176
Craft	0.144	0.122
Operatives, except transport	0.111	0.080
Transport operatives	0.037	0.048
Laborers	0.032	0.030
Service	0.108	0.108
Farm	0.010	0.014
Region:		
New England	0.081	0.091
Middle Atlantic	0.146	0.135
East North Central	0.169	0.160
West North Central	0.095	0.104
South Atlantic	0.153	0.191
East South Central	0.057	0.051

Table 3 (continued):   Means of Explanatory Variables

Explanatory variable	1979	1988
West South Central	0.079	0.083
Mountain	0.089	0.093
Pacific	0.130	0.092
Urban residence:		
SMSA	0.577	0.535
Non-SMSA	0.423	0.465

SOURCE: Authors' tabulations of wage and salary workers who responded to the May 1979 or May 1988 Employee Benefits Supplements to the Current Population Survey, who were 25 years old or older, who had earnings in the previous year, and who were not self-employed or in the military.

Table 4:   Decomposition of Changes in Pension and Health Insurance Coverage, 1979-1988

| Change in coverage attributable to changes in: | Percentage point change in pension or health insurance coverage | | | |
| | Based on 1979 model | | Based on 1988 model | |
	Pension	Health insurance	Pension	Health insurance
Tax-price of fringe benefits	−1.49	−0.67	−1.27	−0.54
Lifetime wage	−0.26	−0.72	−0.61	−0.63
Gender composition	−0.20	0.23	0.15	0.23
Age composition	0.17	0.00	−0.07	−0.04
Ethnic composition	−0.03	−0.02	−0.02	−0.04
Educational composition	0.87	0.21	0.70	0.19
Household composition	−0.44	−0.91	−0.13	−0.81
Full-time/part-time composition	−0.11	−0.12	−0.11	−0.15
Job tenure	−0.01	−0.01	−0.01	−0.01
Employer size composition	0.70	0.58	0.71	0.54
Union membership	−2.22	−1.26	−2.03	−0.90
Industry composition	−0.13	−0.22	0.08	−0.18
Occupational composition	0.02	−0.25	−0.07	0.01
Regional composition	−0.11	−0.03	0.02	0.17
Urban residence	0.01	0.08	0.07	−0.15
Totals:				
Actual change	−4.90	−1.70	−4.90	−1.70
Explained change	−3.25	−3.13	−2.59	−2.33
Residual change	−1.65	1.43	−2.31	0.63

SOURCE: Authors.

coverage model).[19] Hence, the 1979 model and changes in observable variables are able to account for about two-thirds of the total change in pension coverage that occurred during the decade of the 1980s.

Which changes in explanatory variables had the largest impacts on pension coverage during the 1979 to 1988 period? The figures in the first column of Table 4 decompose the total change into its component parts. The decomposition suggests that increases in the tax-price of benefits (that is, decreases in marginal income-tax rates) reduced pension coverage by 1.5 percentage points. Even more important was the influence of declining union coverage, which pulled down pension coverage by over 2 percentage points. Shifts in household composition—mainly an increase in the proportion of the labor force composed of spouses—accounted for a decline of roughly two-fifths of a point. Other negative influences are quite minor. Shifts in the educational and employer-size compositions of employed workers put upward pressure on pension coverage, according to the simulation. The upshot of these negative and positive impacts on pension coverage is an explained decrease in pension coverage of 3.25 percentage points.

The pension simulation based on the 1988 model (third column of Table 4) tells a similar story. Although the 1988 model is able to account for a smaller part of the total change in pension coverage during the 1980s (only 2.59 out of the total decline of 4.9 percent points), this decomposition also points to increases in the tax-price of benefits and declining unionism as the most important negative influences on pension coverage in the 1980s.

Consider next the simulation of health-insurance coverage that is based on the 1979 model (second column of Table 4). The bottom three rows of the column show that health coverage actually dropped by 1.7 percentage points between 1979 and 1988, and that the simulation (that is, the 1979 model and changes in explanatory variables during the 1980s) predicts a drop of slightly over 3 percentage points. The residual in this case is positive (1.43 percentage points); the simulation overestimates the actual decline in health-insurance coverage. The main explanators of the drop in health-insurance coverage are (as with pensions): the increasing tax-price of benefits, the decline in union membership, and shifting household composition.[20] In addition, the modest decline in the lifetime wage had a negative impact on health-insurance coverage. Changes in the educational and employer-size composition of employed workers tended to increase health-insurance coverage, but not by enough to offset the impacts of the negative factors.

The health-insurance simulation based on the 1988 model (fourth column of Table 4) points to the same factors in explaining the drop in health-insurance coverage. The only significant difference is that the simulation based on the 1988 model comes closer to predicting the actual decline in health-insurance coverage (the predicted decline is 2.33 percentage points, the actual was 1.7 points).

There are two possible explanations for the tendency of our health-insurance simulations to overpredict the drop in health coverage during the 1980s. First, it is likely that changes in benefit coverage occur with a lag, and that our simulations suggest a long-run level of health-insurance coverage that is below the currently observed (short-run) level. If so, then in 1988 there was underlying pressure for additional reductions in health-insurance coverage, and we would expect to see further reductions. Second, some factor for which our models do not control may have induced employers to maintain a higher level of health-insurance coverage than they would have absent this uncontrolled factor. The most likely such influence is actual or anticipated regulation of health insurance, including mandating of employer-provided health benefits.

This second point raises a general caveat that should be made about the simulations, which is that the models on which they are based do not control for all factors that may have exerted pressure on benefit provision during the 1980s. For example, changes in benefit regulation and changes in the cost to employers of providing benefits may have influenced benefit coverage, but the cross-sectional framework and data we have used here impedes consideration of such factors (on these points, see Woodbury [1990]). Correcting this shortcoming should be high on the agenda for future work.

The pension and health-insurance coverage simulations are consistent with each other in suggesting that changing tax policy, declining unionism, and shifts in household composition (mainly an increase in the proportion of the labor force composed of spouses) played key roles in reducing benefit coverage during the 1980s. The pension simulations suggest that, absent these three changes, pension coverage would have decreased by only about 1 percentage point between 1979 and 1988, rather than declining by nearly 5 percentage points. Similarly, the health-insurance simulations suggest that, absent the same three changes, health-insurance coverage would not have fallen, and may have increased, rather than falling by 1.7 points.

Some factors that one might expect to be important to the decline of benefit coverage turn out to be rather insignificant. Chief among these perhaps are shifts in the industry and occupational mix of employment, and the reasons for their impotence is clear. The decline of manufacturing industries has not resulted in significant declines in benefit coverage because various nonmanufacturing industries that have grown (finance, insurance, and real estate; professional and health services) also have high-benefit coverage.[21] Regarding occupation, the cross-sectional relationships between benefit coverage and occupation are minor to nonexistent, once other factors are controlled for (see section II.B.3).

IV. Summary and Conclusions

During the 1980s, the percentage of workers over age 24 who were covered by pensions fell by 5 percentage points (from 60 to 55 percent), and the percentage covered by health insurance fell by nearly 2 points (from 74 to 72 percent). Coverage figures shown in Table 1 suggest that certain groups of workers—workers who were younger and less skilled, and unionized workers—bore a larger share of these declines than did others (see Section I).

Models of pension and health-insurance coverage estimated in Section II show that a worker's probability of being covered by employer-provided benefits can be explained by a relatively small number of variables. Especially important is the tax-price of benefits facing a worker, which reflects the degree to which the tax-favored treatment of benefit contributions creates an incentive to receive compensation as benefits. The results suggest strongly that decreases in marginal tax rates on earned income (which translate into an increase in the tax-price of benefits) lead to sharply lower probabilities of coverage by pension and health-insurance plans. The expected lifetime wage also plays a central role in explaining the probability of benefit coverage, with increases in the lifetime wage leading to increases in the probability of coverage. Additional individual characteristics that are important to the probability of benefit coverage include education (for pensions), household status, part-time/full-time status, and job tenure. The features of the labor market that are most important to whether a worker is covered by benefits are employer size and union membership. Several factors that are widely believed to be important to benefit coverage—gender, age, ethnicity, industry, occupation, region of residence, and urban/nonurban residence— turn out to be much less important than the former variables.

Simulations presented in Section III and Table 4 suggest that roughly two-thirds to three-quarters of the decline in pension coverage that occurred during the 1980s can be explained by successive reductions in marginal tax rates on earned income (which reduced the tax advantages of receiving compensation in the form of benefits), and by reductions in union membership. Further, the decline in health-insurance coverage is almost fully explained by these two factors. Shifting household composition (chiefly an increase in the proportion of the labor force composed of spouses) and a modest fall in lifetime expected wages (resulting from the influx of the baby-boom generation) also put downward pressure on health-insurance coverage. In fact, our health-insurance simulations predict a greater decline in health coverage than actually occurred, which we interpret as evidence of underlying pressure for further reductions in health coverage. The reductions in benefit coverage that occurred during the 1980s cannot be attributed to changes in the gender or ethnic composition of the labor force, or to changes in the industrial, occupational, or regional mix of the labor force.

The results have two main implications for labor-market adjustments that occurred during the 1980s and that may occur in the future. First, a clear implication is that the moderate wage growth of the 1980s was not compensated by large increases in benefit coverage. That is, workers were not substituting more rapid growth of benefits for slower wage growth during the 1980s, but rather were accepting slower growth of total compensation.[22]

Second, the decline of benefit coverage during the last decade could be interpreted as an attempt by firms to reduce fixed costs of employment and the degree to which labor represents a quasi-fixed factor.[23] Although the comparative static implications of such changes have been developed and are well understood (Hart [1984]), the dynamic implications are much less well understood.[24] Nevertheless, we could speculate that if benefit coverage is highly correlated with firm-specific human capital, then a decline in benefit coverage is a signal that a smaller proportion of the labor force can expect to be carried through a severe recession because of their long-run value to their employer. This suggests in turn that firms have lowered their costs of labor-force adjustment, so that changes of both employment and compensation may be greater in any future recession than in the past. Of course, it could also suggest that during the recovery of the 1980s firms restructured employment so that continuous adjustment would be less costly and more feasible. The continuous adjustment made possible by such improved flexibility might lessen the need for major cyclical adjustments.

Combined with some unabashed speculation, the results offer suggestions about how benefit coverage might change during the 1990s.[25] The four factors that drove down benefit coverage during the 1980s—tax policy, declining unionism, shifting household composition, and a modest decline in the average lifetime wage—may well behave differently in the 1990s. Since it is highly unlikely that marginal income tax rates will continue to fall, we do not expect changes in tax policy to continue as a source of declining benefit coverage. The future of union membership is difficult to predict, but it is clear that further erosion of membership would pull down benefit coverage. Changes in household composition are notoriously difficult to forecast, and it seems foolish to speculate on how changes in the 1990s might influence benefit coverage. In contrast, it is clear that the birth-dearth cohort that is now entering the labor force will have higher lifetime wages than the baby-boom cohort that preceded it. Hence, changes in lifetime wages, which put a drag on benefit coverage during the 1980s, will start to put upward pressure on benefit coverage during the 1990s.

The simulations suggest that two factors put significant upward pressure on benefit coverage during the 1980s—increasing educational attainment of the work force and the increasing proportion of the labor force employed in larger firms. Both are associated with an increasing level of skill and specialization of labor, and we would expect these and other variables that reflect skills and specialization to increase during the 1990s. Large firms will become increasingly important as competition from abroad stiffens, average job tenure should increase as the baby-boom cohort ages, enhanced educational attainment of new and continuing labor-force participants can be expected, and (as already noted) the birth-dearth cohort will have higher lifetime wages than earlier groups. All of these factors will imply a labor force with increased human capital (both general and firm-specific), and benefits—especially deferred compensation such as pensions—will be used as a means of rewarding workers with greater skill and of retaining workers with greater specialization.

Some labor-force changes did not lead to significant changes in benefit coverage in the past, and probably will not in the future. For example, although the gender, age, and ethnic compositions of the work force are expected to change significantly in the 1990s, the benefit-coverage models suggest that these changes are unlikely to alter significantly pension or health-insurance coverage (that is, the coefficients of the gender, age, and ethnicity variables are small). Similarly, changes in the industrial, occupational, and regional compositions of the work force are unlikely to drive important changes in benefit coverage, for reasons already discussed.

To summarize, we draw three main conclusions from the empirical findings. First, the decline of benefit coverage during the 1980s was based primarily on reductions in tax incentives for workers to receive benefits and on declining union membership. The decline was not a function of a declining manufacturing sector, shifts in occupational mix, or regional movements of labor. Nor was it driven by changes in the gender, age, or ethnic compositions of the labor force. Second, the health-insurance simulations predict an even larger decline in health coverage than actually occurred, which suggests that there may be underlying pressure for further decreases in health-insurance coverage as firms make long-run adjustments. Third, increases during the 1990s in factors closely related to skills and specialization of labor can be expected to place upward pressure on benefit coverage (especially pension coverage). Whether this upward pressure from increased skills and specialization will be enough to outweigh the negative effects of any further declines in union membership and rising costs of benefit provision (due to regulation or higher health-care costs) is an open question.

Acknowledgments

For discussions and comments on an earlier draft, we are grateful to seminar participants at Michigan State University, to conference participants at the Federal Reserve Bank of Cleveland, and to B.K. Atrostic, Barry Chiswick, Daniel S. Hamermesh, Andrew Hogan, the editors, and particularly to Robert A. Hart. We are also grateful to Ellen Maloney and Claire Vogelsong for help in preparing the paper.

Notes

1. This was down from a peak of 8.7 percent of total compensation in 1982. These expenditure figures are derived from published and unpublished National Income and Product Accounts data, and reported in Woodbury and Huang (1988, Table 1). Total compensation is defined as the sum of wages and salaries, legally required nonwages (OASDHI, Unemployment Insurance, and Workers' Compensation), and voluntary nonwages (pensions and health insurance). Voluntary nonwages also include life insurance, supplemental unemployment benefits, and profit sharing, which together are roughly 5 percent of voluntary nonwages.

2. There was also a benefits supplement to the CPS in May 1983, which we do not use here.

3. We will use "coverage" and "inclusion in a plan" interchangeably. That is, coverage by a pension plan means that a worker who continued working for his or her current employer would receive benefits upon retirement. Similarly, coverage by health insurance means that specified medical treatments received by the worker would be paid for by the insurance.

   In recent years, the March Annual Demographic File of the Current Population Survey has also included data on pension and health-insurance coverage. The main advantage of using the May Employment Benefits Supplement is that the May Supplement includes data on job tenure and employer size, which are unavailable in the March file.

4. Available CPS data are insufficient to distinguish voluntary from involuntary exclusion from a plan, although the survey instrument would suggest otherwise. If such a distinction could be made, it might be useful to examine eligibility for inclusion in a benefit plan rather than actual inclusion. In Section III below, we include controls for spouse's coverage by a plan in our probit models of benefit coverage. This is a effort to control for the most important factor that might induce a worker to opt out of a plan for which he or she is eligible.

5. The Survey of Employer Expenditures for Employee Compensation (EEEC) made available firm-level data on fringe-benefit expenditures that were nationally representative, but which ended in 1977. On fringe-benefit data sources, see Antos (1983).

6. The Employee Retirement Income Security Act and the Internal Revenue Service Code have provided for increasingly equal treatment of workers with regard to pension provision. Section 89 of the Internal Revenue Code, which was passed with the Tax Reform Act of 1986 but never became effective, would have done the same for health insurance. Although section 89 never went into effect, many employers have been faced with state regulations that may have a similar impact.

7. Note that equations (1) and (2) are similar to the benefit-coverage models estimated by Mellow (1982), Dorsey (1982), and Andrews (1985).

8. Evidence on benefit contributions in the 1980s suggests that reductions in marginal tax rates during the 1980s blunted the incentive to receive benefits, and played a key role in reducing the proportion of compensation received as benefits (Woodbury and Huang [1988]; and Hamermesh and Woodbury [1990]).

9. Two other possible measures of the tax-price of fringe benefits account for the fact that the social security tax does not apply to benefit contributions. These alternative measures can be written as:

$$\tau^a = 1 - t_f - t_s - t_{ss},$$

where t_{ss} is the social security tax rate (zero for workers over the maximum contribution level, the FICA rate otherwise) and

$\tau^{b} = (1 - t_f - t_s - t_{ss})/(1 + t_{ss})$.

We have used these alternative measures of the tax-price of benefits and obtained results that are virtually identical to those using the equation (3) definition of τ. For further discussion and evidence on these different measures of the tax-price of benefits, see Hamermesh and Woodbury (1990).

10. This approach required us to create a file of married couples, and to use available income and earnings data on each couple to impute the joint filing tax rate.

11. The Lifetime Wage estimate is obtained as follows. First, we regress the natural logarithm of each worker's hourly wage and salary earnings on variables capturing gender, age, ethnicity, education, industry, and occupation. Second, we obtain a predicted wage for each worker at age 55-64 by substituting into the estimated wage equation each worker's characteristics (except age, which we set equal to 55 to 64). Third, we standardize each worker's wage to age 60 by inflating or deflating the predicted wage by 2 percent annually. This last step is necessary to take account of secular growth of wages, and reflects the fact that a worker who is 30 today can expect his or her wage to grow not just because of aging, but because of economywide wage growth as well.

12. Formally, the linear response is the partial derivative of the probability of inclusion in a plan with respect to the independent variable, evaluated at the sample mean. The linear response is obtained by multiplying the probit coefficient (which can be thought of as a z-value from a standard normal density) by the slope of the cumulative normal function at the mean of the dependent variable. See Maddala (1983).

13. Note that the mean (logarithmic) tax-price of fringe benefits was –0.381 in 1979 (implying a 32 percent average marginal tax rate, or a tax-price of fringe benefits of 0.68) and –0.310 in 1988 (implying a 27 percent average marginal tax rate, or a tax-price of fringe benefits of 0.73). It follows that between 1979 and 1988 the tax-price of fringe benefits fell by about 7 percent on average, which implies an expected drop in pension coverage of about 1.5 percentage points (0.21 times 0.07 = 0.015), and an expected drop in health-insurance coverage of about two-thirds of a percentage point.

14. We use the 1979 point estimate of the response of pension coverage to changes in the lifetime wage even though the coefficient is statistically significantly different from zero only at the 10-percent level of confidence. All other lifetime wage coefficients are statistically significantly different from zero at better than the 5-percent level of confidence.

15. As discussed below, spouses have a lower probability of benefit coverage than household heads, and all spouses in the CPS samples are women. It follows that there may be discrimination against *married* women in benefit provision, but not against unmarried women. We are working out a more complete analysis of the response for gender-related differences in benefit coverage.

16. The findings could also be evidence of marital sorting, with individuals who have similar tastes for retirement income and abilities to command a job with a pension selecting each other.

17. As noted above, all spouses in our samples are women, implying that there may be discrimination against married women in benefit provision. It does not follow that there is discrimination against other women, however, as already discussed.

18. Both Chi-square statistics are in excess of that needed to reject equality of coefficients at the 1-percent level of confidence.

19. This method of decomposing changes into explained and unexplained components is due to Blinder (1973) and Oaxaca (1983). The unexplained component can also arise because of factors for which we have been unable to control in our model.

20. The shifts in household composition that tended to pull down health-insurance coverage were the decreased proportion of the labor force composed of spouses and, to a smaller degree, the decreased proportion of the labor force composed of married household heads.

21. To the extent that declining union membership can be attributed to the secular decline of manufacturing, declining unionism may be picking up some of the effects of the changing importance of industries and occupations. But it has not been shown that industry and occupational shifts can account for the decline of unionism (Dickens and Leonard [1986a, 1986b]).

22. Evidence on benefit expenditures also supports this conclusion—see Woodbury and Huang (1988) and Hamermesh and Woodbury (1990).

23. This is especially true of the portion of the decline that can be traced to declining unionism, in that declining unionism seems to stem at least in part from employer resistance to unions (Freeman [1989]). Also, employers could be restructuring employment in response to the falling demand for benefits that has come from reduced tax incentives.

24. See Hamermesh (1988) for a development to what is known about adjustment costs and demand for labor.

25. It goes without saying that such government policies as mandated employer-provision of health insurance or adoption of national health insurance would render the health-insurance model and simulations obsolete, and would make any attempt at forecasting quite useless. Also, we can only speculate on how changes in the costs of providing benefits will influence coverage.

Comments

David Lewin

Stephen Woodbury and Douglas Bettinger (hereafter WB) identify two goals of their chapter, "The Decline of Fringe-Benefit Coverage in the 1980s": to describe and explain patterns of fringe-benefit coverage and to identify the determinants of changes in such coverage over the 1977 to 1988 period in the United States. The two specific categories of fringes treated in their paper are health-care and retirement (or pension) benefits. The apparent motivations for this research are that "fringe benefits may be important to macroeconomic fluctuations" and that "wage and employment adjustments [of firms] are likely to be different in the presence of benefits than would otherwise be the case."

However, a close reading of WB's paper suggests that their research stems not so much from theoretical or even public-policy concerns as from an empirical "fact," namely, that both health-care and pension-benefit coverage of adult workers in the United States declined during the 1980s. Hence, an assessment of WB's research must rest primarily on how well they explain this declining fringe-benefit coverage.

What do the authors find? Using the Current Population Survey (CPS), WB show that the proportion of workers over age 24 that was covered by employer-provided pension plans declined from 60 percent in 1979 to about 55 percent in 1988, and that the proportion covered by employer-provided group health insurance plans declined from about 74 percent to 72 percent over the same period. These declines are nontrivial or, put differently, they are statistically significant in as much as a one percentage point change in coverage by either type of benefit plan represents about one million workers. Note, further, that while benefit coverage declined less over the 1979 to 1988 period among small than among large firms, employee-benefit coverage was far more prevalent in large than in small firms.

With respect to the determinants of changes in fringe-benefit coverage, WB's regression analyses show that increases in the tax-price (that is, the marginal income tax rate) of such benefits are associated with large reductions in the probability of workers being covered by pension plans and health-care plans. Recognize that the effective tax-price of fringe benefits in the United States increased during the 1980s, when marginal rates on earnings via wages and salaries were reduced. Increases in workers' lifetime wages are significantly positively associated with the probability of pension and health-care-plan coverage (especially the latter), which suggests that wages and benefits are complementary goods. At the start of the period examined by WB, 1979, women were as likely as men to be covered by pension and health-care plans, *ceteris paribus;* by 1988, women were more likely to be covered than men. This finding, which WB label "surprising," is claimed to prevail because other factors controlled for in their regression equations (e.g., household status and job tenure) account for ostensible male–female differences in fringe-benefit coverage.

Additionally over the 1979 to 1988 period, younger workers continued to be as likely as older workers to be covered by a health-insurance plan, but became less likely than older workers to be covered by a pension plan; the well-known positive effects of unionization on both types of benefit coverage declined markedly. Unmarried heads of households with a family present became less likely than unmarried heads of households without a family present to be covered by pension and health-care plans; spouses became more likely to be covered by a pension plan when their spouses are so covered, but became less likely to be covered by a health-care plan when their spouses are so covered. The probability of benefit coverage, especially pension coverage, rises with job tenure, but did so more strongly at the end than at the start of the 1979 to 1988 period; and industry differentials in pension coverage decreased, whereas industry differentials in health-care coverage remained about the same. Variables such as ethnicity, region, and residential location had minor effects on *changes* in the pension and health-care benefit coverage of workers in the United States between 1979 and 1988.

To understand better how the aforementioned variables, as well as others, influenced the overall declines in the pension and health-care benefit coverage of adult workers in the United States during the 1980s, WB performed computer simulations in which they constructed 1979 probit linear probability models of pension and health-care coverage and then substituted changes in the explanatory variables for the 1979 to 1988 period. Predictions about changes in benefit coverage in the 1980s could then be compared to changes that actually occurred during the period.

This simulation approach led to a predicted 3.25 percentage point decrease in pension coverage between 1979 and 1988, whereas such coverage actually declined by 4.90 percentage points during these years. The simulations indicated, further, that increases in the tax-price of fringe benefits reduced pension-benefit coverage by 1.5 percentage points, and the decline of union membership reduced pension-benefit coverage by 2.0 percentage points. These two factors dominated the simulation-based predicted increases in pension coverage owing to (predicted) changes in such factors as employee wages, education, and employer size over the 1979 to 1988 period. Concerning health-care coverage, WB's simulations predicted a 3.13 percentage point decrease in coverage between 1979 and 1988, but the actual decline in such coverage was 1.70 percentage points during the period. Here, too, increases in the tax-price of fringe benefits and the decline of union membership had the largest negative effects on health-care coverage of the U.S. work force. These reductions more than offset the putative increases in health-care benefit coverage that were attributed by the simulation to increases in worker education and to changes in the size and composition of company work forces during the 1980s.

The starting point for a critical analysis of WB's research is the lack of theory underlying the work. Although in their introduction to the paper, the authors raise the question of why pension and health-care benefit coverage exist at all, they chose not to take up this question in the remainder of their paper. In fact, such institutional arrangements as pension and health-care plans appear to be inconsistent with a purely competitive labor market; therefore, it is important to understand not only why these arrangements exist, but why they continue to encompass a large majority of the United States work force (more so in the case of health-care benefits than pension benefits). Indeed, the authors tell us that they expect to see increased fringe-benefit coverage of workers during the 1990s. Thus, WB's work is very largely an empirical exercise, albeit an important exercise.

With respect to the empirical analysis, numerous questions and caveats arise. First, the CPS data used by the authors are not capable of shedding light on employer behavior in terms of the rationale underlying employers' decisions to adopt, not adopt, or abandon pension and health-care benefit programs. This is because the CPS elicits responses from employees (as well as the unemployed and those not in the work force), not employers. More will be said about this point later in this discussion. Second, no information or discussion about the nonresponse rates associated with the CPS is provided by the authors, which raises questions about the validity of CPS data for use in this type of research. Third, in a related point, the validity of employee responses about the pension and health-benefit coverages provided by their employers is open to question, especially in light of other evidence showing that large proportions of employees (and employers) are ignorant or misinformed about the provisions, coverages, benefits, and costs of the benefit plans in which they are enrolled.

Fourth, and as noted by WB, their analysis fails to include data about changes in fringe-benefit regulation or changes in the costs to employers of providing fringe benefits to employees. Numerous surveys and other data show that fringe-benefit costs, especially health-care costs, were the most rapidly rising category of costs for U.S. employers during the 1980s. It might well be that changes in these costs were the dominant variable affecting changes in actual pension and health-care coverage in the United States during the 1980s, possibly negating the effects of other variables examined by the authors. At the least, recognition of these omitted variables calls into question WB's specification of their estimating equations and the robustness of their empirical results.

Fifth, the construction of certain independent variables is open to question, especially variables that are insufficiently discussed by the authors. For example, employer size is restricted to three categories, the largest of which is the category "more than 99 workers." Yet, because benefit coverage has been shown in several studies to be strongly positively correlated with employer size, it would be helpful to have had a more stratified, parsimonious categorization of this variable. Similarly, the union-coverage variable is specified in simple dichotomous form, yet strong arguments can be made for using either or both a percentage-of-workers-organized or a percentage-of-workers-covered-by-collective-bargaining-contracts form of this variable. The latter specifications would seem to be especially appropriate in light of the importance of declining union membership to pension and health-care coverage in the United States during the 1980s, as shown by WB.

Sixth, WB speculate that the decline of pension and health-care benefit coverage during the 1980s resulted from "attempts by firms to reduce fixed costs of employment and the degree to which labor represents a quasi-fixed factor." This is a plausible speculation, especially if it is connected to another of the authors' speculations, namely, that "moderate wage growth of the 1980s was not compensated by large increases in benefit coverage" (a connection not made by the authors). The problem with, or limitations of, these speculations, however, is that the authors provide absolutely no data by which the reader can assess the behavior of employers concerning fringe-benefit coverage of workers. A modest survey of employers or even a case study or two could shed some light on this presumably important "variable." In this respect, WB's work continues a long tradition of research by economists that treats the firm (employer) as a black box. Put differently, it simply is not enough to "control" for the firm's industry and size when researchers study a problem that they themselves believe is subject to firm (as well as worker) behavior—as WB clearly believe is the case with fringe benefits. Thus, WB should enlarge their research design, which uses CPS data on large numbers of workers, to encompass methods for eliciting data from employers.

Seventh, the authors treat their data as though they pertained to a cohort of workers, but, of course, the CPS does not provide cohort data. Rather, and as with virtually all government surveys, the CPS yields data on different samples of workers at various points in time—in the present case, 1979 and 1988. Therefore, it is not possible for WB to "control" for changes in the CPS databases over time, and it is possible—perhaps likely—that the apparent changes in pension-benefit and health-care-benefit coverage between 1979 and 1988 are due to differences in the extent of such coverage among CPS samples of workers. Because the decline in pension and health-care-benefit coverages that WB say has occurred in the United States is relatively small percentagewise (and would be smaller still if reported for all workers, including those 24 years old and younger), the absence of cohort data concerning the pension and health-care-benefit coverage of workers appears to be a major limitation of the type of study conducted by WB. At the least, the authors owe the reader a discussion of this point.

Finally, while WB indicate that they also are concerned about the consequences of changing fringe-benefit coverage, they devote little actual attention to such consequences. Their main conclusion in this regard seems to be that the future direction of pension and health-benefit coverage in the United States will depend upon future changes in tax policy, the incidence of unionism, and other factors. For their part, the authors do not expect to see further reductions in marginal income tax rates in the near future, but they do expect to see a continued decline in the incidence of unionism. However, they also expect some of the other variables included in their analyses (e.g., worker education) to change in such ways that pension and health-benefit coverage in toto will increase modestly during the 1990s.

The "problem" with these conclusions is that they focus almost solely on changes attributable to the determinants of fringe-benefit coverage that were studies by WB, not on the consequences of changes in such coverage. Consider, for example, whether labor-market mobility in the United States is, or will be, hindered by changes in fringe-benefit coverage. (The authors say that their prediction of increased pension and health-care-benefit coverage in the 1990s implies a labor force with increased human capital, but they avoid the issue of whether this increase will be so firm-specific [general] as to retard [enhance] labor mobility.)

Or, consider how the authors' findings bear on questions of pension portability, national health insurance, and direct foreign investment in plants and facilities in the United States. A wide variety of consequences and public-policy implications can be drawn from WB's work, but because the authors do little of this the reader will have to do it for himself. In conclusion, WB have produced a competent and interesting empirical exercise, but one that is markedly limited by the lack of theoretical, consequence-oriented, public-policy perspectives.

6

Indexation and Contract Length in Unionized U.S. Manufacturing

Mark Bils

I. Introduction

About 10 years ago, several papers exploited long-term labor contracts with incomplete wage indexation to build model economies where nominal disturbances have important effects on employment and output, and where real disturbances have larger impacts than in the presence of a spot labor market (e.g., Fischer [1977]; Gray [1976]; and Taylor [1979]). In much of this literature, the length of contracts was taken as exogenous. Gray (1978) and later others, however, stressed that the length of labor contracts and the amount of indexation should depend on the uncertainty of real and nominal factors faced in setting future wage rates. These authors were particularly concerned with the implications of endogenous contract length for an activist monetary policy.

I examine whether contract durations and indexation in United States manufacturing in the postwar period have been reasonably consistent with the implications of the Gray literature. I will argue that neither the time-series nor the cross-sectional patterns in U.S. manufacturing support this standard view of contracting. Failure to find behavior consistent with the Gray model indirectly questions the validity of the models discussed above in which long-term contracts have important implications for employment behavior. The same assumptions that give rise to important costs of long-term contracts suggest that contract length should respond to changes in the contracting environment.

Selective Literature Review

The literature on optimal length of labor contracts can be traced to the monopoly pricing problem examined by Barro (1972). Barro considered the rule a monopolist follows in changing price in an uncertain environment where it is costly to change price. He found that price changes will be less frequent if they are costly, and more frequent if the amount of uncertainty is large.[1] There is an immediate roadblock when applying this model to labor contracts, particularly union contracts. In the monopoly pricing problem, the actual duration of a price is stochastic; it is the size of the price change that is deterministic. In labor contracts, however, the reverse is typically true. Most contracts explicitly state a contract duration; and contracts typically do end according to the date agreed upon at signing.[2]

Gray allows for a predetermined contract length by simply excluding the possibility of contracts of contingent duration. At the same time, she relaxes the assumption of a constant nominal price during a contract. Limited wage indexation is considered in the form of costless indexation to the aggregate price level. Optimal wage indexation to the price level is generally not one to one. It is less than one to one if inflation is negatively correlated with the market-clearing real wage. (This is the case for her model economy.) Optimal wage indexation is more than one to one if inflation and the market-clearing real wage are positively correlated. (See Blanchard [1979], for example.) Given the optimal degree of indexation, the implications for contract length parallel the predictions for average price duration depicted by Barro. Higher costs of contracting imply longer contracts. Higher uncertainty, either about the aggregate price level or about real factors driving labor supply or demand, are associated with shorter contracts.

A number of subsequent papers have extended the Gray model or made the results more precise. Dye (1980) solved for optimal contract length more exactly than Gray by adopting a dynamic programming approach. Blanchard (1979) and Canzoneri (1980), among others, solve for endogenous monetary policy. Fethke and Policano (1984) and Ball (1987) have examined implications for how contract dates are distributed across bargaining units. A number of papers, including Calvo and Phelps (1977), Hall and Lilien (1979), and Fethke and Policano (1986) have considered indexation to more than the price level. With the exception of Fethke and Policano, however, these papers do not explicitly treat contract length as well as indexation.

More recently, some authors have begun to address the more fundamental question of why contracts actually have an explicit duration. In the environments specified in most of the literature, an exogenous or predetermined contract duration is strictly dominated—in the sum of payoffs to the firm and workers—by a contract with endogenous duration. Papers by Cantor (1985), Huberman (1985), and Huberman and Kahn (1986) show how various forms of asymmetric information can provide the need for a noncontingent upper bound on contract length. Contract length is implicitly partially contingent. Contracts can, and do, end prematurely when both parties agree to do so. Contracts also occasionally remain in effect beyond a scheduled ending. (See the data section to follow.) The joint decision to shorten or extend a contract reflects realizations of labor supply and demand; and so length is, to an extent, endogenous.

Although the literature on contract length lends itself directly to testing, it was rather slow in generating an empirical literature. Much of this literature has focused on the effects of price-level uncertainty.

Christofides and Wilton (1983) examine a sample of about 1,500 union contracts in Canada for the years 1966 to 1975. They find a significantly negative impact on contract length of a time-series estimate for price-level uncertainty. Their finding is largely driven by a significant fall in contract lengths in the years 1974 to 1975. Christofides (1985) examines a longer sample period, 1966 to 1981, and finds results generally consistent with Christofides and Wilton. Cousineau, Lacroix, and Bilodeau (1983) similarly studied Canadian union contracts, finding negative effects of both inflation and inflation uncertainty on contract length.

Union contracts in the United States have also been studied. Ehrenberg, Danziger, and San (1984) find little relation between inflation uncertainty, as measured from survey data used to construct the Livingston Index of expected inflation, and contract length for a sample of about 1,000 contracts on file at the Bureau of Labor Statistics in 1981. Cecchetti (1987) finds no relation between inflation and contract length over the period 1960 to 1978 for a relatively smaller sample of about 200 contracts. By contrast, in a recent paper, Susan B. Vroman (1988) finds that inflation uncertainty, as measured by the Livingston survey data, has a significantly negative impact on contract length. She examines a sample of about 2,500 contracts in unionized manufacturing for the years 1957 to 1984. Although my sample is similar to Vroman's, I find little or no significant time-series relation between contract length and inflation or inflation uncertainty. Thus my results are more consistent with the earlier findings of Ehrenberg, Danziger, and San, and Cecchetti.

Several papers have focused on the determinants of indexation. For Canadian contracts, Cousineau, Lacroix, and Bilodeau find increased indexation in periods with either higher inflation or more variable inflation. Card (1986) finds that industries whose output prices are highly correlated with the aggregate price level are more likely to index to aggregate prices. By contrast, Ahmed (1987) finds little support for the Gray model in the cross-industry pattern of indexation in Canadian union contracts.   Some of the above-mentioned studies have also tested for effects of federal wage-price controls and guidelines on contract length. Results vary from clearly negative effects of incomes policies on contract length (Christofides [1985], and Cecchetti [1987]) to mixed effects (Cousineau, Lacroix, and Bilodeau [1983], and S. B. Vroman [1988]).

Results for this Study

I examine contract length and indexation for 2,684 major collective bargaining agreements in U.S. manufacturing for the years 1957 to 1983 to test whether the cross-industry or time-series patterns in contract length and indexation are consistent with the Gray literature. I conclude that, for the most part, they are not. The pattern of contract lengths across industries is inconsistent with the Gray model. And the model does not help to explain the cross-industry pattern in indexation. It is true that indexation has increased with increases in inflation and inflation uncertainty, but there are no significant corresponding decreases in contract length. Periods of greater real uncertainty have not been associated with significantly shorter contracts.

Table 1:   Manufacturing Contracts with Stated Duration by Beginning Year

Year	Number of contracts	Year	Number of contracts	Year	Number of contracts	Year	Number of contracts
1955	7	1963	100	1971	110	1979	84
1956	44	1964	117	1972	73	1980	116
1957	67	1965	122	1973	107	1981	77
1958	109	1966	75	1974	123	1982	88
1959	126	1967	105	1975	77	1983	108
1960	103	1968	105	1976	92	1984	59
1961	110	1969	81	1977	119	1985	2
1962	122	1970	98	1978	74		

TOTAL (1955 through 1985)   = 2,800

            (1957:Q2 through 1983:Q4) = 2,684

SOURCE: Author.

II. Description of Contract Data

The contract data were put together under the direction of Wayne Vroman at the Urban Institute. The data were constructed from reports on contract settlements contained primarily in the Bureau of Labor Statistics (BLS) monthly publication Current Wage Developments. Most contracts in the data set are from manufacturing. I restrict attention solely to manufacturing contracts, of which there are 3,081, with effective beginning dates from the years 1955 through 1985. (The distribution of contracts by year is discussed momentarily.) These data represent a large majority of major collective bargaining agreements in manufacturing during this period.[3] Detailed description of the data is found in W. Vroman (1984) and in W. Vroman (1986, Section 3).

Of principal interest, the data detail provisions for contract length, that is, for duration agreed upon at signing, as well as for the duration realized. In most cases, as discussed momentarily, these two are equivalent. The data also state whether the negotiated contract contains an escalator clause indexing the contract wage to realizations of inflation.[4] The quantitative response dictated by these escalators is discussed at length in the next section.

Not all of the contracts have a preset duration; of the 3,081 manufacturing contracts, 281 have no stated duration at signing. I eliminate these in all subsequent exercises. If duration of these contracts is truly determined ex post, they provide an interesting source for future empirical work.[5]

Table 1 breaks down the remaining 2,800 manufacturing contracts by year the contract begins. I was concerned that there could be a selectivity bias against recording data on short contracts at the beginning of the sample and against recording data on long contracts at the end. This concern was heightened by the fact that the years 1956 and 1984, and the first quarter of 1957, have fewer contracts

Table 2:   Contracts by Length and by Indexation Status

Negotiated length in months	Number of contracts	Number of contracts with escalators	(As percentage)
Up to 12	400	15	(3.8)
13 to 23	117	5	(4.3)
24	661	62	(9.4)
25 to 35	157	71	(45.2)
36	1,221	619	(50.7)
More than 36	128	74	(57.8)
Totals	2,684	846	(31.5)

SOURCE: Author.

than that dictated by the bargaining cycle for the sample period as a whole; and the years 1955 and 1985 have only a few contracts. For this reason, throughout the paper, I include only contracts that begin in the second quarter of 1957 through the end of 1983. This reduces the number of contracts examined to 2,684.[6]

Not all of the remaining contracts actually ended according to schedule. Seven percent of the contracts reopened prior to schedule. For about one-fourth of the sample, there occurred a gap between one contract's scheduled end and agreement on a subsequent contract. These periods were typically short. One-third of these occurrences were associated with strikes. For these contracts, length is measured by how many months the contract would have been in effect had it ended on schedule.

The distribution of lengths for the 2,864 manufacturing contracts is presented in Table 2. The average contract length is 28.61 months; and the standard deviation is 9.72 months. Contracts exactly one year in length are 12.3 percent of the table; 24.6 percent are exactly two years; and 45.5 percent are exactly three years.

The contracts vary widely in terms of the number of workers represented.[7] The average number is 9,370. Contracts for fewer than 2,500 workers are 35.8 percent; 15.9 percent are for more than 10,000 workers. Contracts between a union and more than one firm total 21.5 percent.

III. Cross-Industry Patterns

Much of the empirical literature has focused on the time-series behavior of contracting, in particular how contract length and indexation have responded to price-level uncertainty. Although I turn to these issues momentarily, I begin by examining cross-sectional patterns in contracting. I test whether industries with more variable employment (e.g., durable goods industries) write shorter contracts, and whether industry patterns in indexing are related to the correlation between industry employment and inflation. On both issues, I find no support for the predictions of the Gray literature.

Contract Length

The contracts are from 87 three-digit industries. To obtain industry effects for contract length, I regressed contract duration on 87 industry dummy variables as well as on 107 time-period dummies representing each of the quarterly periods in the sample period. The resulting industry dummies are comparable (and quantitatively similar) to average contract duration by industry; but they control for the fact that some industries disproportionately signed contracts in periods where contracts generally were shorter or longer than usual. The industries vary considerably in their typical durations. The mean industry contract length is 29.33 months; the standard deviation across the industries is 5.15 months. The industry-effects explain about one-fourth of the total variance in contract lengths in the sample (based on partial sums of squares).

To obtain a measure of industry employment variability, I take annual production-worker employment for the years 1958 to 1985 and regress its rate of growth on a constant and linear time trend. Employment variability is then measured by the standard error for rate of growth for each industry. Employment data are from the BLS Establishment Survey. Employment data are not available for one of the 87 industries. For 14 of the industries employment data are only available for 1972 and after. I regressed the standard errors for these industries to reflect the extent that employment growth in manufacturing was more variable for 1972 to 1985 than for 1958 to 1972.[8]

Regressing the log of industry contract length on this measure of employment variability yields:

(1) Log (Contract   =   3.256   +   1.759 Std. Error Employ Growth
        Length)   (67.09)   (2.39)
      $R^2 = 0.064$; SEE = 0.197.

T-statistics are in parentheses. More variable industries on average write somewhat longer contracts. The coefficient predicts that contracts in the most-variable industry in the sample, Railroad Equipment (with a standard error of employment growth of 17.8 percent), would be 30 percent longer than contracts in the least-variable industry, Dairy Products (with a standard error of 1.1 percent).

By itself, this positive correlation does not refute the standard theory of contract length. Causality could run from length of contracts to employment variability, with long contracts being the cause of variable employment. That this is not the answer, however, is somewhat clear from the fact that the durable-goods industries, which predictably have higher employment variability for accelerator reasons, also write longer contracts. Employment is almost twice as variable in durables; yet contracts are nine percent longer.[9]

To address causality, I use a set of industry-specific variables as instruments for industry equipment variability. I assume that those variables are unrelated to contract length, except through their impact on employment variability. The instruments are a dummy variable for whether the industry produces durables, labor's share in industry value added, value added as a share of value of shipments, and the ratio of inventories to shipments. Data on the latter three variables are from the 1977 Census of Manufactures. Marshall's laws predict greater employment variability with a greater share of labor in value added. Value added's share in output has no clear prediction. The importance of inventories also has an ambiguous prediction, which depends on the source of disturbances and on whether industries without inventories can smooth production through variations in unfilled orders. Regressing employment variability on these variables for the 86 industries yields:

The coefficient on employment variability actually increases relative to its ordinary

$$(2) \quad \widehat{\text{Std. Error}} = 0.0685 + 0.0318 \, \text{Durable} + 0.0181 \, \text{Log} \left(\frac{\text{Labor}}{\text{ValAdd}} \right)$$
$$\text{Employ Growth} \quad (4.95) \qquad (6.13) \qquad\qquad (2.16)$$

$$- \; 0.0140 \; \text{Log} \left(\frac{\text{Val Add}}{\text{Output}} \right) + 0.0106 \; \text{Log} \left(\frac{\text{Invent}}{\text{Ship}} \right);$$
$$\quad (-1.54)$$
$$\qquad\qquad\qquad\qquad\qquad\qquad (2.17)$$

$$R^2 = 0.492; \; \text{SEE} = 0.0206.$$

Regressing contract length on this instrument yields:

$$(3) \; \text{Log (Contract} = \quad 3.215 \quad + \quad 2.441 \; \widehat{\text{Std. Error Employ Growth}} \, ;$$
$$\text{Length)} \qquad (48.54) \qquad (2.32)$$

$$R^2 = 0.054; \; \text{SEE} = 0.193.$$

least squares (OLS) estimate and remains statistically different from zero. This is a rather paradoxical result. Not only the Gray model predicts a negative coefficient, but presumably any model in which bargainers dislike uncertainty, and in which greater contract length increases uncertainty, would also suggest a negative coefficient.

There are factors beyond uncertainty that should influence contract length. In the Gray model, the other critical factor is the fixed cost of contracting. It is difficult to say how costs of negotiating should vary cross-sectionally. If there are increasing returns to negotiating for a large group of workers, this would suggest that larger bargaining units should have shorter contracts. In addition to the measure of employment variability, in Table 3 I relate industry contract length to two dummy variables reflecting bargaining-unit size. One variable is for industries where bargains, on average, cover fewer than 2,500 workers; the other is for industries where bargains, on average, cover more than 10,000 workers.

Table 3:   Explaining Cross-Industry Contract Length and Indexation[a]

	Dependent variable			
	Log (contract length)		Propensity to index	
	OLS	IV[b]	OLS	IV[b]
Intercept	2.156	2.138	−2.306	−2.886
	(3.28)	(3.23)	(−2.68)	(−2.87)
Std. error of	1.943	2.714		
employ growth	(2.78)	(2.67)		
Co-movement of employ.			−0.0531	−0.1994
growth and inflation			(−1.36)	(−1.95)
< 2,500 workers	0.014	0.015	−0.0101	−0.146
	(0.31)	(0.33)	(−1.72)	(−2.08)
> 10,000 workers	0.059	0.058	0.153	0.171
	(1.12)	(1.10)	(2.26)	(2.29)
More than one	0.242	0.252	−0.125	−0.155
firm	(4.11)	(4.20)	(−1.66)	(−1.84)
Industry	0.075	0.067	0.047	0.019
bargaining pattern	(1.38)	(1.21)	(0.67)	(0.25)
Avg. industry	0.155	0.150	0.412	0.500
wage	(1.49)	(1.44)	(3.04)	(3.17)
Trend industry	2.23	2.21	2.76	2.59
employ. growth	(2.53)	(2.48)	(2.42)	(2.08)
R^2	0.302	0.291	0.432	0.329
SEE	0.172	0.173	0.222	0.241

a. N equals 86; t-statistics are in parentheses.
b. Instrumental variables.
SOURCE: Author.

The regression includes two other variables reflecting the bargaining environment. One is the fraction of industry contracts that are agreements with more than one firm in the industry; the other is the fraction of industry contracts that are part of an industry bargaining pattern. Both fractions tend to take values of either zero or one. Arguments can be constructed yielding either positive or negative predictions for how these variables should affect contract length.[10] The regression also includes two variables reflecting industrywide conditions: the average hourly wage of production workers in 1977, and the average growth in production worker employment for the years 1958 to 1985.[11] I anticipated no particular signs for these variables.

The first column in Table 3 gives OLS results and can be compared to the results in equation (1). Including the additional variables slightly increases the coefficient on employment variability. The variables for bargaining size are insignificant. In addition to employment variability, the two significant variables are the fraction of contracts with multiple firms and the industry's trend employment growth. Contracts with more than one firm are 24 percent longer. Contracts are somewhat longer in growing industries. (The cross-industry standard deviation in trend growth is 2.2 percent per year; this is associated with an effect on contract length of 5.0 percent.) An industry bargaining pattern and the average industry wage are not significantly related to contract length.

The second column in Table 3 gives results instrumenting for employment variability. The instruments include the variables from equation (2), plus the variables that appear as second-stage regressors in columns one and two of Table 3. The coefficient for employment variability is slightly larger than in equation (3) without the additional regressors, and is larger than the OLS estimate in column one. The estimated coefficients for the remaining variables are all essentially unchanged from their OLS values.

In sum, factors related to greater employment variability, most noticeably the production of durable goods, paradoxically bear a small positive relation to contract length.

Indexation

Next consider the cross-industry pattern of indexing. The Gray model assumes that indexation to the price level is costless; therefore, indexation does not depend on contract length. At any contract length, the degree of indexation depends solely on the anticipated co-movement between the price level and the desired real wage rate. If there is no correlation between the two, then the optimal degree of wage indexation to the price level is one to one.

In practice, however, many contracts are not indexed at all; and longer contracts are much more likely to be indexed. This behavior suggests that bargainers associate some fixed costs with introducing indexation. Contracts totaling 31.5 percent of the sample contain some escalator clause indexing the wage at least partially to a price index.[12] Table 2 gives the number of contracts containing escalator clauses by negotiated contract lengths. Two years appears to be a critical length. Only 9.4 percent of contracts up to and including two years in length were indexed; 50.7 percent of contracts over two years in length were indexed.

Of the 846 indexed contracts, 93 percent actually realized a wage increase due to indexing. For these 93 percent, the total indexed wage increases during the contract averaged 9.13 percent, which equaled 3.22 percent per year the contract was in effect.

Table 4 presents estimates describing how real wage growth differed between indexed and nonindexed contracts for contracts that are more than two years long. Wage growth is per year and is relative to straight-time wages for total manufacturing adjusted for interindustry shifts (from the BLS). Column 1 shows that wages,

Table 4: Wage Behavior by Indexation Status for Contracts Over Two Years Long[a]

	Equation 1	Equation 2	Equation 3
Not indexed	−0.139	0.041	−0.406
	(1.70)	(0.24)	(−1.89)
Indexed	1.335	0.289	0.533
	(16.49)	(1.55)	(2.34)
(Not indexed)∗ Inflation		−0.036	
		(−1.21)	
Indexed∗ Inflation		0.177	
		(6.22)	
(Not indexed)∗ E(Inflation)			0.042
			(1.12)
Indexed∗ E(Inflation)			0.135
			(3.71)
(Not indexed)∗ [Inflat − E(Inflat)]			−0.175
			(−3.45)
Indexed∗ [Inflat − E(Inflat)]			0.243
			(5.33)
R^2	0.155	0.177	0.185
SEE	2.237	2.209	2.200

a. Wage behavior is relative to straight-time wages for all manufacturing. E(Inflation) denotes expected inflation at the beginning of a contract. There are 742 nonindexed and 764 indexed contracts. T-statistics are in parentheses.
SOURCE: Author.

on average, grew much faster in indexed contracts. Indexed contracts gained 1.3 percent per year relative to manufacturing as a whole, whereas nonindexed wages fell slightly. Over a three-year contract, these numbers imply that indexed wages, on average, grew 4.5 percent relative to nonindexed wages.

Column 2 in Table 4 represents an interaction of indexation with the realized annual rate of Consumer Price Index (CPI) inflation during the life of the contract. Not surprisingly, indexed wages have gained on nonindexed wages, primarily when inflation has been high. Column 3 is more meaningful; it breaks inflation into expected and unexpected components. Expected inflation is the average rate of inflation expected in the Consumer Price Index over the next three years at the time the contract goes into effect. The forecast of the three-year-ahead CPI (in logs) is based on 12 monthly seasonal dummies, on linear and quadratic time trends, and on the CPI for each of the six months prior to the first month the contract goes into effect.[13] Column 3 shows that indexation is much more important for unexpected inflation. A one percent increase in expected inflation per year increases indexed wages by less than one-tenth of one percent per year relative to nonindexed wages. Nonindexed contracts are responding to expected inflation by building in higher fixed wage increases during the contract; therefore wages do not decline with expected inflation relative to manufacturing wages in general. By contrast, a one-percent increase in unexpected inflation is associated with an increase of 0.42 percent in indexed wages relative to nonindexed wages. The 0.42 quantity could be interpreted as the average effective marginal degree of indexation for the indexed contracts in the sample.[14]

The literature on indexing does not suggest that higher average wage growth will be associated with greater indexing. I view it as genuinely puzzling that the decision to index is so skewed toward contracts with expected real-wage growth. It is as if, upon receiving a large wage increase, the first good that workers choose to purchase is wage indexation against nominal uncertainty.

Although many contracts are not indexed at all, it is still possible to ask whether the Gray model is helpful in understanding the cross-industry pattern in indexing. In particular, are industries in which the desired real wage and aggregate prices move together more likely to index than industries in which they move counter?

To explain how indexation varies across industries, I proceed much as I did in defining industry effect for contract length, except I also control for the length of contracts. I created a dummy variable that takes the value of 1 when a contract contains an escalator clause and 0 when it does not. I also created dummy variables for the 87 industries in the sample, for the 107 time periods, and for six categories of contract length, as shown in Table 2. I then regressed the dependent variable against these explanatory variables. The resulting industry dummies for indexation vary considerably. The mean industry propensity to index equals 0.293; the standard deviation equals 0.282. For 40 of the 86 industries, the probability of indexing is less than 0.2; for 26 industries it is less than 0.1. On the other hand, for 20 industries the probability of indexing is above 0.5, and for 10 industries it is above 0.75.

The co-movement between the aggregate price level and the desired real wage is not observable because the ex post desired real wage is unobserved. In lieu of this, I examine the relation between prices and an industry's rate of employment growth. I examine whether industries for which periods of inflation typically accompany growing employment are more likely to index wages.

To measure co-movement of employment and inflation for each of the 86 industries for which employment data are available, I regress annual rates of growth in production-worker employment for the years 1958 to 1985 on the year's rate of growth in the Consumer Price Index, as well as on a constant and linear time trend. Co-movement is then measured by the coefficient on the rate of inflation.[15] For 62 of the 86 industries, the coefficient is negative—periods of high inflation are periods of lower-than-normal employment growth. The mean coefficient is −0.340 and its standard deviation is 0.653, implying a good deal of variation across the industries.

The cross-industry OLS relation between propensity to index and the co-movement coefficient is:

(4) Propensity to   = 0.299   +   0.0183 Co-move Employ Growth
         Index   (8.69)   (0.39)   and Inflation;

$R^2 = 0.002$; SEE = 0.283.

This relation is slightly positive, but not different from zero.

The co-movement of industry employment and the CPI could clearly be influenced by the propensity of an industry to index wages to the CPI. For this reason, it is necessary to instrument for the co-movement variable with industry variables that are unrelated to the desire to index, except through their effect on the correlation between employment and aggregate prices. For instruments, I use the same industry variables used above to instrument for variability of industry employment. This yields the following instrument for co-movement of aggregate prices and industry employment:

(5) $\hat{\text{Co-move}}$ Employ = −0.0827 − 0.300 Durable − 0.549 Log$\left(\dfrac{\text{Labor}}{\text{Val Add}}\right)$
       Growth and Inflation   (−0.20)   (−1.92)   (−2.18)

       +   0.012 Log$\left(\dfrac{\text{Val Add}}{\text{Output}}\right)$ + 0.294 Log$\left(\dfrac{\text{Invent}}{\text{Shipment}}\right)$;
           (0.05)   (2.02)

$R^2 = 0.142$; SEE = 0.620.

These instruments explain much less of the cross-industry variability in this variable than they do for cross-industry employment variability. Regressing propensity to index on this instrument yields:

(6) Propensity to   =   0.242   −   0.150 $\hat{\text{Co-move}}$ Employ Growth
         Index   (4.32)   (−1.12)   and Inflation;

$R^2 = 0.150$; SEE = 0.304.

The relationship now becomes negative (the reverse of that expected from the Gray literature), but is still not statistically different from zero.

In the final two columns of Table 3, I relate an industry's propensity to index to six additional variables. These are the same variables examined for effects on contract length: two dummy variables reflecting bargaining unit size, the fraction of industry contracts that are agreements with more than one firm, the fraction of contracts that are part of an industry bargaining pattern, the average industry wage, and average growth in employment for 1958 to 1985.

The third column gives OLS results and can be compared to the results in equation (4). Including the additional variables decreases the coefficient on the co-movement variable slightly, but it remains insignificantly different from zero.

Turning to the other variables, the more workers involved, the more likely a contract will be indexed. This is consistent with the notion of a fixed cost to indexing; with more workers, this fixed cost is spread more and is less likely to prevent indexing. Higher wage industries are more likely to index. This is also consistent with a fixed cost to indexing if the benefit of real wage stability is increasing in the absolute size of the wage. The final significant variable is employment growth— growing industries are more likely to index. I do not know why this should be. It is presumably related to the finding above, that is, contracts with higher wage growth are more often indexed. Together, the variables in Column 3 explain a good deal of the cross-industry variation in indexing of contracts of a given length.

The final column of Table 3 illustrates the results of instrumenting for co-movement between industry employment growth and CPI inflation. The instruments include the variables from equation (5), plus the second-stage regressors in Table 2. The coefficient on co-movement now becomes more negative than it was without the additional regressors, and becomes marginally statistically significant. The standard deviation in the co-movement variable across the 86 industries is 0.65; this is associated with an effect on propensity to index of 0.13. The estimated coefficients for the remaining variables are similar to their OLS values.

I conclude that the cross-industry behavior of indexing, as well as contract length, is at odds with predictions from the Gray literature.

IV. Time-Series Patterns

Contracting and Inflation

In constructing time series for contract length, I regressed contract length for the sample of 2,684 contracts against 107 quarterly time-period dummies, as well as 252 dummy variables for each of 252 separate bargaining match-ups in the data. (For instance, the United Auto Workers [UAW] and Chrysler is one match-up, while the UAW and Ford constitutes another.) This regression yields a time series that controls for the continually changing makeup of bargaining parties. I proceeded similarly to construct a time series for indexing. I regressed the zero/one variable for whether the contract contains an escalator clause against the 107 time dummies, against the 252 bargaining match dummies, as well as against the six dummies reflecting contract length that correspond to the categories in Table 2.

The resulting time series for contract length is pictured in Figure 1, together with the quarterly inflation in the Consumer Price Index adjusted to an annual rate. Christofides and Wilton (1983) and Christofides (1985) note that union contracts became shorter in Canada when both inflation and price level uncertainty rose in the early to mid-1970s. This finding is consistent with the Gray model; more price-level uncertainty reduces the value of the price level as a signal for indexing real wages, thereby reducing the optimal length of contracts.

Figure 1 shows that this was clearly not the case in the United States. In the United States, contracts grew considerably longer during the 1960s. With increased inflation in the 1970s, contract length continued to grow, though at a slower pace. Regressing contract length on the rate of inflation from the prior quarter shows that, when inflation has been higher by a percentage point, contracts have typically been about 1.7 percent higher. I also regressed contract length on the standard deviation of inflation during the prior eight quarters. An increase of one percentage point in this standard deviation was associated with time periods with 4.3 percent longer contracts.

At the same time, indexation has been closely positively associated with periods of inflation. Figure 2 presents the time series for propensity to index, together with the inflation rate. Bargainers were much more likely to index contracts of a given length in the 1970s and 1980s than before. Regressing the propensity to index on the rate of inflation during the previous quarter shows that contracts written following periods with a one percentage point higher inflation rate have had a 0.024 higher probability of being indexed. Contracts written when the standard deviation of inflation over the past eight quarters has been a percentage point higher have had a 0.118 higher probability of being indexed. Later in this section, I explore the effects of an estimate of price-level uncertainty on contract length and indexation.

These long-run patterns in contract length and indexing are both consistent with some fixed cost to indexing. Greater price-level uncertainty could cause bargainers to go from zero indexing to some positive amount. This switch could then cause contract length to increase because bargaining is more costly and because wages are better indexed.

The remainder of Section IV focuses on what I consider the two primary predictions of the Gray model: that greater real uncertainty is associated with shorter contracts; and that a more positive correlation between prices and desired real wages is associated with greater indexation.

Real Uncertainty and Contract Length

To be consistent with the cross-industry evidence, I again measure real uncertainty by variability of production-worker employment. I test whether contract length is negatively affected by the expected variance in forecasting future employment. Length of contracts should be affected if there is conditional variance in forecasting employment.

I first construct time series for an eight-quarter-ahead employment forecast, and for the realized squared errors from this forecast. I choose an eight-quarter horizon because the median contract length in the sample is near two years. This suggests

Figure 1: Contract Length and Inflation Rate

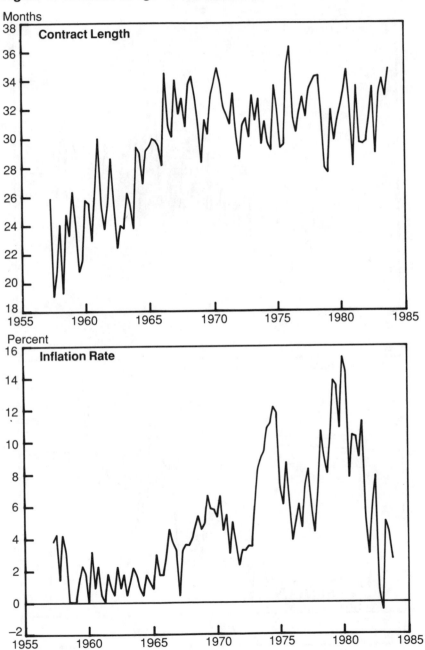

Figure 2: Fraction Indexed and Inflation Rate

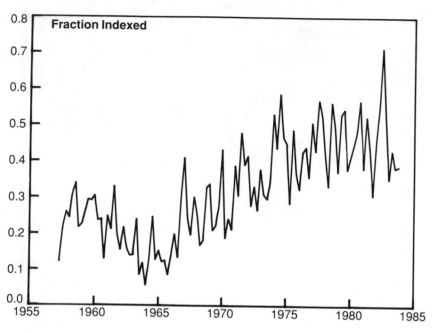

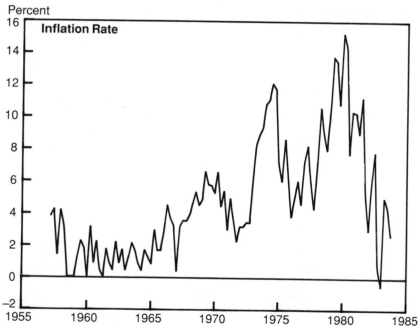

Figure 3: Squared Employment Errors and Expected Squared Errors

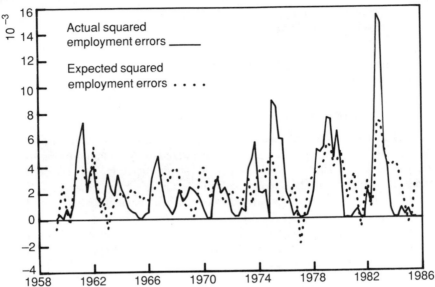

that employment uncertainty approximately two years ahead is relevant for marginal decisions on contract length. I then relate length of contracts that begin in period t to the squared error in the employment forecast for period $t + 7$, the final period of an eight-quarter contract.

$$(7) \quad \text{Log (Contract Length}_t) = \text{Constant} - a\, E_t\, [L_{t+7} - E_t\, (L_{t+7})]^2$$

L denotes the natural log of production-worker employment for total manufacturing. Of course, contract signers at time t cannot respond to the realized squared error at time $t + 7$, but only their expectation of this squared error. Therefore, I instrument for the squared forecast error with a set of variables dated up through period $t - 1$. This instrument is denoted by the expectation operator E_t.[16]

I base a forecast of employment for period $t + 7$ on seasonal dummies, on linear and quadratic trends, on four lags of employment, and on the rate of growth in real GNP in period $t - 1$. In constructing the forecast, I use a sample period for t of 1954 through 1983 (the last year any contracts begin in my sample). After squaring the forecast errors, I then instrument for them with all the variables used in forecasting employment, plus the four most recent squared forecast errors prior to t, and the standard deviation of employment growth over the eight quarters $t - 8$ to $t - 1$. Figure 3 shows the behavior over time of both the squared employment forecast errors and the expected squared forecast errors. The expectation is formed eight periods (two years) prior to a period in the figure. The instruments explain a third of the variance of the squared forecast errors.

Results for equation (7) are:

(8)   Log (Contract $=$ 17.15 $E_t[L_{t+7} - E_t(L_{t+7})]^2$;
        Length $_t$)   (1.89)

R^2 $=$ 0.073; SEE = 0.148; D–W = 0.48; t = 1957:Q3 to 1987:Q4.

This equation also includes four seasonal dummies, as do all equations estimated in Section IV. Rather than being negatively related, periods with greater employment-forecast variance are associated with longer contracts. This effect is only marginally significant. The standard deviation in the right-hand variable is 0.00214; an increase in the forecast variance of 0.00214 is associated with an increase in contract length of 3.7 percent.

The errors in explaining contract length in equation (8) are highly autocorrelated. Including trend terms and the previous quarter's contract length in the equation gives the following results:

(9)   Log (Contract $=$ 0.00168(t – 72:1)   –   0.0000543 $(t – 72:1)^2$
        Length $_t$)   (4.68)   (–4.67)

        +   0.270 Log (Contract   +   2.53 $E_t[L_{t+7} - E_t(L_{t+7})]^2$;
        (2.73)   Length $_{t-1}$)   (0.51)

        R^2 $=$ 0.712; SEE = 0.078; D–W = 1.81; t = 1957:Q3 to 1987:Q4.

Filtering the lower-frequency variations in the data this way eliminates most of the relation between employment variability and contract length. The sign of the relation remains perversely positive.

As discussed above, uncertainty in predicting prices can also decrease contract length in the Gray model by reducing the value of prices as a variable for indexing real wages. For this reason, I included forecast variance of the price level (measured by the natural log of the CPI) in period $t +7$ as an additional regressor.

In constructing a time-series for variability of prices, I proceed in the same manner as above for employment variability. I first construct a forecast for price in $t +7$ based on seasonal dummies, linear and quadratic trends, four lags of prices, and the rate of growth in the monetary base in period $t -1$.[17] I then squared the errors from this forecast. I instrument for these squared errors and the squared errors in forecasting employment with a common set of variables. These are all the variables used in forecasting employment, all the variables used in forecasting

Figure 4: Squared Price Errors and Expected Squared Errors

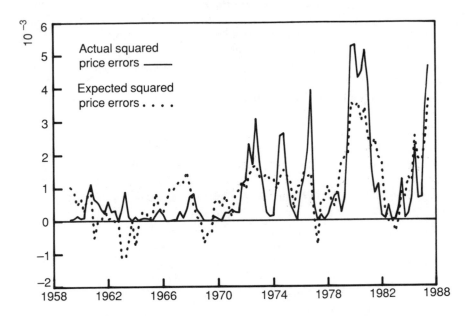

prices, the four most recent squared forecast errors prior to t for both employment and prices, and the standard deviations of employment growth and inflation over the eight quarters $t - 8$ to $t - 1$. These instruments explain 57 percent of the variance of the squared employment forecast errors and 58 percent of the variance of the squared price level forecast errors. Figure 4 shows time series for both the squared price forecast errors and the expected squared forecast errors. Measured price-level uncertainty is much greater in the 1970s than in the earlier part of the sample.

Incorporating this measure of expected price uncertainty in equation (7) yields the following results for contract length:

$$(10) \quad \text{Log (Contract Length}_t) = 10.76 \ E_t \left[L_{t+7} - E_t (L_{t+7}) \right]^2$$
$$(1.60)$$

$$+ \ 58.08 \ E_t \left[P_{t+7} - E_t (P_{t+7}) \right]^2;$$
$$(4.04)$$

$$R^2 = 0.021; \ \text{SEE} = 0.142; \ \text{D–W} = 0.58; \ t = 1957{:}Q3 \text{ to } 1987{:}Q4.$$

As discussed with regard to Figure 1, contract length behaves perversely with regard to inflation uncertainty. Periods with higher inflation uncertainty are periods with longer contracts. From the coefficient in equation (10), the standard deviation of the expected squared price error of 0.000898 has an effect on contract length of 5.2 percent. The significantly positive coefficient reflects that contracts were longer in the latter half of the sample period despite much greater price uncertainty. The expected squared price forecast error was almost four times larger in the second half of the sample than in the first half; yet contracts were 14 percent longer in the second half. Examining only nonindexed contracts yields a similar picture.[18]

The coefficient on employment variability remains positive, but is quantitatively less important.

$$(11) \quad \text{Log (Contract Length}_t) = 0.00185 \; (t - 72{:}1) - 0.0000550 \; (t - 72{:}1)^2$$
$$\phantom{(11) \quad \text{Log (Contract Length}_t) =} (4.54) \phantom{(t - 72{:}1) -} (-4.82)$$

$$+ \; 0.259 \; \text{Log (Contract Length}_{t-1}) - 3.44 \; E_t \; [L_{t+7} - E_t \, (L_{t+7})]^2$$
$$ (2.66) \phantom{\; \text{Log (Contract Length}_{t-1})} (-0.88)$$

$$- \; 3.53 \; E_t \; [P_{t+7} - E_t \, (P_{t+7})]^2$$
$$ (-0.36)$$

$$R^2 = 0.726; \; SEE = 0.076; \; D\text{–}W = 1.83; \; t = 1957{:}Q3 \text{ to } 1987{:}Q4.$$

Including trend terms and the previous quarter's contract length in the equation eliminates the impact of both employment and price-level uncertainty. The variability terms now have the expected negative signs; but they are quantitatively and statistically not different than zero.

The predictions of the Gray literature, in sum, are not helpful in understanding the time-series behavior of contract length.

Price/Employment Behavior and Indexation

Finally, I examine whether bargainers are more likely to index contracts of a given length when they expect price-level surprises to move in conjunction with employment surprises. Failure to do so would cause real wages to predictably decline with surprise increases in employment.

I examine the following relation between indexing and a time-varying covariance for employment and prices:

$$(12) \quad \text{Propensity to Index}_t = \text{Constant} + b \, E_t \, [L_{t+7} - E_t \, (L_{t+7})][P_{t+7} - E_t \, (P_{t+7})].$$

Figure 5: Employment and Price Forecast Errors

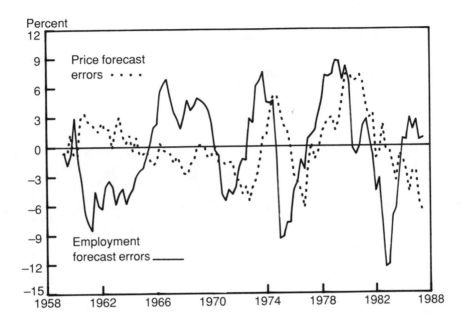

Propensity to index is the time series presented in Figure 2. It controls for the greater indexing in longer contracts. The forecasts for period $t+7$, manufacturing employment (L_{t+7}), and consumer prices (P_{t+7}) are those described in the prior subsection. Time series for both forecast errors are illustrated in Figure 5. The right-hand variable is then constructed by multiplying the employment errors by the price-forecast errors. I instrument for this realized co-movement with all variables used in forecasting employment and prices, with the four most recent realizations for multiplied employment and price forecast errors prior to t, and with the covariance of employment growth and inflation over the eight quarters $t-8$ to $t-1$. These instruments explain 24 percent of the variance of the realized multiples of employment and price errors. Figure 6 shows time series for the realized covariance of employment and prices, as well as the expectation of this covariance given the set of instruments.

Results for equation (12) are:

(13) Propensity $=$ $104.90\, E_t\, [L_{t+7} - E_t\,(L_{t+7})][P_{t+7} - E_t\,(P_{t+7})]$.
        to Index $_t$ (4.01)

$R^2 = 0.477$; SEE $= 0.171$; D–W $= 0.78$; $t = $ 1957:Q3 to 1987:Q4.

Figure 6: Co-movement of Employment and Price Errors and Expected Co-movement

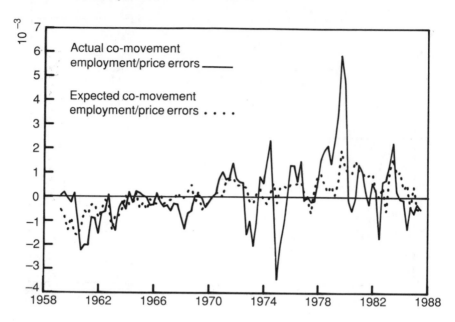

Consistent with theory, contracts were more often indexed in periods that bargainers could expect the CPI and employment to vary together. The standard deviation in the right-hand variable is 0.000673; an increase in the expected covariance of 0.000673 is associated with an increase in probability of indexing of 0.071. This is fairly large relative to the overall probability of indexing in the sample of about 0.315.

Including trend terms and the previous quarter's tendency to index eliminates this significant effect.

$$(14) \quad \text{Propensity} \quad = \quad 0.00200 \ (t - 72{:}1) + 0.0000154 \ (t - 72{:}1)^2$$
$$\text{to Index}_t \qquad (3.76) \qquad\qquad (1.35)$$

$$+ \ 0.404 \ \text{Propens. to} \ + \ 5.83 \ E_t[L_{t+7} - E_t(L_{t+7})][P_{t+7} - E_t(P_{t+7})];$$
$$(4.29) \quad \text{Index}_{t-1} \qquad (0.27)$$

$$R^2 = 0.628; \ \text{SEE} = 0.087; \ \text{D–W} = 2.02; \ t = 1957{:}\text{Q3 to } 1987{:}\text{Q4}.$$

Higher-frequency movements in the covariance show no impact on the higher-frequency movements in indexing.

As discussed above in connection with Figure 2, indexation increased in the second half of the sample period at the same time price-level uncertainty increased. This is predicted by the Gray model. Therefore, I additionally included price-level uncertainty in equation (12).

Price-level uncertainty is measured, as in the prior subsection, by the squared errors from the equation forecasting the CPI in $t+7$. I instrument for these squared price errors and the multiplied employment and price errors with a common set of variables. These include all variables used in forecasting employment and prices, the multiplied employment and price forecast errors, and the squared price forecast errors for $t-4$ to $t-1$, the covariance of employment growth and inflation over $t-8$ to $t-1$, and the standard deviation of inflation over $t-8$ to $t-1$. These instruments explain 27 percent of the variance of the realized multiples of employment and price errors and 66 percent of the variance of the squared price-level forecast errors.

Incorporating the instrument for expected price uncertainty in equation (12) yields the following results for indexing:

(15) $\begin{array}{ll} \text{Propensity} \\ \text{to Index}_t \end{array}$ = $\underset{(2.72)}{70.17}\ E_t\,[L_{t+7}-E_t\,(L_{t+7})][P_{t+7}-E_t\,(P_{t+7})]$

$+\ \underset{(1.73)}{28.49}\ E_t\,[P_{t+7}-E_t\,(P_{t+7})]^2\ ;$

$R^2 = 0.099;\ \ \text{SEE} = 0.148;\ \ \text{D–W} = 0.88;\ \ t = 1957\text{:Q3 to }1987\text{:Q4.}$

Adding price uncertainty somewhat reduces the coeffcient on the employment-price covariance; but it remains quantitatively important. The standard deviation for expected price level uncertainty of 0.00099 has an implied effect on probability of indexing of 0.028.

Finally, I include trend terms and the lagged indexing variable.

(16) $\begin{array}{ll} \text{Propensity} \\ \text{to Index}_t \end{array}$ = $\underset{(3.96)}{0.00207}\,(t-72\text{:}1)\ +\ \underset{(1.26)}{0.0000144}\,(t-72\text{:}1)^2$

$+\ \underset{(4.28)}{0.404}\ \begin{array}{l}\text{Propens. to}\\ \text{Index}_{t-1}\end{array}\ +\ \underset{(0.05)}{1.08}\ E_t\,[L_{t+7}-E_t\,(L_{t+7})][P_{t+7}-E_t\,(P_{t+7})]$

$-\ \underset{(-0.03)}{0.32}\,E_t\,[P_{t+7}-E_t\,(P_{t+7})]^2\ ;$

$R^2 = 0.632;\ \ \text{SEE} = 0\ .087;\ \ \text{D–W} = 2.02;\ \ t = 1957\text{:Q3 to }1987\text{:Q4.}$

This eliminates any significant effect of either the employment-price covariance or price uncertainty on indexing.

The long-term increase in indexing that occurred roughly in the 1970s is consistent with the Gray model; but, as with contract length, the model has no success in explaining the detrended behavior of indexing.

V. Conclusions

To briefly summarize, I do not find that contracting practices in U.S. manufacturing support predictions by Gray (1978), or by others whose models show the benefit of longer contracts as reduced contracting costs, and the cost of longer contracts as greater deviation of wages from a desired level. Contracts are not shorter and, in fact, are longer in industries facing more uncertainty—durable goods industries, for example. Greater employment and price-level uncertainty in the latter half of the postwar period have been associated with somewhat longer, rather than shorter, contracts.

As for indexing, industries where employment moves in conjunction with the aggregate price level are not more, and are perhaps less, likely to index to the price level. As models suggest, indexation has increased with greater price uncertainty and greater price-employment co-movement in the 1970s and 1980s. But, more generally, movements in indexing bear no resemblance to these predictions. There are other puzzling features of indexing. Most contracts up to two years in length, and half of all longer contracts, are not indexed at all. The decision to index is closely related to wage growth—a contract that specifies higher wage growth is much more likely to be indexed.

What directions does this behavior suggest for modeling contracting? A richer description of the benefit of long contracts is probably needed. In particular, if contracts are not shorter where and when uncertainty is greater, this suggests there is a component to the benefit of long contracts that increases with uncertainty. It has been suggested that one benefit of writing longer contracts is that they may reduce strikes (e.g., Ball [1987]). Asymmetric-information explanations for strike behavior (Kennan [1986]) might associate greater uncertainty with a greater concern for strikes. S.B. Vroman (1988) does find a positive relation between the occurrence of a strike and subsequent contract length. But this correlation may reflect causality in the opposite direction, from duration to striking—it is much more profitable to strike to affect a long contract than a short contract. In fact, this effect suggests that longer contracts may not reduce strikes.[19] Some recent work (Danzinger [1988], and Ragan [1989]) suggests that longer contracts are designed to insure workers and possibly employers against uncertainty. My findings of longer contracts in more uncertain settings might be considered support for these models.

I have suggested that introducing an important fixed cost associated with indexing could explain several observed features of indexing—in particular, the failure of many contracts to index and the greater propensity to index with larger bargaining units and higher-wage workers. But, important costs to indexing, at least to the CPI, do not seem very plausible.

An alternative explanation for the failure to index is that it simply does not matter very much in writing a good contract if the wage is off its optimal value. This would be true, for instance, if the labor-supply schedule of workers is very elastic, if the labor-demand schedule of firms is very inelastic, and if firms largely dictate employment during the contract. It could also be true if firms and workers arrive at decisions for employment during the contract in a fashion at least partially divorced from the contract wage. Hall (1980) suggests that much of the labor force is described by long-term firm-worker attachments, in which decisions on employment and hours are probably chosen with reasonable efficiency despite lack of wage movements that would be required in a spot labor market. Whether this is an appropriate picture for bargaining in unionized manufacturing is debatable. At any rate, it provides little guidance for explaining the systematic patterns in indexing that do occur, such as greater indexing, for example, in contracts with higher wage growth.

I have focused on the period 1958 to 1983 covered by the panel data set on bargaining in manufacturing. I conclude by pointing out how average contract length and indexation have continued through the 1980s. The 1980s have displayed a decline in indexation to inflation. For all contracts settled in the private sector (manufacturing and nonmanufacturing) in the years 1980 to 1983, contract length averaged 31.5 months, with 55.2 percent of workers covered by wage indexation. (Data are from various issues of the BLS Current Wage Developments.) In the years 1984 to 1988, contracts averaged 31.9 months, only a slight increase over the early 1980s, but with only 36.8 percent of wages indexed. Thus indexation declined as inflationary uncertainty lessened in the 1980s. The decline in indexing occurred at the same time labor contracts became increasingly detailed on other issues. This is further evidence that bargainers associate important costs with indexing; and it suggests that the historical U.S. tendency for not indexing labor contracts cannot be explained by lack of experience either with inflationary episodes or with indexing.

Acknowledgments

I have benefited from comments by Randall Eberts, Erica Groshen, and Paul Wachtel. I am grateful for research support from the National Science Foundation, the Graduate School of Business at the University of Chicago, and the Hoover Institution.

Notes

1. The frequency of changes will also depend on the persistence of disturbances to the market. For instance, if the disturbances to the optimal price are white noise, then no updating of price is desirable. Barro, as well as Gray (1978), however, only consider random-walk disturbances.

2. For the manufacturing contracts I consider, over 90 percent have a stated duration. Of these, 70 percent end according to schedule; many of the others end within a month or two of the scheduled date.

3. Their relative importance can be determined by reference to the BLS bulletin *The Bargaining Calendar*, which is also periodically reported in the *Monthly Labor Review*.

4. Essentially none of the approximately 3,000 contracts are indexed to factors other than inflation.

5. One could examine in what characteristics these firms and unions differ from those that write duration into contracts. The size and timing of wage changes in these matches could be compared to the predictions of the monopoly-pricing problem (Barro [1972]), as well as compared with behavior for contracts that explicitly state duration.

6. The first quarter of 1957 contained only four of the 67 contracts for 1957, whereas, for the entire 1958 to 1983 period, first quarters contained 20 percent of the sample contracts. There is a three-year cycle in the bargaining pattern, with the most contracts being in years 1958, 1961, and so forth. The pattern in the Vroman data reflects a pattern in manufacturing more generally. (See the data source in note 4.) The heavy bargaining years generally coincide with years the auto industry and UAW have signed three-year agreements.

7. The Current Wage Developments provide benchmark numbers on the number of workers covered by an agreement. They reflect membership, rather than workers actually employed.

8. Running the stated regression for total manufacturing for 1972 to 1985 yields a standard error for annual employment growth of 5.86 percent, compared to a standard error of 4.61 percent for the years 1958 to 1985.

9. The comparison between durables and nondurables would imply a coefficient of 2.35 in the first column of Table 2. This is very close to the coefficient I find momentarily when instrumenting for employment variability.

10. Contracts with multiple firms or that follow a pattern would presumably occur where bargaining costs are high—this suggests a positive relation to contract length. On the other hand, a bargaining pattern may sufficiently lower the cost of negotiation so that it leads to more frequent bargains.

11. For the 14 industries where employment data begin in 1972, I adjust rate of growth to reflect that manufacturing employment grew more slowly during 1972 to 1985 than from 1958 to 1972.

12. These typically take one of two forms: either a fixed number of reviews during the contract, where each time the magnitude of increase is linked to past price behavior; or adjustments triggered by a critical amount of inflation, with the magnitude of increase then again related by formula to prior price increases.

13. The price forecast is based on 1954 to 1983 for the date the contract begins. Therefore the prices being forecast are for 1957 to 1986.

14. This is reasonably close to the degree of marginal indexing that Card (1983) finds in Canadian union contracts.

15. For the 14 industries for which employment data are available beginning in 1972, I increased the

coefficient to reflect the fact that growth of manufacturing employment was more negatively correlated with inflation during 1972 to 1985 than during 1958 to 1972.

16. This would be equivalent to fitting an ARCH model (Engle [1982]) and using the eight-quarter-ahead variance estimates to explain contract length if the only variables used as instruments were past squared errors.

17. Monetary base data are taken from various issues of the *Federal Reserve Bulletin* of the Board of Governors of the Federal Reserve System.

18. Examining time-period effects only for contracts that are not indexed yields:

$$(10') \quad \text{Log (Contract Length }_t\text{)} = \underset{(1.02)}{8.03} \; E_t \left[L_{t+7} - E_t (L_{t+7}) \right]^2$$
$$+ \underset{(3.04)}{51.41} \; E_t \left[P_{t+7} - E_t (P_{t+7}) \right]^2 .$$

These results parallel those for all contracts. Results for equation (11) are also similar when only nonindexed contracts are considered.

19. In Bils (1988) I argue that, when firms have a dynamic labor demand, longer contracts are beneficial because they can allow more efficient employment outcomes. Longer contracts allow unions to react to the fact that the wages they are expected to demand in the future affect current employment. Longer contracts also lessen firms' incentive to reduce employment in order to affect future wage agreements. The model does not suggest, however, that these benefits should be related to uncertainty.

Comments

Michael L. Wachter

Mark Bils presents a strong negative assessment of one version of the neoclassical model of contract formation in the union sector. Specifically, he argues that the neoclassical explanation of contract length, which predicts shorter contracts in times of greater economic uncertainty, is fundamentally in conflict with the data. Contracts are longer in industries marked by greater employment uncertainty, rather than shorter as predicted by the theory. Bils also tests for the causes of the propensity to index contracts. Here again he discovers more puzzles that are unexplained by the theory. In particular, he notes that "the decision to index is closely related to wage growth—a contract that specifies higher wage growth is much more likely to be indexed."

There is always a tendency to discard negative empirical results as being a function of imperfect data, rather than of an imperfect theory. There are some legitimate worries that the data are imperfect. First, Bils has 2,864 pooled, time-series, cross-section data contracts. The contracts, however, are only in manufacturing. That is a serious limitation. Much of the richness or independent variation in the economic statistics of unions only appears when comparing manufacturing unions with construction unions or retail trade unions, etc. This variation is lost when focusing on manufacturing.

Secondly, the contracts in the study are from 87 three-digit manufacturing industries. Although there are some notable exceptions, most of the myriad contracts in each three-digit industry (and sometimes even in the two-digit industry) are being written by a few unions with different firms or by the same firm with different unions representing different craft workers. These contracts are not independent events; that is, they are not different observations. Attempting to buy additional observations by pooling cross-sectional with time-series observations also is limited. Contracts change relatively little over time; hence, much of the additional richness created by the pooling of time-series observations does not buy commensurate independent variation.

Having criticized the data, I would still conclude that Bils's negative evidence is too strong to write off as a creation of bad data. Bad data are more likely to result in statistically insignificant coefficients rather than in incorrectly signed coefficients. For some reason, industries marked with greater uncertainty in employment (as measured by Bils) write longer contracts.

173

Since the theory being tested posits the opposite result, the theory is incorrect, or more likely, fundamentally incomplete. Although Bils identifies puzzles in the theory and data, he does not seek to provide answers. This leaves the reader with a clear field to solve the puzzles.

I would argue that the incompleteness is due to the fact that the labor-contract theory being disproved has no features that make it recognizable as a labor contract. Instead, the model being tested is recognizable as a generic commercial contract. Linking increased uncertainty with decreased contract duration would probably prove to be correct if tested on commercial contract data.

Labor contracts, however, are different than commercial contracts, and the differences are not captured by the theory being tested. The major difference, of course, is that a commercial relationship can be terminated at contract duration if the parties do not agree on a new contract. In the labor-union setting, the parties have a continuing statutory obligation to "bargain in good faith." At contract expiration, if the parties cannot agree on a new contract, the union can strike the firm.

If all contracts were equally likely to end in a strike and have similar strike costs, then the omission would not be important. On the other hand, if employment uncertainty and strike hazard were correlated, then there would be a problem. Indeed, if greater uncertainty increased the probability of a strike, which is not an implausible assumption, then Bils's results might be explained in that fashion. The importance of strike uncertainty is discussed by Bils in the conclusion of his paper, but should be elevated to the theory to be tested.

In addition, correlates of union power are likely to affect contract duration (as well as strike hazards). A more-complete theory would attempt to control for the venerable Hicks-Marshall conditions that describe union power. Hicks-Marshall variables, however, are not included in the theory being tested and are not included in the regression equations. Industries with greater employment variability, such as autos and steel, bargain with strong unions. It has frequently been argued that these unions preferred longer contracts in order to average over the business cycle. Whatever the exact explanation, employment variability or uncertainty may turn out to be a proxy for union strength.

The issue of union strength is not stressed in Bils's paper. It explains, however, an important point that he raises about the hazard of writing long contracts in uncertain economic environments. Namely, he mentions that the parties do not appear to be disturbed when the "wage is off" due to long contracts. Paying too low a wage, for example, would be very costly if the contract wage were the competitive wage. But, of course, it is not a competitive wage. The union premium insulates the contract from changes in the market-clearing wage. In other words, the "wage is wrong" to begin with.

In this environment, the unions' concern is to avoid losing the golden egg. Strikes are not only costly in terms of lost wages to the workers and production for the firm, they are also a threat to the union. Strikes could prove a disaster if the firm decides to take a tough stand against the premium. It could mean a sharply lower premium if the firm wins, or it could mean a much weaker firm, unable to afford to pay the premium, if the strike drags on for a long period. The uncertainty generated by a strike is a major factor. The extra deviation of the wage from the competitive (or target) wage resulting from "too long a contract" is a small factor.

For the above reasons it is not surprising that contract length is not shorter in industries marked by greater employment variability. Moreover, any possible puzzle over the result is reduced by the fact that contracts are indexed in industries with greater employment variability. Instead of shortening the contract, the parties insert an index clause such as a cost-of-living clause (COLA).

But this raises the second puzzle identified by Bils; namely, the fact that indexed union contracts are those with greater wage growth. Alternatively stated, unions with COLA clauses had increasing premiums over the period. This is a topic that I have researched with some of my colleagues. More specifically, we have identified the fact that high premium industries also had increasing premiums over the period 1960 to 1988. The higher premiums, in turn, were also responsible for declining union employment.[1]

This empirical fact about the union sector is what Bils has discovered in his data. I do not, however, have a particularly neat explanation for this puzzling rise in union premiums. I believe that they were partly unintended. In keeping with Bils's finding, I also believe that the unintended increases were located in union contracts with COLA clauses.

The inflation of the 1970s and early 1980s was the result of supply shocks. The inflation was marked by a divergence of the Consumer Price Index (CPI) from domestic prices (GNP deflator). The typical view is that the GNP deflator is the appropriate price variable that affects the demand for labor in competitive sectors. Union contracts use the CPI as the index; hence, workers are overcompensated for the inflation of the period. In other words, the source of the puzzle is a failure of the index to correctly compensate the workers.

There is a separate issue as to why the parties did not more quickly reform the contract to adjust general wage increases for the unexpectedly high payout of the COLA clause. I believe that the answer here is contract rigidity. Contract clauses are Nash equilibria. They are infrequently changed. This relates back to the fact that the firm-union relationship is ongoing. At contract expiration, the parties update the contract by making small changes. Larger changes, such as altering the COLA clauses or undoing the effects of the COLA clause, are not undertaken lightly.[2]

To conclude, Bils has provided a damaging test of a simple model of union contract behavior. In so doing, he has moved the debate forward by showing the need to enrich the theory with those factors that differentiate union contracts from commercial contracts.

Notes

1. See Peter D. Linneman, Michael L. Wachter, and William H. Carter, "Evaluating the Evidence of Union Employment and Wages," *Industrial and Labor Relations Review,* Vol. 44, No. 1 (October 1990).

2. Michael L. Wachter, "Union Wage Rigidity: The Default Settings of Labor Law," *American Economic Review,* Vol. 76, No. 2 (May 1986), pp. 240-244.

7

Gender Differences in Cyclical Unemployment

Sanders Korenman and Barbara Okun

I. Introduction

The high and persistent unemployment rates of the 1970s have often been attributed to the entry of large numbers of women and baby-boom youth into the labor force. The historically high unemployment rates and low job-attachment of these groups are thought to have increased the overall unemployment rates at all stages of the business cycle, and made it less responsive to government policy.

Overlaid on the impact of demographic changes on labor supply are the shifts in labor demand associated with the business cycle. Following the recession in the early 1980s, the U.S. economy has experienced seven years of economic expansion. The last two years of this expansion have witnessed employment growth accompanied by relatively low and constant unemployment rates, and slow wage growth.

The increase in employers' demand for labor, which is characteristic of an expansion, can be met in three ways: unemployed workers may be hired (lowering the unemployment rate), wages may be bid up (increasing wage inflation), or people may be drawn from other activities into the labor market (increasing labor-force participation). Since the unemployment rate and wage growth have both been low and stable during this period, attention centers on the supply-side role of entry into the labor market. Could demographic changes during this expansion explain the recent pattern in labor-market conditions? During the 1980s, as in the 1960s and 1970s, a majority of new entrants have been women. After rising five percentage points in the 1960s, and seven and one-half percentage points in the 1970s, female labor-force participation rates once again rose by five percentage points in the 1980s (*Economic Report of the President,* 1990, Table C-37).[1] What does increased labor-force participation among women portend for the future performance of the economy?

As noted, women have been characterized as being less attached to the labor force than are men; on average, women are more likely to enter the labor force during expansions and more likely to exit during recessions. Economists since Perry (1970) have maintained that this procyclical labor-force participation behavior acts to dampen cyclical changes of the unemployment rate (e.g., Feldstein [1973]; Clark and Summers [1981]; Baily [1982]; and Keifer and Neumann [1982]), as it leads women to have less cyclically volatile unemployment rates than men. This chapter considers whether women's increased presence in the labor market can be expected to dampen or amplify business-cycle swings in unemployment rates. There are a number of possibilities.

If women in the 1980s and 1990s have the traditional low attachment to the labor force, then cyclical wage and unemployment changes will be further muted because the labor force will be increasingly composed of workers with low labor-force attachment who are more likely to respond to cyclical unemployment by leaving the labor force. Alternatively, women's higher participation rates may signal increasing labor-force attachment, so that the economy is losing a buffer and may suffer wider swings in the future. Finally, neither of these alternatives may be true if the labor-force participation behavior of women does not act as an important buffer to macro-economic shocks.

We explore these possibilities and conclude that lower labor-force attachment is not the primary explanation for greater cyclical stability of the female unemployment rate over the business cycle. We examine three types of data representing three distinct statistical "experiments" to arrive at this conclusion. Aggregate time-series data presented in the next section suggest that, despite what appears to be a convergence in male and female cyclical participation response, there is little evidence of a convergence in the cyclical behavior of female and male unemployment rates. This finding calls into question the idea that the principal explanation for gender differences in cyclical unemployment rate movements can be found in different cyclical patterns of labor-force participation. In the third section of the paper, we explore additional explanations for the lower cyclical responsiveness of female unemployment by examining data on individuals' movements into and out of employment, unemployment, and the labor force. These data also do not support the hypothesis that gender differences in labor-force attachment are the driving force behind gender differences in cyclical unemployment response. Rather, much of the difference in unemployment volatility appears to be explained by the distribution of men and women across industries and occupations.

Men, more than women, are employed in industries and occupations in which employment responds dramatically to the business cycle. Therefore, increased labor-force participation among women may indeed be associated with smaller business-cycle amplitudes and more stable unemployment rates. However, our analysis suggests that this stability is most likely the result of growth of employment in less cyclically sensitive occupations and industries (perhaps fueled by the availability of large numbers of female employees), quite apart from any issues of "labor-force attachment."

II. Aggregate Time-Series Evidence

A. *Background*

The argument that weak labor-force attachment of women is responsible for the low cyclical responsiveness of their unemployment rates is supported by a number of empirical studies,[2] the most detailed of which is Clark and Summers (1981). Clark and Summers quantify the contribution made by differences in participation behavior to differences in the unemployment rate cyclicality of different demographic groups. In contrasting the cyclical employment variation of men and women, they conclude— at least for younger women—that greater cyclical participation response (compared to men) lowers unemployment response. Thus, Clark and Summers find that "Were participation to remain constant, it is clear that aggregate demand could eliminate serious unemployment problems for most demographic groups" (p. 75).

Blank and Blinder (1984) present findings that are strikingly similar to those of Clark and Summers in documenting the lower cyclical responsiveness of female unemployment. Blank and Blinder conclude that "...white female unemployment is least affected by changes in the general unemployment rate. This finding almost surely reflects the 'discouraged worker' effect among women—a high propensity to drop out of the labor market in response to increases in unemployment" (pp. 191-192).

In summarizing their results, Blank and Blinder remark that "...female and older workers (especially those over 65)—who are also typically low wage workers—are not as sensitive to changes in general unemployment levels. This probably reflects the availability of other income sources for these workers—either transfers or earnings of other family members—that make job search less mandatory, allowing them to drop out of the labor market more easily in times of high unemployment. In addition, it might also reflect the comparative cyclicality of the occupations and industries in which women tend to work relative to men" (p. 192). Although they do not pursue the last explanation, different occupations and industries turn out to be important in accounting for gender differences in cyclical movements of unemployment (Williams [1985]; and Rives and Turner [1987]). We return to this point below.

Since 1976, the last year covered by the Clark and Summers study, female labor-force participation rates have continued to rise steadily. In the next section, we update the Clark and Summers figures to the 1980s to determine whether women's labor-force attachment has increased, and to examine whether increased attachment is associated with increased cyclical unemployment response as predicted by the "labor-force attachment" hypothesis.

B. Gender Differences in Cyclical Unemployment and Employment: An Update

A standard way to measure the cyclical responsiveness of the unemployment rate of a demographic group is to relate its unemployment rates statistically to the overall unemployment rate (e.g., Blank and Blinder), or to the prime-age male unemployment rate (e.g., Clark and Summers). Similarly, the group's labor force participation rate can be regressed on the male or overall unemployment rate to obtain a measure of its cyclical rates.

Clark and Summers employ the following identity in order to relate cyclical changes in unemployment and participation rates:

(1) $E/P = E/L * L/P,$

where E is the number of people employed, L is the labor force, and P is the population. Taking natural logs and differentials yields:

(2) $dLn (E/P) = dLn (E/L) + dLn (L/P),$

or, rearranging

(3) $dLn (1 - UR) = dLn (E/P) - dLn (L/P),$

where UR (the unemployment rate) is the fraction of the labor force that is unemployed, equal to one minus the employment rate. Changes in a group's employment rate can thereby be decomposed into a part resulting from changes in the employment to population ratio, and into a part caused by changes in the participation rate.

The first term on the right side of (3) is the percent change in the employment rate or the percentage point change in the unemployment rate that would occur "...in the absence of labor force participation adjustment," while the term on the left represents the percentage point change in the unemployment rate that results "net" of changes in participation.[3] Thus, Clark and Summers simulate changes in unemployment that would take place in the absence of labor-force participation adjustments. Cyclical behavior of labor-force participation rates and unemployment rates of various age and gender groups are estimated from regressions of these rates on current and lagged values of the prime-age male unemployment rate, on two time trends, and on a constant.[4]

In order to explore whether higher labor-force participation is associated with increased or decreased cyclical unemployment response, the sample is divided into two periods: 1950 to 1966 and 1967 to 1987, chosen to correspond to the two time trends employed by Clark and Summers (i.e., one running from 1950 to 1976, and a second starting in 1967). The log of the employment rate or participation rate of a group is regressed on a time trend, on the prime age (45 to 54) male unemployment rate, on a one-period lagged value of this variable, and on a constant. A simple first-order serial correlation correction was carried out using the standard iterative Cochrane-Orcutt procedure (Cochrane and Orcutt [1949]). The coefficients reported in Table 1 are the sums of the coefficients of the current period and one-period lagged male unemployment rates. These sums represent the percent increase in the labor force participation rate or employment rate due to a one percentage point decline in the prime-age male unemployment rate.[5] Standard errors appear in parentheses below regression coefficients.[6]

The first two columns of Table 1 present estimates of cyclical participation rate response for men and women by age group. Positive values denote procyclical participation (participation that falls as unemployment rises) and are generally evident for younger women in the early period, and for all but the oldest group of women in the later period. Negative values denote countercyclical participation, and are often interpreted as an "added worker" effect: women enter the labor force during a recession to compensate for income lost due to the unemployment of a family member. For men, there is very little association between labor-force participation rates and the prime-age male unemployment rate, with the exception of the youngest and oldest men.

Table 1: Cyclical Unemployment and Participation Response, 1950 to 1987

	Labor-force participation rates		Unemployment rates	
	1950 to 1966	1967 to 1987	1950 to 1966	1967 to 1987
Women aged:				
16 to 19	2.94	1.93	1.87	2.04
	(1.24)	(0.63)	(0.49)	(0.41)
20 to 24	−0.38	0.99	1.60	1.48
	(0.87)	(0.28)	(0.17)	(0.18)
25 to 34	1.49	0.25	1.21	1.19
	(0.83)	(0.49)	(0.20)	(0.16)
35 to 44	0.70	0.43	0.97	0.94
	(0.36)	(0.29)	(0.19)	(0.12)
45 to 54	−0.45	0.67	0.86	0.87
	(0.59)	(0.34)	(0.17)	(0.14)
55 to 64	−0.55	0.18	0.74	0.85
	(0.84)	(0.42)	(0.21)	(0.15)
65+	−2.15	−0.12	0.54	0.56
	(2.63)	(1.10)	(0.22)	(0.19)
Men aged:				
16 to 19	1.85	1.90	2.76	2.82
	(0.73)	(0.49)	(0.44)	(0.47)
20 to 24	−0.26	0.48	2.36	2.52
	(0.27)	(0.32)	(0.21)	(0.35)
25 to 34	0.14	0.31	1.25	1.43
	(0.10)	(0.05)	(0.11)	(0.16)
35 to 44	0.03	0.10	0.97	1.20
	(0.08)	(0.07)	(0.07)	(0.11)
45 to 54	0.05	0.00	1.04	1.04
	(0.07)	(0.11)	(0.00)	(0.01)
55 to 64	−0.14	0.36	1.14	1.12
	(0.23)	(0.30)	(0.11)	(0.08)
65+	0.59	1.63	1.11	0.71
	(0.82)	(1.02)	(0.15)	(0.19)

NOTES: Responses are the percent change in the employment rate (1 − UR) or labor-force participation rate associated with a 1 percentage point increase in the prime-age male unemployment rate. A 1 percent increase in the employment rate of a group is approximately equal to a 1 percentage point decrease in the unemployment rate of that group. Also included in the regressions are a linear time trend and a constant.

SOURCE: U.S. Department of Labor, Bureau of Labor Statistics (BLS), 1988, various tables. Data are annual averages.

There appear to be some notable differences between the two periods. First, net countercyclical participation among women seems to have disappeared by the later period, i.e., on balance, "added worker" effects are disappearing (Lundberg [1985]; and Williams [1985]). Second, age groups for whom participation rates were highly procyclical appear to show much less procyclicality. These figures suggest to us that women's labor-force attachment has increased and their labor-force participation behavior has moved toward the male pattern.[7] There is also evidence suggesting that male participation rates became slightly more cyclically responsive, perhaps the result of increased labor-force participation of married women.

The figures reported in the first two columns of Table 1 would lead to predictions of greater cyclical responsiveness of women's unemployment rates in the second period, due to their increased labor-force attachment. This would be especially true for women whose participation responses became less procyclical (i.e., ages 16 to 19, 25 to 34, and 35 to 44). Surprisingly, the figures in the third and fourth columns of Table 1 indicate very little change between periods in the association between women's unemployment rates and the prime-age male rates. For example, despite what appear to be large drops in the cyclical responsiveness of the participation rates of the three age groups just mentioned (and therefore of increases in their labor-force attachment), their cyclical unemployment responses did not budge. These estimates do not lend support to the hypothesis that differences in labor-force attachment are the principal force driving differences in cyclical behavior of male and female unemployment rates.[8]

How can we explain the finding that procyclical labor-force participation dropped, yet cyclical unemployment response did not increase accordingly? One mechanical explanation is that women who today remain in the labor force when unemployment increases (and who would have dropped out under similar circumstances in the earlier period) have unemployment risks that are comparable to those of other women in the labor force. In this case, increased attachment need not give rise to increased unemployment responsiveness.[9]

Although the results presented in this section indicate that gender differences in labor-force attachment probably do not account for gender differences in the cyclical behavior of unemployment rates, we have limited faith in the ability of these time-series estimates alone to resolve the issue. Instead, the findings could be taken as indicating that the statistical experiment conducted here (and elsewhere by other researchers) is somewhat flawed. One reason is that the flows of persons between the states of employment, unemployment, and out of the labor force are masked by aggregate data, and therefore do not distinguish among persons in a given state according to the reason for their entry into that state. The unemployed, for example, include labor-force entrants as well as job losers. On the other hand, the hypothesis that weak labor-force attachment leads to lower cyclical unemployment response implies that unemployment rates should be lower among female job losers specifically because they are more likely to leave the labor force than are their male counterparts. Aggregate time-series data can provide only indirect tests of this hypothesis.

A more promising approach is to use data that allow us to evaluate directly the labor-force attachment hypothesis. Therefore, in the next section, we examine data that capture individuals' movements into and out of employment, unemployment, and the labor force, including data on workers who are displaced from their jobs.

III. Evidence from Microdata

In this section, we present results from a more explicit statistical evaluation of the importance of labor-force participation behavior in determining gender differences in cyclical unemployment.

The most direct tests are provided by information on workers who are displaced from their jobs. These data capture the essence of cyclical unemployment: job loss. If gender differences in labor-force attachment determine gender differences in cyclical unemployment, then:

1) the unemployment rate at a given time after job loss should be lower for women than men;

2) women who lose their jobs should be more likely than their similarly displaced male counterparts to drop out of the labor force; and

3) women's greater propensity to drop out of the labor force following displacement should be the principal explanation for women's lower unemployment rates after displacement.

Although data on displaced workers allow us to examine directly the labor-force attachment hypothesis, a limitation is that displaced workers make up only a portion of unemployed workers, so that their experience cannot be generalized to the entire unemployed population. Therefore, we also present data concerning the unemployment experience of all workers at the height of the early 1980s recession. Data on all workers complement those on displaced workers by representing a broader segment of the work force. However, being broader, they also cover unemployment experience during the early 1980s that should not be attributed to strictly cyclical factors. Although the two types of data are complementary, their strengths and weaknesses should be kept in mind when evaluating what follows.

A. *Displaced Workers, 1984 and 1986*

Data come from the Displaced Workers Survey, 1984 and 1986, a supplement to the January Current Population Survey (CPS).[10] We restrict our sample to persons aged 20 to 61 who were full-time workers on the job from which they were displaced, and exclude students and construction workers. A worker is "displaced" if he or she lost a job due to a plant closing, employment cutback due to slack work, elimination of a shift or position, or layoff from a job to which he or she has not been recalled.

For our purposes, data on displaced workers have an important advantage over other types of data that follow workers across labor force or employment states (e.g., "gross flows" data). With data on displaced workers, we can be fairly certain about the reason for workers changing states (they lost their jobs). Finding out what happens after job loss is essential for testing the labor-force attachment hypothesis.

The first panel of Table 2 reports unemployment rates and labor-force participation rates as of January 1986 for workers who were displaced from their jobs within the previous year. In 1986, with the exception of the oldest group, women's unemployment rates are lower (less responsive to job loss), and their labor-force participation rates are lower, than men of the same age. These figures would appear to lend support to the labor-force attachment hypothesis because the first two criteria listed above are fulfilled. However, female unemployment rates would have remained well below male unemployment rates even if male and female labor-force participation behavior had been identical. This is shown in the last column of Table 2 (headed UR'), which demonstrates that even if female labor-force participation rates were brought up to male levels by placing the appropriate fraction of women who were out of the labor force into unemployment, female unemployment rates would remain below the corresponding male unemployment rates.[11] This extreme assumption, of course, leads to a gross overstatement of what the female unemployment rate would be in the counterfactual world where women's labor-force attachment is as high as men's.

The objection could be raised that 1986 was not a recession year and hence does not properly simulate cyclical unemployment. In Table 2's lower panel, we present unemployment rates and labor-force participation rates as of January 1984 for workers who were displaced in 1983. Unlike the results for 1986, displaced women have *higher* unemployment rates than their male counterparts despite women's lower participation rates. The higher female unemployment rates in 1984 after displacement might be taken as evidence that higher attachment increases unemployment response. Proponents of this hypothesis might argue that, by definition, persons at risk of displacement have high labor-force attachment. Moreover, the higher unemployment rate for displaced women stands in contrast to the lower unemployment rate for all women found in official unemployment statistics (11.3 percent of the male labor force and 10.4 percent of the female labor force was unemployed as of January 1983; BLS, 1988, Table A7). While this is a plausible alternative interpretation of the data, recall that we also found women's labor-force attachment to be lower than that of their male counterparts in 1986, but female unemployment rates following displacement were lower in that year than the corresponding male rates (and were lower to a degree that could not be explained by differences in labor-force attachment). Therefore, evidence from the Displaced Workers Surveys is perhaps inconclusive, but nonetheless suggests that the labor-force attachment hypothesis provides an incomplete explanation for gender differences in cyclical unemployment-rate movements.

A remaining issue is how to reconcile our findings of higher female unemployment rates for workers displaced in 1983 with the lower overall female unemployment rates in 1983. There are several potential explanations. First, women may be less likely than men to be displaced workers. In our samples, men comprised nearly two-thirds of the displaced workers, whereas they made up only slightly more than half of the labor force. If unemployment rates among workers who are not displaced are lower

Table 2: **Unemployment and Labor-Force Participation Rates for Workers Displaced During the Previous Year, January 1984 and January 1986**

	Men			Women			
	Percent	LFPR	UR	Percent	LFPR	UR	UR'
Jan. 1986							
Age:							
20 to 24	19.6	90.9	42.8	21.9	86.9	37.4	40.2
25 to 34	37.4	93.0	45.2	33.4	89.3	36.9	39.4
35 to 44	23.2	95.5	46.0	22.3	88.8	40.8	45.0
45 to 61	19.8	89.4	49.1	22.1	80.0	58.7	63.0
All ages	100.0	92.5	45.7	100.0	86.6	42.4	46.1
Jan. 1984							
Age:							
20 to 24	18.2	93.2	47.9	23.9	87.5	48.7	51.8
25 to 34	40.0	95.1	41.5	33.2	84.7	45.0	50.0
35 to 44	19.6	94.8	43.6	22.7	81.4	44.8	52.6
45 to 61	22.2	92.6	58.0	20.2	87.8	60.4	62.5
All ages	100.0	94.2	46.6	100.0	85.2	49.2	54.1

NOTES: For definition of "displaced" see text. UR' is the female unemployment rate that would result from bringing the female labor-force participation rate up to the corresponding male rate by reclassifying the appropriate fraction of women into unemployment. Sample sizes: 974 men and 565 women in 1984; 954 men and 521 women in 1986.

SOURCE: Displaced Workers Survey, January 1984 and 1986.

than those who are displaced, this alone would lower women's unemployment response relative to men's. There are, in turn, three reasons that women may be less likely to be "displaced." First, they may face lower probabilities of being displaced from any type of job. Second, for definitional reasons, they may not be at risk of displacement (e.g., women are less likely to work full time). Third, women may be less likely to be employed in industries that account for a large percentage of displaced workers, such as durable manufacturing or mining (Horvath [1987]).

The second reason that comparisons of overall unemployment rates may differ from comparisons of unemployment rates among displaced workers is that among workers who are not displaced, unemployment rates may be lower for women than for men.

Since displaced workers make up a small fraction of all unemployed workers, we expand our analysis in the next section to include a broader segment of the labor force.

B. Data from the March 1983 Current Population Survey

We analyze data from March 1983 because of its proximity to the trough of the early 1980s recession. (Unemployment rates peaked for men at 12.0 percent in February 1983, and, for women, at 10.4 percent in January 1983.) In effect, we are assuming this unemployment represents cyclical unemployment (primarily unemployment resulting from job loss) even though only a portion of it should be attributed to strictly cyclical factors. Thus, the March CPS data have the advantage of representing the entire population and labor force, while the Displaced Workers Survey data allow us to restrict our attention to workers who lost jobs within the previous year.

We consider four samples from the March 1983 CPS: (1) all persons who participated in the labor force (LF) for one week or more in the 12 months preceding the survey ("last year" or LY); (2) those in the first group who are also in the labor force as of the survey week; (3) those who experienced one week or more of unemployment over the same period; and (4) those in the third group who are also in the labor force as of the survey week. We also study two measures of unemployment: unemployed in the survey week and unemployed for one week or more in the previous 12 months ("experienced any unemployment last year").

Our purposes are twofold. First, we seek to compare gender differences in unemployment between two groups: that is, between all persons who worked in the previous year and current labor-force participants. If labor-force exits among un-employed women lower women's unemployment rates relative to men's, then gender differences in unemployment among current participants should be greater than among those who participated at all in the previous year. Second, we seek to explore alternative explanations for gender differences in unemployment.

Listed in Tables 3 and 4 are coefficients and standard errors from ordinary least squares (OLS) linear probability models of unemployment.[12] The samples are re-stricted to persons between the ages of 20 and 61 (inclusive) who participated in the labor force at least one week in the previous year, and who were either private- or public-sector nonagricultural workers.

The first and second columns of Table 3 present coefficients of female indicator variables representing gender differences in the probability of experiencing unemploy-ment in any week of the previous 12 months. These coefficients are for all persons in the labor force last year, and for the subset of persons who are also currently in the labor force, respectively. If procyclical labor-force participation plays a major role in explaining gender differences in cyclical unemployment, we would expect the figures in the second column to be greater than those in the first column. If female job losers are more likely than their male counterparts to leave the labor force, thus driving down female unemployment rates, then women who remained in the labor force would be

Table 3: Coefficients (SEs) of Female Indicator Variables from Linear Probability Models, March 1983

| | Dependent variable = any unemployment LY | | Dependent variable = currently unemployed persons | | | |
| | | | All persons | | UNE 1+ Weeks LY | |
	All	Currently in LF	All	Currently in LF	All	Currently in LF
Controls						
1. None	−4.3	−4.4	−3.7	−3.4	−11.0	−9.8
	(0.4)	(0.4)	(0.3)	(0.3)	(1.1)	(1.2)
2. Age, age^2, education (4), urban, black, married	−4.9 (0.4)	−4.9 (0.4)	−4.0 (0.3)	−3.8 (0.3)	−10.4 (1.1)	−9.1 (1.2)
3. Industry (12), occupation (7), and controls in specification 2	−0.4 (0.5)	−0.2 (0.5)	−1.4 (0.3)	−1.1 (0.3)	−6.2 (1.3)	−5.0 (1.4)
Mean of dependent variable	18.5	18.2	7.9	8.5	29.3	32.1

NOTES: All models contain an intercept. LF = labor force; LY = last year; UNE = unemployed. The sample is restricted to persons aged 20-61 who participated in the labor force one week or more in the previous year, and who were nonagricultural private- or public-sector employees. Data are weighted. Weights are rescaled to sum to the original sample size of 60,441: 31, 690 men to 28,751 women.
SOURCE: Annual Demographic Files, CPS, 1983.

less likely than all women who participated last year to have experienced a spell of unemployment, while there would be a much smaller difference for men.

As can be seen from the top two rows of the first and second columns, women are four to five percentage points less likely than men to have experienced unemployment in the previous year, whether or not the sample is restricted to current labor-force participants (i.e., there are no differences between the first and second columns). This holds regardless of whether controls are included for urban residence, education (four dummy variables), age and age squared, marital status, and race, despite the fact that all of these characteristics are strong predictors of unemployment. Evaluated at the sample mean, four and one-half percentage points represent a 25 percent lower probability of experiencing unemployment.

Strikingly, when controls for broad occupations and industries are entered into the models (third row), there are no longer sizable or statistically significant differences between men and women in the probability of experiencing unemployment.[13]

Similar conclusions emerge from comparisons of current labor-force status (rather than incidence over the previous year) between men and women, presented in the

Table 4:   Gender and Marital Status Differences in Unemployment Probabilities, Linear Probability Models, March 1983

	Coefficients (standard errors)					
	Dependent variable = any UNE LY		Dependent variable = currently unemployed persons			
			All persons		UNE 1+ weeks LY	
	All	In LF	All	In LF	All	In LF
1. Without occupation or industry controls						
Unmarried men	5.8 (0.6)	5.4 (0.6)	3.7 (0.4)	4.2 (0.5)	2.3 (1.5)	3.8 (1.6)
Unmarried women	−1.4 (0.6)	−1.6 (0.6)	−1.6 (0.4)	−1.4 (0.4)	−7.5 (1.7)	−6.2 (1.8)
Married women	−3.7 (0.5)	−3.7 (0.5)	−3.3 (0.4)	−2.7 (0.4)	−11.0 (1.5)	−8.2 (1.8)
2. With occupation and industry controls						
Unmarried men	5.0 (0.6)	5.0 (0.6)	3.7 (0.4)	4.2 (0.5)	3.7 (1.5)	5.0 (1.6)
Unmarried women	2.9 (0.6)	2.9 (0.6)	1.0 (0.4)	1.3 (0.5)	−2.8 (1.8)	−1.6 (1.9)
Married women	0.8 (0.6)	1.0 (0.6)	−0.6 (0.4)	0.1 (0.4)	−5.9 (1.7)	−3.4 (1.9)

NOTES: All models contain an intercept. LF = labor-force; LY = last year; UNE = unemployed. The sample is restricted to persons aged 20-61 who participated in the labor force one week or more in the previous year, and who were nonagricultural private- or public-sector employees. Data are weighted. Weights are rescaled to sum to the original sample size of 60,441: 31,690 men and 28,751 women.
SOURCE: Annual Demographic Files, CPS, 1983.

third through sixth columns. Again, women are found to have substantially and statistically significantly lower unemployment probabilities than men, whether or not the sample is restricted to those currently in the labor force, and whether or not controls for race, education, marital status, age, and urban residence are included in the regressions. There are no significant differences between figures in the third versus fourth columns, nor between the fifth and sixth. As above, this suggests that women's procyclical participation was not a major determinant of gender differences in unemployment during the 1982 to 1983 recession. Note that the fourth column of the table corresponds roughly to the differences between published unemployment rates of women and men: i.e., in the fraction of the labor force that is unemployed. Differences in occupations and industries (third row), can account for a large portion (over two-thirds) of the estimated gender difference in unemployment.[14]

A promising avenue for explaining gender differences in cyclical unemployment and participation is the role played by the presence of other family or household members. In fact, it is sometimes argued that lower labor-force attachment among women is a function of the availability of income via the husband's employment. This hypothesis suggests a more direct consideration of marital status in explaining unemployment differences. Table 4 presents results from such a consideration. Reported are coefficient estimates from linear probability models, where the effect of gender on unemployment probabilities is allowed to vary by marital status. (The specifications reported in Table 4 correspond to the second and third rows of Table 3.)

The first and second columns of the first panel of Table 4 indicate that unmarried men are the most likely to experience unemployment, followed by married men (the reference category), unmarried women, and married women. All differences between married men and others are statistically significant at conventional levels. However, controlling for occupation and industry markedly alters the rankings of the four groups in terms of their probabilities of experiencing unemployment (panel 2). For instance, controlling for occupation and industry, married men have the lowest unemployment rates, and there no longer are sizable or significant differences between married men and married women. Unmarried men and women are more likely to experience unemployment than married men and women.

Similar results appear for gender and marital status differences in the probability of being currently unemployed (columns 3 and 4). When occupation and industry are not controlled, married women have the lowest unemployment probabilities, followed by unmarried women, married men, and finally, by unmarried men. However, when occupation and industry are included in the linear probability models, the differences between married men and both groups of women are reduced substantially, and are generally not statistically significant.

Recall that the fourth column of the table roughly corresponds to differences in unemployment rates. There are two points to note about these figures. First, the unemployment rate during the 1982 to 1983 recession was higher for men than for women. For our sample, the fourth column of Table 3 puts this difference at about 3.4 percentage points at the mean, and about 1.1 percentage points after controlling for occupation, industry, and individual characteristics. The remaining differential of 1.1 percentage points could be attributed to differences in labor-force attachment. But, second, the fourth column of Table 4 demonstrates that, controlling for occupation and industry, men as a group only have higher unemployment rates than women because of the very high unemployment rates of unmarried men (also controlling for age, race, urban residence, and education). These figures make it difficult to argue that the higher cyclical responsiveness of male unemployment is primarily due to men's higher labor-force attachment, because the relatively small group of unmarried men (about one-third) that is responsible for the high male unemployment rate has *lower* labor-force attachment than other men. Similarly, married men, who have by far the highest labor-force attachment, have the lowest unemployment rates of all.[15] In no way do we mean to suggest that their exits from the labor force do not lower the cyclical responsiveness of female unemployment. For example, the figure in the fifth column for married women implies that, even after controlling for occupation and industry, married women who experience unemployment are less likely than married men to be currently unemployed (roughly 20 percent less likely, evaluated at the sample mean).

However, the estimates presented in Tables 3 and 4 do indicate that the bulk of the difference in male and female unemployment rates can be accounted for without resorting to differences in labor-force attachment as an explanation. Differences in the occupations and industries in which men and women work and the high unemployment rates of unmarried men (who do not have particularly high labor-force attachment) can explain the well-known fact that male unemployment rates rise more in recession years than female unemployment rates.

IV. Conclusion

We have explored the hypothesis that women's low labor-force attachment (procyclical labor-force participation) serves to dampen the cyclical movements of unemployment rates. First, aggregate time-series data suggest that there has been growing labor-force attachment among women, but stronger attachment has not been associated with increased cyclical unemployment response, contrary to the predictions of the labor-force attachment hypothesis.

Second, data on displaced workers from 1984 and 1986 indicate that differences in labor-force attachment provide an incomplete explanation for differences in unemployment rates between men and women. First, in both 1984 and 1986, we found evidence that women were more likely to leave the labor force following displacement. In 1984, however, female unemployment rates following displacement were higher than the corresponding male rates, whereas the opposite was the case in 1986. Even though women's unemployment rates following displacement were lower than those of their male counterparts in 1986, we showed that this difference was too large to be explained by differences in labor-force participation following displacement.

Data from the March 1983 Current Population Survey indicated that the differential distribution of men and women across industries and occupations appears to be the most important reason that the male unemployment rate is more cyclically volatile: men, to a greater degree than women, are employed in cyclically sensitive industries and occupations.

What, then, are the implications of continued increases in female labor-force participation rates? If differences in the occupations and industries in which men and women work persist, then even substantial convergence of female labor-force participation behavior to the male pattern will not guarantee convergence in the cyclical responsiveness of female and male unemployment rates. If less cyclically sensitive sectors of the economy (such as the service sector) continue to expand as women comprise a larger part of the labor force, we can expect smaller unemployment rate responses to macroeconomic shocks of given magnitudes. This lower volatility may be the silver lining around the cloud of recent concern over the shrinking share of manufacturing employment.

Acknowledgments

We thank the editors, Katharine Abraham, Larry Ball, Doug Kruse, Phil Levine, and the participants in the Macroeconomics Lunch Seminar at Princeton for helpful suggestions. We are grateful to Doug Kruse for providing data on displaced workers.

Table A1: Cyclical Changes in Unemployment and Labor-Force Participation, 1950 to 1976

Women aged:	Labor-force participation		Unemployment	
	Clark and Summers	Korenman and Okun	Clark and Summers	Korenman and Okun
Women aged:				
16 to 19	2.53	2.31	1.88	1.91
	(0.62)	(0.78)	(0.29)	(0.31)
20 to 24	0.71	0.50	1.52	1.59
	(0.66)	(0.61)	(0.20)	(0.12)
25 to 34	1.31	0.93	1.13	1.17
	(0.46)	(0.56)	(0.18)	(0.13)
35 to 44	0.55	0.47	0.95	0.97
	(0.25)	(0.28)	(0.15)	(0.13)
45 to 54	0.13	−0.21	0.83	0.86
	(0.56)	(0.43)	(0.13)	(0.11)
55 to 64	−0.79	−0.45	0.73	0.75
	(0.58)	(0.59)	(0.09)	(0.13)
65 +	−1.50	−1.08	0.59	0.62
	(1.25)	(1.58)	(0.10)	(0.14)
Men aged:				
16 to 19	1.91	1.77	2.62	2.79
	(0.45)	(0.49)	(0.51)	(0.29)
20 to 24	−0.41	0.06	2.26	2.35
	(0.30)	(0.28)	(0.59)	(0.19)
25 to 34	0.04	0.15	1.27	1.28
	(0.10)	(0.07)	(0.26)	(0.07)
35 to 44	0.01	0.06	1.05	1.00
	(0.05)	(0.06)	(0.18)	(0.04)
45 to 54	0.00	0.04	1.01	1.04
	(0.07)	(0.06)	(0.02)	(0.00)
55 to 64	−0.04	0.07	1.11	1.11
	(0.24)	(0.22)	(0.12)	(0.08)
65 +	1.68	1.21	1.02	1.06
	(0.02)	(0.73)	(0.08)	(0.10)

NOTES: See footnotes to Table 1. Specifications include two time trends, one beginning in 1950 and a second in 1967. Clark and Summers's data are quarterly and include seven lagged values of unemployment. Both sets of estimates employ a correction for first-order serial correlation.

SOURCE: U.S. Department of Labor, Bureau of Labor Statistics (BLS) 1988, various tables; and Clark and Summers (1981).

Table A2: Cyclical Unemployment Response with and without Labor Force Participation Responses, 1950 to 1966 and 1967 to 1987

	1950 to 1966		1967 to 1987	
	Full participation response	No participation response	Full participation response	No participation response
Women aged:				
16 to 19	1.87	4.81	2.04	3.97
20 to 24	1.60	1.22	1.48	2.47
25 to 34	1.21	2.70	1.19	1.44
35 to 44	0.97	1.67	0.94	1.37
45 to 54	0.86	0.41	0.87	1.57
55 to 64	0.74	0.19	0.85	1.03
65 +	0.54	−1.62	0.56	0.48
Men aged:				
16 to 19	2.76	4.62	2.82	4.72
20 to 24	2.36	2.10	2.52	3.00
25 to 34	1.25	1.39	1.43	1.74
35 to 44	0.97	1.00	1.20	1.30
45 to 54	1.04	1.09	1.04	1.04
55 to 64	1.14	1.00	1.12	1.48
65 +	1.11	1.70	0.71	2.35

NOTE: Responses are the percent change in the employment rate (1 − UR) of a particular group associated with a 1 percentage point increase in the prime-age male unemployment rate.
SOURCE: U.S. Department of Labor, Bureau of Labor Statistics (BLS) 1988, various tables.

Notes

1. After enormous increases in the 1970s, the share of youth in the labor force (e.g., ages 16 to 24) has shrunk considerably in the 1980s as the baby-boom cohorts were absorbed into the labor force, albeit at reduced wages (e.g., Bloom, Freeman, and Korenman, [1987]).

2. We will refer to this as the "labor-force attachment hypothesis" at times throughout the remainder of the paper.

3. We employ the following approximation throughout the paper: for small values of UR, $Ln(1 - UR)$ is approximately equal to $-UR$.

4. Our specifications differ slightly from those used by Clark and Summers; also, we use annual rather than quarterly data, and we study different periods. Nevertheless, Table A1 (appendix) documents that with our data (and the Clark and Summers specifications) we are able to replicate nearly exactly Clark and Summers's unemployment results, and to replicate reasonably well their labor-force participation results.

5. A positive value in the third or fourth column of the table indicates that a group's unemployment rate increases with increases in the prime-age male unemployment rate.

6. The coefficients reported in Table 1 are most easily related to the equations presented in the text as follows: the difference between the labor-force participation response and the unemployment response is equal to the percent change in the employment to population ratio associated with a one percentage point decline in the prime-age male unemployment rate, as indicated by equation (2).

7. We also run all models using the labor-force participation rate or the employment rate as the dependent variable, rather than the natural logs of these variables. Our conclusions were unchanged.

8. Although the labor-force attachment hypothesis is not the focus of his paper, the findings reported by Levine (1990) are consistent with ours. Using differences between current and retrospective unemployment as a measure of labor-force attachment, he finds that women's labor-force attachment increased markedly between 1967 and 1987, but he finds no evidence of increasing cyclical responsiveness of the female unemployment rate relative to the male rate over the same period.

9. An alternative way to present the data in Table 1 is to carry out the Clark and Summers's simulation for the two periods. The results of this exercise are reported in Table A2 (Appendix). The "full participation response" column (corresponding to the terms on the left side of equation [3]) shows little change between the two periods. More specifically, little change is observed in the "full participation responses" of women whose participation became less procyclical (16 to 19, 25 to 34, and 35 to 44-year-olds), because their unemployment rates with "no participation response" and their participation rates both became less procyclical.

10. See Kruse (1988) for further discussion of these data, as well as references to other studies using the Displaced Workers Survey.

11. UR' is the unemployment rate that would result if female and male participation rates were made equal, and if the additional women who are added to the labor force are all categorized as unemployed. It is calculated in the following manner: the difference between the male and female labor-force participation rates is added to the proportion of the female population (not labor force) that is unemployed. The resulting sum is divided by the male labor-force participation rate (which also equals the "new" female labor-force participation rate).

12. We present linear probability model coefficients and the corresponding "incorrect" standard errors

because they are easily interpreted (i.e., coefficients represent changes in probabilities). We have also estimated logit models corresponding to several of the specifications presented here. Our conclusions were not affected.

13. The industrial categories are: forestry and fishing; mining; nondurable manufacturing; durable manufacturing; transport, communication, and public utilities; trade; FIRE; low-wage services; higher-wage services; public administration; construction; and missing. The occupational categories are: managers and professionals; technical; sales and support; service; precision production, craft and repair; operators, fabricators, and laborers; forest and fishery workers; and missing. A dummy variable for public-sector workers was also included. We use Freeman's (1988) definition of low-wage services.

14. We also ran specifications that included, in addition to all of the variables listed in the table, the (log of) the average weekly earnings of workers (annual earnings divided by weeks worked). The results did not differ markedly from those reported in the third row of the table. Gender differences in unemployment rates increased slightly, and gender differences in unemployment incidence were unchanged.

15. Labor-force participation rates at survey (among those who participated at least one week in the previous year) are: 98.0 percent of married men, 92.1 percent of unmarried men, 92.1 percent of unmarried women, and 87.5 percent of married women.

Comments

Katharine G. Abraham

The central motivation underlying Sanders Korenman and Barbara Okun's analysis is to assess the effect of growing female labor-force participation on the cyclical behavior of unemployment in the United States. Historically, female unemployment has been less cyclically sensitive than male unemployment. This has been attributed to the fact that female labor-force participation has risen more during economic upturns, and fallen more during economic downtowns, than has male participation. These swings have made female unemployment higher during good times, and lower during bad times, than it would have been had female labor-force participation been less cyclically sensitive. The net effect, it is argued, has been to reduce the cyclical volatility of female unemployment.

This analysis suggests the possibility that, insofar as today's working women are more attached to the labor market than their predecessors, the economy may be losing a buffer. Alternatively, if women's labor-force attachment remains weaker than men's, the continued influx of women into the labor force may be reducing the cyclical volatility of aggregate unemployment.

To address these issues, Korenman and Okun begin with an analysis of the cyclical sensitivities of labor-force participation and unemployment during the 1950 to 1966 and 1967 to 1987 time periods for various age/sex groups. This may be as good a place as any at which to raise one criticism of the approach they have adopted. In their analysis, the prime-age male unemployment rate serves as the indicator of cyclical conditions. If prime-age men's behavior or vulnerability to economic downturns has changed over time, this measure's relationship to underlying economic conditions may have changed as well. This does not pose serious problems for comparisons between men and women during a given time period; in regressions of either labor-force participation or unemployment measures on the prime-age male unemployment rate, those labor-market aggregates for which larger responses are estimated can reasonably be concluded to be more cyclically sensitive. It does, however, complicate the interpretation of cross-time-period comparisons. The reduced procyclicality of female labor-force participation that Korenman and Okun report for a number of age groups, for example, might reflect either a change in female behavior or a change in the cyclical behavior of prime-age male unemployment. While the findings reported in the first part of the chapter are certainly of interest, I personally would have preferred the use of an alternative cyclical indicator, such as the deviation of ln(GNP) from trend, in place of the prime-age male unemployment rate.

Turning to the findings reported, one complication that becomes apparent when one looks at the numbers is that women's labor-force behavior has, in fact, always been rather heterogeneous. Korenman and Okun's results indicate that, during the 1950 to 1966 period, female labor-force participation among most younger age groups (ages 16 to 19, 25 to 34, and 35 to 44) was highly procyclical, but that among other age groups (ages 20 to 24, 45 to 54, 55 to 64, and 65+) it was, if anything, countercyclical. Moreover, even groups of women whose labor-force behavior has not conformed to the stylization outlined above—those in the age groups for which labor-force participation has fluctuated countercyclically rather than procyclically—have had unemployment rates that were less cyclically sensitive than those of men the same age. These numbers make clear that labor-force participation behavior on its own cannot fully account for male/female differences in the cyclical sensitivity of unemployment, since, all else the same, countercyclicality in labor-force participation should be associated with *greater* unemployment volatility.

Furthermore, the evolution of labor-force behavior over time has not had the expected association with the evolution of unemployment rates. In all of the age groups that have exhibited procyclical labor-force participation, Korenman and Okun demonstrate that women's labor-force participation has become less procyclical over time, but that their unemployment has not become more cyclically sensitive. These findings imply that one must look beyond the behavior of labor-force participation to explain the continued discrepancy between the cyclical volatility of male and female unemployment.

The missing link in all of this is the cyclical behavior of employment. Consider the following identity offered by the authors:

$$(1) \quad \Delta UR = -\Delta ln\,(E/P) + \Delta ln\,(L/P),$$

where UR is the unemployment rate, E is employment, L is the labor force, and P is the population, all for a particular age/sex group. This identity implies that unemployment for any group may rise either because the number of group members participating in the labor force rises, holding employment constant, or because group employment falls, holding the size of the labor force constant.[1] This same identity must also hold with respect to the responsiveness of UR, $ln\,(L/P)$, and $ln\,(E/P)$ to other variables. For example, the cyclical sensitivity of unemployment reflects not just the cyclical sensitivity of labor-force participation, but also the cyclical sensitivity of employment. While Korenman and Okun do not explicitly discuss differences in the cyclical sensitivity of employment across age/sex groups or across time periods, what they refer to as "cyclical unemployment responses without labor-force participation responses" (Table A2) could equally well be labeled "cyclical employment responses"; by equation (1), they equal the percentage changes in employment associated with a change in the prime-age male unemployment rate.

Taking employment explicitly into account helps to make sense both of differences in unemployment volatility across groups in any particular time period and of changes in unemployment volatility across time periods. For example, during the 1950 to 1966 period, the reason that female unemployment in age groups exhibiting countercyclical labor-force participation was less cyclically sensitive than male unemployment in the same age groups is that, as can be seen in Table A2, net cyclical changes in these women's employment were extremely small.

Turning to the issue of changes in the behavior of unemployment over time, if the cyclical sensitivity of female labor-force participation has fallen, but women's unemployment is no more cyclically sensitive than previously, female employment must have become less cyclically sensitive. The numbers in Table A2 of the Korenman and Okun chapter confirm that, in the relevant age groups, the responsiveness of female employment to changes in the prime-age male unemployment rate has in fact fallen, in some cases substantially.

Having concluded that labor-force participation responses cannot fully account for cross-group and cross-time-period differences in the cyclicality of unemployment and that the behavior of employment must therefore be important, the most obvious next step would be to try to explain male/female differences in the cyclical sensitivity of employment and changes in those cyclical sensitivities over time. These are not issues that Korenman and Okun tackle directly. The second part of their paper uses Current Population Survey (CPS) microdata to establish that, during the early 1980s, women's and men's occupational and industry attachments were the primary proximate determinants of their different unemployment rates. This was true both among samples of persons who had been displaced from their jobs and among the labor force as a whole. Because these findings refer only to the trough of a particular business cycle, however, one cannot conclude from them that occupational and industry attachment explain male/female differences in the cyclical sensitivity of employment. Drawing any such conclusion would require, at a minimum, similar evidence for the corresponding business-cycle peak.

Data from the payroll employment survey might also help to shed some light on male/female differences in the cyclical sensitivity of employment. While these data offer no disaggregation by age or occupation, they do provide time-series information on employment by sex and industry. They could be used to determine the relative contributions of differences in the industrial distribution of male and female employment, versus differences in the cyclical sensitivities of male and female employment within particular industries, toward explaining the overall male/female difference in the cyclical sensitivity of employment.

The point-in-time evidence in the second section of the paper also fails to illuminate the factors underlying the apparent decrease in the cyclical sensitivity of female employment. Again, I suspect that payroll-employment data might prove to be of some use. They could be used to study whether aggregate female employment elasticities have changed because women are distributed differently across industries than they used to be, as Korenman and Okun seem to suggest, or because female employment in particular industries responds differently to aggregate conditions, at least as proxied by the prime-age male unemployment rate, than used to be the case.

In short, as is true of most research endeavors, this paper raises a good many questions that it leaves unanswered. I am persuaded that female labor-force participation alone can account neither for male/female differences nor for cross-time-period differences in the cyclical behavior of unemployment. By implication, differences in the cyclical behavior of employment merit further study. Korenman and Okun's finding that occupational and industry attachment play at least as important a role as gender *per se* in the determination of unemployment during the 1980s is provocative, but further work would certainly aid our understanding of these issues. Somewhat ironically, given that the paper is billed as a study of gender differences in the cyclical behavior of unemployment, perhaps the major contribution of the Korenman and Okun study is to draw the attention of those who would attempt to identify the structural determinants of cyclical volatility in the economy away from gender to focus on the characteristics of jobs.

Note

1. In an open system, one would also have to take changes in population into account.

8

Macroeconomic Implications

Olivier Jean Blanchard

Let me start with one slightly off-the-wall comment before turning to the central issues. Quite apart from the effects lump-sum bonuses may have on employment and wage determination, they may go some way towards solving the problem of the low saving rate in the United States.

Lump-sum bonuses are, in most cases, paid in large chunks, usually with a "ratification payment" after a contract is signed and with annual installments thereafter. While an uneven path of income should not affect a rational consumer, there are good reasons to think that, in fact, it does. It is often argued, although my attempts to track down quantitative proof have failed, that in countries in which workers receive a large payment once a year (such as the payment of a 13th month), some of the money is permanently saved. The idea that workers may gear consumption to the usual level of monthly income, using bonuses partly for extraordinary expenses and partly for savings, is highly plausible.

Even if only a fraction of bonuses was saved, the effects would not be inconsequential. Bonus payments range from 2 percent to 10 percent of annual pay. Taking a midrange value of 6 percent, and assuming that one-third was saved, would lead to an increase in workers' savings of 2 percent. What is saved is eventually dissaved so that this does not translate to a 2 percent increase in the savings rate, but it is far from negligible.

Let me now return to the main topic. Before one can say anything about macro implications of the new forms of labor contracts, one must answer two questions. What do lump-sum bonuses (LSB for short in what follows) and profitsharing schemes (PS) really do? What change in the environment has led to the widespread adoption of LSBs in the 1980s? Then one can ask whether those presumably privately optimal arrangements will affect the macroeconomy for better or for worse. This is a tall agenda, but it is worth trying.

I. What Do LSB and PS Schemes Really Do?

What profitsharing schemes do is clear: they share profit and risk. But the real purpose of lump-sum bonuses is far less clear. We have heard a number of hypotheses at this conference. One, argued most forcefully by Ken Ross in his comments on Bell and Neumark, is that they have been introduced to affect wage concessions, making them more palatable and/or more obscure to the workers. The formal evidence, however, suggests another interpretation. Put a bit formally, it suggests that the introduction of lump-sum bonuses, instead of standard increases in the base wage, is the purchase of an option by firms not to increase wages in the next contract if economic conditions are bad.

Two pieces of evidence argue in favor of this interpretation. The first comes from Bell and Neumark, who find little evidence that LSBs matter for anything they can measure. The second comes from the work of Erickson and Ichino (1989), who construct measures of total compensation growth in contracts with and without LSBs, using a data base of 455 contracts, including 66 with LSB provisions, over the period 1982 to 1988. The rate of growth in contracts with LSBs is 3.4 percent annually versus 3.5 percent for contracts without LSBs. Even this small difference is misleading because LSBs are often introduced in concessionary environments. Controlling for other factors, such as regional and industry characteristics, Erickson and Ichino find that contracts with LSBs have actually paid (statistically) significantly more than those without LSBs. A natural interpretation of these findings is that these excess payments represent the purchase of an option by firms.

Under that interpretation, there is an interesting difference between PS plans and LSBs. Profitsharing plans imply sharing of both small and large risks, and can be thought of as a more or less linear sharing rule. LSBs may be very nonlinear. Workers get their wage increases unless things are very bad, such as when the firm, for example, is facing a high risk of bankruptcy and all jobs are thus at stake. LSBs may be aimed at decreasing bankruptcy risk, not at sharing profit. For that reason, it may well be that LSBs are not, as has been argued by some at this conference, the first step towards explicit profit sharing, but rather a different animal.

II. Why Have LSBs Been So Popular in the 1980s?

The chapter by Mark Bils reminds us of the difficulty of explaining institutional changes by changes in the environment. Why contracts are designed the way they are often appears to have little to do with the current environment, but more to do with the accidents of history. Nevertheless, the increase in the proportion of contracts with LSBs in the 1980s appears too large to be dismissed as just a fad. Under my interpretation of LSBs, the natural culprit is any factor that led to an increase in the risk of bankruptcy under standard wage arrangements. And, at this stage, one cannot help but remember that new forms of labor contracts are only one of the changes in risk-sharing arrangements that have taken place in the 1980s. Another change, which has received much attention, although it is of smaller quantitative macroeconomic magnitude (see for example Bernanke and Campbell [1988]), has been the increase in leverage and the increase in risk, including bankruptcy risk, facing shareholders and managers.

Surprisingly, studies of the causes of the introduction of new financial arrangements and of new forms of labor contracts have proceeded independently. The explanations usually given for the increased leverage range from the existence of "free cash flow," to changes in the technology of financial intermediation (see, for example, Jensen [1988]). The explanations given for new labor contracts emphasize instead higher uncertainty and higher competition in product markets. The schizophrenia is intellectually unappealing, and the tensions between the two strands of research are obvious. The first strand tries hard to explain why financial arrangements that, among other things, increase the risk of bankruptcy, may be privately optimal. The second strand tries just as hard to explain why, given the new environment, new forms of labor contracts are desirable precisely because they decrease the risk of bankruptcy. One is tempted, if only for the sake of intellectual simplicity, to look for an integrated explanation. A number of possibilities come to mind.

Leveraged buy-outs (LBOs) or management buy-outs (MBOs) increase the stake of managers in the ups and downs of companies, which is widely thought to be good. They also increase bankruptcy risk, which, if bankruptcy and reorganization costs are substantial, can be quite bad. If my interpretation of LSBs as labor contracts that decrease bankruptcy risk without otherwise introducing much risk-sharing is correct, then managers of companies that have gone through LBOs will find LSBs highly appealing because they will decrease bankruptcy risk without affecting their incentives very much. Under that interpretation, LBOs and LSBs are then part of a restructuring of claims that leads to a better incentive structure without much of an increase in the probability of bankruptcy.

One can also think of a more cynical interpretation. Under that interpretation, increased leverage works as an incentive device mostly because it increases the risk of bankruptcy, which managers will then try hard to avoid. That is, they will try hard to avoid bankruptcy unless they can reduce this risk by getting workers to accept wage cuts in bad times by introducing LSBs. Under this interpretation, LSBs partly cancel the effects of the changes in financial structure. The net effect of changes in financial structure and labor contracts then is a transfer of fixed claims from the workers to the debt holders, without much effect on the incentives of managers. (The net effect on the firm need not, however, be unproductive, because the increase in debt leads to a bigger tax break.)

All this is pure speculation. But the basic point must be correct, that looking at both sets of changes in isolation cannot be right. At a minimum, it suggests looking at whether there has been any relation between firms that have experienced major changes in financial structure, and those that have offered profitsharing or lump-sum bonuses to their workers.

If LSBs are really designed mainly to reduce bankruptcy risk, another interesting question is why unions appear to be so opposed to their adoption. After all, a decrease in bankruptcy risk could be beneficial to both the firm and its workers, and, as we have seen, workers seem to be compensated anyway for the introduction of LSBs. One possible explanation, which I find appealing, is that the unions do not quite know what option the firm has bought, and what the "bad times" are under which the firm will ask to exercise the option. Put another way, what happens when contracts with LSBs are renegotiated is still, at this stage, anybody's guess.

III. What Might the Macro Implications Be?

The fact that new labor contracts are presumably privately optimal surely does not imply that they are socially optimal. Let me focus on LSBs and assume, as I have argued, that LSBs in effect allow for automatic wage slowdowns or reductions when a firm is close to bankruptcy. What then are the likely macro implications?

To the extent that they lower the risk of bankruptcy, and ignoring the incentive effects I discussed earlier, LSBs are almost unambiguously good from the point of view of short-run stabilization. Here again, the parallel with the macroeconomic research on the effects of new financial arrangements is striking. There, the theme is that increased bankruptcy risk is socially bad, as it may lead to multiplier effects, Minsky crises, and other bleak scenarios. (For a discussion, see Bernanke [1989]. Most of the arguments there are directly applicable to new forms of labor contracts, with the sign changed.)

To the extent that they lead to wage decreases rather than to plant closings in sectors in difficulty, LSBs will affect the pattern of labor mobility in response to sectoral shocks. Under fixed wages, unemployment is the signal that leads workers to leave declining sectors. Under LSBs, signals will come from both wage differentials and unemployment. The evidence, however, is that workers respond much more to unemployment than to wage differentials. Thus, LSBs may not have much of a quantitative effect there.

Finally, with respect to aggregate shocks, LSBs will lead to more wage flexibility. In a recession, some wages will fall not because of unemployment but because of poor profit conditions, leading to a stronger effect of aggregate conditions on wages and on inflation. While recent papers (DeLong and Summers [1986], for example), echoing an old theme from Keynes, have pointed out the dangers of excessive nominal wage flexibility, I have little doubt that, starting from the current situation, such an increase in wage flexibility is likely to be stabilizing. It suggests, however, modifications in the specification of the Phillips curve. Profitsharing schemes and the widespread adoption of LSBs suggest a direct effect of profit on wage determination, a theme emphasized in particular by Ed Kuh in the early work on the Phillips curve.

Under my suggested interpretation of LSBs, a better variable than profit may be a variable more closely associated with bankruptcy risk. Candidates for bankruptcy may be the proportion of firms with poor profit performance, or with more indirect indicators, such as various premia on private versus government bonds in financial markets. In unpublished work, Pierre Fortin has reported that the financial "crunch" variable developed by Eckstein and Sinai appears to play an important role in recent wage developments in Canada. A similar examination for the United States would clearly be worthwhile.

Acknowledgments

These comments rely heavily on work done by Chris Erickson and Andrea Ichino at MIT, and I thank them for providing me with information and insights. I also thank Ben Bernanke and Julio Rotemberg for a stimulating discussion.

Macroeconomic Implications

Finn E. Kydland

My main focus will be on what the chapters in this book have to offer that can influence the answers to, or the way we approach, interesting business-cycle questions. Frisch (1933) made a distinction between impulse and propagation. This distinction is still useful. An important question that has occupied business-cycle theorists for decades is: What are the main sources of shocks that lead to business-cycle fluctuations? And given the nature of these shocks, how much of business-cycle fluctuations do they account for?

For each source of shocks, the answer to the latter question clearly depends on the propagation mechanisms as well as on the magnitudes of the shocks. The propagation of shocks over time has to be intimately related to the ability and willingness of households and businesses to substitute time as well as goods intertemporally. Thus, business-cycle theorists are interested in labor-market facts that may influence their thinking both with regard to the sources of shocks and about the nature of the propagation. An understanding of these issues is a necessary precondition for obtaining reliable answers to policy questions.

I. Organization of Empirical Knowledge

The neoclassical growth (NG) model has become the established framework for addressing questions in aggregate economics. Its emergence in this role changes the way empirical knowledge about national income and product accounts data is organized. The NG model framework has replaced the system-of-equations (SE) approach that had gathered momentum in the 1950s and that became predominant in the 1960s. Perhaps the most prominent example of the SE approach can be found in the large macroeconometric models of that period. A central component of SE models, in addition to identities, institutional rules, and technology constraints, was *behavioral relations,* such as consumption function, investment equation, labor-demand function or wage equation, money-demand function, and so on, with parameters to be estimated using time-series methods.

The SE empirical approach of determining relations between aggregate variables appeared to be a reasonable one and had parallels in the natural sciences. A serious blow to the SE approach, however, was the demonstration by Lucas (1976) that, not only was the theoretical foundation incomplete, but that these models were inconsistent with dynamic economic theory. Lucas showed that such behavioral relations are not invariant to changes in the paths of policy variables or in the rules governing their motion. This is a serious problem for policy evaluation, which was a major purpose for which the models had been designed. It is true that, at that time, the requisite dynamic economic theory was lacking in general. That is no longer the case, however, as major advances in the development of tools for dynamic aggregate analysis have been made (see, e.g., Stokey and Lucas [1989]).

The current view, with which I sympathize, is that business-cycle theory cannot be separated from growth theory. Neoclassical growth theory clearly got a head start in the 1950s and, by the 1970s, had to be regarded as the established framework for aggregate analysis. This is reflected, for example, in the fact that Lucas (1977) defined the cycle as the deviations in real output from trend, which one can interpret as the deviations from established growth theory. Much of business-cycle theory represents extensions of the NG model to address questions related to the cyclical behavior of aggregate national income and product accounts data. This framework is now being used also to address questions in public finance and in international trade, with the aim of obtaining *quantitative* answers.

Central to NG growth theory is the neoclassical production function. Solow (1956, 1957) pioneered its use in growth theory, and proposed a method for measuring technological change as the residual in output growth after the capital and labor inputs have been accounted for. In his overview of growth theory, Solow (1970, p. 2) talks about the influence that the growth regularities, which he attributes to Kaldor, had on this development. For the questions asked in growth theory, however, the time-allocation decision did not play an important role. For business-cycle questions, in contrast, this decision is essential.

Listed below are some cyclical regularities of aggregate labor markets (see Kydland and Prescott [1990]). The cyclical variability of aggregate hours of work is almost as large, in percentage terms, as that of real GNP. Only about one-third of the quarterly variability of aggregate hours of work comes from variation in hours per worker, while about two-thirds is in the form of employment changes. Both measures are highly procyclical, the former perhaps with a slight lead relative to real GNP, while employment lags the cycle by a quarter or so. Average labor productivity also is procyclical, but much less so, with a lead of a quarter or two depending on whether the hours data are taken from the household or the establishment survey. Average real compensation in the business sector displays cyclical behavior that is not much different from that of productivity.

The organization of empirical knowledge implied by the NG framework is very different from that of the SE approach, where the focus was on parameters or elasticities in behavioral equations. In the NG framework, empirical knowledge is organized around the parameters of technology, preferences, information structure, and institutional arrangements. Most parameters in a model within that framework simply follow from the growth facts, namely average noncyclical relations in the data that change little from cycle to cycle. Examples include the long-run fractions of each aggregate component to GNP, including factor shares and other elements such as stock-to-output ratios of various types. These are the same facts that influenced Solow and others in the development of NG theory and that are important today in public finance.

Other NG parameters are related to elasticities of substitution. In some cases, for example, the relative price has changed substantially, sometimes over several decades, with little or no change in the corresponding quantity or in its share of expenditures. Historical experiments of this type suggest strongly that unitary elasticity of substitution is not far off the mark.

In some instances in the development of NG theory, panel data have been used to determine parameter values. For example, the long-run share of discretionary time allocated to market activity has played an important role for some business-cycle questions. Ghez and Becker (1975) used panel data not only to compute an average value of the numerator of this fraction, but also provided values of the denominator for major demographic groups. In so doing, they measured and excluded average sleeping time, as well as time spent for personal care.

There are many other interesting measurements that would be valuable inputs into business-cycle modeling. In business production, for example, employers often vary the number of hours plants are operated, occasionally closing down a plant while operating the remaining ones with approximately the same number of workers as before. A potentially important question is: Do most short-run changes in hours take this form? Or is there a significant portion of the economy with more variation in the number of workers per machine, thus implying a greater extent of decreasing returns?

Household production is also gaining attention in the business-cycle literature. More needs to be known about the interaction between the two wage earners in two-worker families. Various forms of durables in the household may play a role for cyclical behavior of the hours allocated to market activity. Speaking broadly, one could include among such durables health, quality of children, and other things, in the accumulation or maintenance of which one should expect considerable willingness to substitute intertemporally.

The implication for the discussion of the papers in this volume is that their usefulness for analyzing business-cycle questions depends crucially on whether the results have been organized in such a way that they fit in with or can be translated into the NG framework used in aggregate theory. As the Ghez-Becker example shows, labor economics can serve a useful role in imposing discipline on aggregate economics and on the experiments used to provide numerical answers to the questions addressed. This function can be served, for example, by providing new or better measurements, either of parameter values directly, or of magnitudes from which parameter values can be inferred.

Unfortunately, many of the results in the papers in this volume are in fact in the context of equations of the type that one finds in system-of-equations models. Several papers focus on wage equations or on Phillips-curve equations. For example, Vroman and Vroman look for evidence of effects from trade variables in nominal-wage equations that also include the effects of expected inflation and of contract agreements in the steel and auto industries. But these are all endogenous variables that may be associated with the nominal and real wage in complicated ways depending on the source and propagation of the shocks. The authors are puzzled by the net export share of GNP having a negative coefficient in the wage equation. Similarly, they are puzzled by the import share having a positive coefficient on wages in their regression equations. With both imports and exports being procyclical, and with exports having a lag of two or three quarters, the net-export share of GNP is slightly negatively correlated, and more so with a lead. As already noted, aggregate real labor compensation is procyclical with a lead, so it is not surprising to find such associations, at least for the component of wages not accounted for by inflation.

Presenting the results in terms of estimated equations of that type limits, in my opinion, the usefulness of some of the other papers as well. There also is a tendency to focus on unemployment, either as the variable of interest or as an indicator of the status of aggregate or local labor markets. For many questions, of course, the unemployment rate is the variable of interest. To use it as an indicator of the "demand" situation, or of activity in general in the economy, or in a sector thereof, is questionable practice. For example, when some authors focus on differences in the behavior of unemployment rates among age-sex groups in the postwar period, they fail to take into account factors such as the draft or changes in unemployment benefits that may have played a significant role for unemployment of some groups over this period.

II. Demographic Changes

As central as the neoclassical production function is to aggregate theory, a challenging task is to measure the inputs of capital and labor, the latter being particularly important for the measurement of Solow residuals and for business-cycle questions in general. It is well known that aggregate hours is not a good measure of the labor input. This measure gives equal weight to workers with very different human capital. In this sense, a standard principle in national income and product accounting is ignored. Standard practice for most other real series is to weight by some measure of long-run prices, usually for some base year. In contrast, aggregate hours as a measure of labor input gives equal weight, for example, to the hours of the orderly and those of the brain surgeon. It is not obvious, however, what quantitative difference it makes. This measurement problem would not be important, cyclically, if the cyclical variability of different skill groups were quite similar. Kydland (1984) finds, however, that there are sizable cyclical differences among skill groups even for prime-age males.

Some studies have quantified the difference between standard aggregate hours and quality-adjusted hours from the point of view of growth accounting. Examples are Darby (1984), Jorgenson, Gollop, and Fraumeni (1987), and Dean, Kunze, and Rosenblum (1988), all of whom classify workers by demographic groups. They all find that quality adjustment makes a significant difference for growth accounting. From a cyclical accounting point of view, as reported in Kydland and Prescott (1989), their adjustments still make a difference, but not nearly as much as when a separate weight is used for each individual worker. We found for a panel of nearly 5,000 people from the Panel Study of Income Dynamics over the period 1969 to 1982, with all major demographic groups of the labor force represented, that the cyclical variability of our quality-weighted measure of the labor input was only about two-thirds as high as that of the standard measure of aggregate hours obtained by simply adding the hours. As a byproduct, we found that the correlation between the aggregate quantity of labor input and its real compensation is 0.52, substantially higher than between aggregate hours and the average real wage. The main reason for these findings is that the hours of the relatively less-skilled workers on the average are substantially more variable than those of the high-skilled workers.

After late 1982, there was a long string of quarterly increases in real GNP in the United States, except for a brief period in 1986 with below-average growth and even a one-quarter decline. If this were a normal upturn, one should indeed expect the average real-wage growth, conventionally measured, to be lower than that in compensation per unit of labor input. That is a finding that seems to emerge from a couple of the studies in this volume. Unfortunately, because the results are presented mostly in the form of wage equations, it is difficult to tell whether, quantitatively, the behavior of the real wage in the 1980s is much different than in the average postwar upturn.

Vroman and Vroman mention that unemployment among prime-age males remained unusually high during the 1980s and suggest that this fact may have contributed to low wage growth. They do not, however, pursue the question of the compositional effect. This is unfortunate, as a careful quantitative study of this effect for the 1980s easily could have been the most interesting part of their paper. Towards the end, the authors present some facts on employment in major industries for the period 1982 to 1988, some according to age-sex classifications, and contrast them with 1963 to 1969 data. It is not obvious, however, what to make of these facts. They are not presented in a form that lends itself easily to interpretation. Moreover, examination of short periods can be deceptive. The authors suggest, for example, that employment growth in the service sector relative to manufacturing was much larger in the 1980s than in the earlier upturn. This finding does not appear consistent with what is reported in Keane (1990). His Figure 1, covering the period 1947 to 1988, and using BLS data for all employees on nonagricultural payrolls, displays a steady employment-share increase in services and a corresponding decrease in manufacturing over this entire period, with no obvious difference in the 1960s or the 1980s.

Korenman and Okun have produced an interesting study of the effect of demographics on unemployment rates. They focus on sex differences as well as on differences between the married and unmarried. Also, they present statistics that shed light on the interaction within two-worker families. To represent their results as findings about *cyclical* responsiveness, however, is perhaps reaching too far when their data cover only two years, 1984 and 1986.

III. What Is the Wage Rate?

An interesting aspect of labor markets is the extent to which compensation takes the form of fringe benefits. According to Ehrenberg and Smith (1987, p. 138), "...total fringe benefits as a percent of payroll (which does not include pension and insurance costs) rose from 20.3 percent to 38.8 percent during 1957-84." According to their table, most of this increase had already taken place by the late 1970s. The trend may have picked up in the last half of the 1980s.

It is useful to note that the neoclassical framework by itself puts few restrictions on short-term wage payments, whether in terms of the form of payments or the allocation over time. There does not have to be a close correspondence between the quarter in which payment takes place and that of the effort. There may be risk-sharing arrangements that are outside the scope of the abstraction used to address a particular question. Recently, Danthine and Donaldson (1989) and Gomme and Greenwood (1990) have investigated whether risk-sharing contract agreements affect the findings obtained from business-cycle models. One could also mention the suggestion by Hall (1980), as paraphrased by Bils, that "...much of the labor force is described by long-term firm-worker attachments, in which decisions on employment and hours are probably chosen reasonably efficiently despite lack of wage movements that would be required in a spot labor market."

The large fraction of compensation in the form of fringe benefits raises questions about the appropriate wage concept. Consider three workers receiving the same wage rate, one who works a regular 40-hour week, one who works only half-time, and one who works 48 hours, the last eight at a rate of time-and-a-half. Looking only at the direct wage compensation may lead one to conclude that the second worker earns half as much per week as the first, and the third 30 percent more. It may very well be, however, that the second earns little or no fringe benefits, while the third worker earns the same fringes whether he works overtime or not. In this case, which is probably not atypical, the straight wage gives a misleading account of labor compensation associated with different lengths of the workweek.

IV. Final Comments

A fully articulated model economy is just as important for policy questions as it is for the study of business cycles. The neoclassical growth model is the established framework also in public finance. Mostly relying on presenting empirical labor-market results in the form of Phillips-curve relations means that less can be inferred about policy implications. In those studies, I see little that has a bearing, for example, on the interesting question: Are there short-run costs in terms of reduced output that offset the long-run benefits of a policy of low and stable inflation? To answer that, well-thought-out model experiments are needed. If the new policy regime is credible and well understood by the public, it is difficult to see wherefrom the major cost would come.

Acknowledgments

I have benefited from comments by Michael Keane.

Contributors

Katharine G. Abraham is Associate Professor of Economics at the University of Maryland. Her past research includes work on alternative measures of labor-market tightness. Professor Abraham is currently engaged in comparative analysis on labor-cost flexibility in the United States, Germany, and Japan. She received her Ph.D. from Harvard University.

Linda Bell is currently a Visiting Assistant Professor at the John F. Kennedy School of Government at Harvard University. She formerly served as an economist in the Research Department of the Federal Reserve Bank of New York. Dr. Bell received her Ph.D. from Harvard University in 1986. Her research focuses on the importance of relative wage flexibility for comparative macroeconomic performance in the United States and Western Europe.

Douglas R. Bettinger is a Research Assistant at the W. E. Upjohn Institute for Employment Research. He is currently working on issues in unemployment and wage benefits. He has a B.S. in economics from the University of Wisconsin.

Mark Bils is Assistant Professor of Economics in the Graduate School of Business at the University of Chicago. Before taking that position, he was on the faculty at the University of Rochester. Professor Bils was an Olin Fellow at the National Bureau of Economic Research during 1987-88 and is currently a National Fellow at the Hoover Institution. His research focuses on the responses of labor markets and firms' pricing to cyclical fluctuations. His Ph.D. is from the Massachusetts Institute of Technology.

Olivier Jean Blanchard is Professor of Economics at the Massachusetts Institute of Technology. He is also a Research Associate at the National Bureau of Economic Research and a member of the Brookings Panel on Economic Activity. In the past, he has held faculty posts at Harvard and Columbia Universities and has been a National Fellow at the Hoover Institution. He has published numerous books and articles on macroeconomic theory and policy. Professor Blanchard is co-editor of the *Quarterly Journal of Economics*. He received his Ph.D. in economics from Massachusetts Institute of Technology.

Randall W. Eberts is an Assistant Vice President and Economist at the Federal Reserve Bank of Cleveland, where he heads the research unit for applied microeconomics and regional economic analysis. Dr. Eberts received his Ph.D. from Northwestern University. Before joining the bank, he was an associate professor of economics at the University of Oregon.

215

Erica L. Groshen is an Economist in the Research Department at the Federal Reserve Bank of Cleveland, where she is primarily responsible for researching regional and national labor-market issues. Dr. Groshen also studies service-sector expansion and wage differences among employers. She earned her Ph.D. from Harvard University.

W. Lee Hoskins is President of the Federal Reserve Bank of Cleveland. Prior to joining the Bank in 1987, he was Chief Economist and Senior Vice President for Economics and Corporate Affairs at PNC Financial Corporation. Before that, he was Senior Vice President and Director of Research at the Federal Reserve Bank of Philadelphia. Mr. Hoskins received his Ph.D. from the University of California, Los Angeles.

Louis Jacobson is Senior Economist at the Upjohn Institute for Employment Research. He has recently been a Senior Economist with the National Commission for Employment Policy in Washington, D.C., where he studied the role of Employment Service in aiding dislocated workers. His past research includes an examination of the earnings losses of workers displaced by foreign competition. Dr. Jacobson holds a Ph.D. from Northwestern University.

Sanders Korenman is Assistant Professor of Economics and Public Affairs and Faculty Associate in the Office of Population Research at Princeton University. His current research focuses on relationships between demographic behavior and labor-market outcomes. Professor Korenman holds a doctorate in economics from Harvard University.

Douglas Kruse is Assistant Professor of Industrial Relations and Human Resources at Rutgers University. His research has focused on the areas of profit sharing, worker displacement, employee ownership, and worker rights. He received his Ph.D. in economics from Harvard University.

Finn E. Kydland is Professor of Economics at Carnegie-Mellon University and Visiting Scholar at the Institute for Empirical Macroeconomics at the Federal Reserve Bank of Minneapolis and the University of Minnesota. His current research interests include the behavior of employment and hours worked over the business cycle. He holds a Ph.D. from Carnegie-Mellon University.

David Lewin is Professor of Business in the Graduate School of Business at Columbia University. Professor Lewin is also a member of the Executive Board of the Industrial Relations Research Association. He is currently studying the effects of human resource policy and practice on firm performance and is analyzing the consequences of dispute-resolution systems in union and nonunion firms. He holds a Ph.D. from the University of California, Los Angeles.

David Neumark is Assistant Professor of Economics at the University of Pennsylvania. Prior to joining the faculty, he was an Economist at the Board of Governors of the Federal Reserve System. His current research interests include the effects of the declining strength of unions on wage inflation and the relationship between minimum wage laws and unemployment. He received a Ph.D. in economics from Harvard University.

Barbara Okun is currently pursuing her Ph.D. from the Department of Economics at Princeton University. Her areas of specialization are labor economics, econometrics, and demography.

Ken Ross is Co-Executive Director of The Alliance for Employee Growth and Development, Inc., a not-for-profit corporation owned by AT&T, the Communication Workers of America, and the International Brotherhood of Electrical Workers. Before co-founding the Alliance, Mr. Ross was Division Staff Manager of Labor Relations for AT&T, with responsibilities in job evaluation, work design, and work force training and retraining. He was also a part of the AT&T National Bargaining Team with responsibilities for using economic models to determine the cost of contract proposals.

Sharon P. Smith is Dean of the College of Business Administration at Fordham University. Prior to accepting this position, she was Visiting Senior Research Economist at Princeton University and Associate Director of the Project on Faculty Retirement, where she analyzed the impact of the elimination of mandatory retirement for tenured faculty. She has also been a labor economist for the AT&T Corporate Headquarters Labor Relations Department, and was responsible for developing wage positions for bargaining and for estimating actual and potential contract costs. She was also a Senior Economist at the Federal Reserve Bank of New York. Dr. Smith received her Ph.D. from Rutgers University.

Susan Vroman is Associate Professor of Economics at Georgetown University. She has also held economist positions at the Board of Governors of the Federal Reserve System and at the Council on Wage and Price Stability. Her current research focuses on the analysis of unemployment duration. She received her Ph.D. from Johns Hopkins University.

Wayne Vroman is a Senior Research Associate at The Urban Institute. He has held faculty positions at Oberlin College and the University of Maryland. His current research interests include relative earnings of minorities, unemployment trust funds, and regional labor-market performance. He holds a doctorate in economics from the University of Maryland.

Michael L. Wachter is Professor of Economics, Law, and Management and is Director of the Institute for Law and Economics at the University of Pennsylvania. Professor Wachter has served as a consultant to the Joint Economic Committee, the Department of Labor, and the Council of Economic Advisors. He is currently a Senior Advisor to the Brookings Panel on Economic Activity. His most recent research focuses on the economic analysis of labor law and industry wage and price determination. He received his Ph.D. in economics from Harvard University.

Stephen A. Woodbury is Associate Professor of Economics at Michigan State University and Senior Economist at the W. E. Upjohn Institute for Employment Research. He has authored several articles on the economics of nonwage benefits and a forthcoming book entitled *The Tax Treatment of Fringe Benefits*. His Ph.D. is from the University of Wisconsin.

References

Ahmed, S. July 1987. "Wage Stickiness and Non-neutrality of Money." *Journal of Monetary Economics,* 20: 25-50.

Alpert, William T. June 1983. "Manufacturing Workers' Private Wage Supplements: A Simultaneous Equations Approach." *Applied Economics*, 15: 363-378.

Andrews, Emily S. 1985. *The Changing Profile of Pensions in America.* Washington, D.C. Employee Benefits Research Institute.

Antos, Joseph R. 1983. "Analysis of Labor Cost: Data Concepts and Sources," in Jack E. Triplett, ed., *The Measurement of Labor Cost.* Chicago. University of Chicago Press: 153-181.

Antos, Joseph R., and Sherwin Rosen. May 1985. "Discrimination in the Market for Public School Teachers." *Journal of Econometrics,* 3: 123-150.

Baily, Martin. 1982. "Labor Market Performance, Competition, and Employment," in Martin Baily, ed., *Workers, Jobs, and Inflation.* Washington, D.C. The Brookings Institution: 15-44.

Ball, Lawrence. September 1987. "Externalities from Contract Length." *American Economic Review:* 615-629.

Barro, Robert J. 1972. "A Theory of Monopolistic Price Adjustment." *Review of Economic Studies,* 39: 17-26.

Becker, Gary S. 1975. *Human Capital,* second edition. New York: National Bureau of Economic Research.

Bell, John P. August 1980. "Preliminary Results Show Contribution Levels, Rates of Return Up over 1987." *Profit Sharing,* 37. Newsletter of the Profit Sharing Council of America (Chicago, IL).

Bell, Linda A. 1989. "Union Concessions in the 1980s." *Federal Reserve Bank of New York Quarterly Review,* Summer: 44-58.

Bernanke, Ben. September-October 1989. "Is There Too Much Corporate Debt?" Federal Reserve Bank of Philadelphia. *Business Review:* 3-13.

Bernanke, Ben, and J. Campbell. 1988. "Is There a Corporate Debt Crisis?" *Brookings Papers on Economic Activity,* 1: 83-125.

Bils, Mark J. December 1988. "Labor Market Behavior with Labor as a Quasi-fixed Factor." Proposal to National Science Foundation.

Blanchard, Olivier J. August 1979. "Wage Indexing Rules and the Behavior of the Economy." *Journal of Political Economy,* 87: 798-815.

Blanchflower, David G., and Andrew J. Oswald. February 1987. "Shares for Employees: A Test of Their Effects." Discussion Paper No. 273. London: Centre for Labour Economics, London School of Economics.

_____. September 1988. "Profit-Related Pay: Prose Discovered?" *The Economic Journal,* 98: 720-730.

Blank, Rebecca, and Alan S. Blinder. 1984. "Macroeconomics, Income Distribution, and Poverty," in Sheldon Danziger and Daniel Weinberg, eds., *Fighting Poverty: What Works and What Does Not.* Cambridge, MA. Harvard University Press: 180-208.

Blasi, Joseph. 1986. *Employee Ownership: Revolution or Ripoff?* Cambridge, MA: Ballinger Books.

Blau, Francine D., and Andrea H. Beller. July 1988. "Trends in Earnings Differentials by Gender, 1971-1981." *Industrial and Labor Relations Review,* 41 (4): 513-529.

Blinder, Alan S. Fall 1973. "Wage Discrimination: Reduced Form and Structural Estimates." *Journal of Human Resources,* 8: 436-453.

Bloom, David, Richard Freeman, and Sanders Korenman. 1987. "The Labor Market Consequences of Generational Crowding." *European Journal of Population,* 3: 131-176.

Bloom, Steven. 1988. "Employee Ownership and Firm Performance." Ph.D. Dissertation, Harvard University.

Bound, John, and George Johnson. May 1989. "Changes in the Structure of Wages During the 1980s: An Evaluation of Alternative Explanations." National Bureau of Economic Research, Working Paper No. 2983.

Bradley, Keith, and Saul Estrin. April 1987. "Profit Sharing in the Retail Trade Sector: The Relative Performance of the John Lewis Partnership." Draft. London School of Economics.

Brown, Charles, and James Medoff. October 1989. "The Employer-Size Wage Effect." *Journal of Political Economy,* 97: 1027-1059.

Bureau of National Affairs, Inc. 1988. *Changing Pay Practices: New Development in Employee Compensation, a BNA Special Report.* Washington, D.C.

Calvo, Guillermo A., and Edward S. Phelps. Supplement 1977. "Employment Contingent Wage Contracts," in Karl Brunner and Allan Meltzer, eds., Carnegie-Rochester Conference, *Journal of Monetary Economics,* 5: 160-168.

Cantor, R. March 1985. "Work Effort and Contract Duration." Manuscript. Ohio State University.

Canzoneri, Matthew B. April 1980. "Labor Contracts and Monetary Policy." *Journal of Monetary Economics,* 6: 241-255.

Card, David. October 1983. "Cost-of-Living Escalators in Major Union Contracts." *Industrial and Labor Relations Review,* 37: 34-48.

_____. Supplement, June 1986. "An Empirical Model of Wage Indexation Provisions in Union Contracts." *Journal of Political Economy,* 94: S144-175.

Cardinal, Laura B., and I.B. Helburn. 1987. "Union Versus Nonunion Attitudes Toward Share Agreements." *Thirty-Ninth Industrial Relations Research Association Proceedings.* Madison, WI. Industrial Relations Research Association: 167-173.

Cecchetti, Stephen G. 1987. "Indexation and Incomes Policy: A Study of Wage Adjustment in Unionized Manufacturing." *Journal of Labor Economics,* 5: 391-412.

Chamber of Commerce of the United States. Employee Benefits. (Various issues: 1951-79, 1980, 1981, 1982, 1983, 1984, 1985, 1986, 1987.) Washington, D.C.: Economic Policy Division, Chamber of Commerce of the United States.

Chelius, James, and Robert Smith. February 1990. "Profit Sharing and Employment Stability." *Industrial and Labor Relations Review,* 43, 3: 256S-273S.

Christofides, L. N. March 1985. "The Impact of Controls on Wage Contract Duration." *Economic Journal,* 95: 161-168.

Christofides, L. N., and D. A. Wilton. August 1983. "The Determinants of Contract Length: An Empirical Analysis Based on Canadian Micro Data." *Journal of Monetary Economics,* 12: 309-319.

Clark, Kim B., and Richard Freeman. November 1980. "How Elastic Is the Demand for Labor?" *Review of Economics and Statistics,* 62: 509-520.

Clark, Kim B., and Lawrence Summers. 1981. "Demographic Differences in Cyclical Employment Variation." *Journal of Human Resources,* 16 (1): 61-79.

_____. 1982. "Unemployment Insurance and Labor Market Transitions," in M. Baily, ed., *Workers, Jobs, and Inflation.* Washington, D.C. The Brookings Institution: 279-318.

Cochrane, Donald, and Guy Orcutt. 1949. "Application of Least Squares Regression to Relationships Containing Autocorrelated Error Terms." *Journal of the American Statistical Association,* 44: 32-61.

Conte, Michael A., and Jan Svejnar. 1990. "The Performance Effects of Employee Ownership Plans," in Alan Blinder, ed., *Paying for Productivity: A Look at the Evidence.* Washington, D.C. The Brookings Institution.

Cousineau, Jean-Michel, Robert Lacroix, and Danielle Bilodeau. May 1983. "The Determination of Escalator Clauses in Collective Agreements." *Review of Economics and Statistics,* 65: 196-202.

Cymrot, Donald J. July 1980. "Private Pension Saving: The Effect of Tax Incentives on the Rate of Return." *Southern Economic Journal,* 47: 489-509.

Danthine, Jean-Pierre, and John B. Donaldson. 1989. "Risk Sharing Labor Contracts and the Business Cycle." Working Paper. Columbia University.

Danzinger, Leif. May 1988. "Real Shocks, Efficient Risk Sharing and the Duration of Labor Contracts." *Quarterly Journal of Economics,* 103: 435-440.

Darby, Michael R. 1984. "The U.S. Productivity Slowdown: A Case of Statistical Myopia." *American Economic Review,* 74: 301-322.

Dean, Edwin, Kent Kunze, and Larry S. Rosenblum. 1988. "Productivity Change and the Measurement of Heterogeneous Labor Inputs." Paper presented at the Conference on New Measurement Procedures for U.S. Agriculture Productivity.

DeBoer, Larry, and Michael Seeborg. 1989. "The Unemployment Rates of Men and Women: A Transition Probability Analysis." *Industrial and Labor Relations Review,* 42 (3): 404-414.

De Long, J. Bradford, and Lawrence H. Summers. December 1986. "Is Increased Price Flexibility Stabilizing?" *American Economic Review,* 76(5): 1031-1044.

Dickens, William T., and Jonathan S. Leonard. April 1986a. "Accounting for the Decline in Union Membership, 1950-1980." *Industrial and Labor Relations Review,* 38: 323-334.

_____. April 1986b. "Structural Changes in Unionization: 1973-1981." NBER Working Paper No. 1882.

Dornbusch, Rudiger, and Stanley Fischer. 1986. "The Open Economy, Implications for Monetary and Fiscal Policy," in Robert Gordon, ed., *The American Business Cycle: Continuity and Change.* Chicago, Ill. University of Chicago for NBER: 459-516.

Dorsey, Stuart. October 1982. "A Model and Empirical Estimates of Worker Pension Coverage." *Southern Economic Journal,* 49: 506-520.

Dye, Ronald A. 1980. *Contract Complexity and Length.* Ph.D. dissertation. Graduate School of Industrial Administration, Carnegie-Mellon University.

Economic Report of the President. 1990. Washington, D.C.: Government Printing Office.

Ehrenberg, Ronald G. 1971. *Fringe Benefits and Overtime Behavior.* Lexington, MA. D.C. Heath.

Ehrenberg, Ronald G., Leif Danziger, and Gee San. 1984. "Cost-of-Living Adjustment Clauses in Union Contracts," in R.G. Ehrenberg, ed., *Research in Labor Economics,* 6: 1-63.

Ehrenberg, Ronald G., and Robert S. Smith. 1987. *Modern Labor Economics.* Glenview, IL: Scott, Foresman.

Engle, Robert F. July 1982. "Autoregressive Conditional Heteroscedasticity with Estimates of the Variance of United Kingdom Inflation." *Econometrica,* 50: 987-1007.

Erickson, C., and A. Ichino. September 1989. "Lump Sum Bonuses in Union Contracts: Semantic Change or Step Toward a New Wage Determination System?" Mimeo. Massachusetts Institute of Technology.

Estrin, Saul, Paul Grout, and Sushil Wadhwani. April 1987. "Profit Sharing and Employee Share Ownership." *Economic Policy.*

Estrin, Saul, and N. Wilson. May 1989. "Profit Sharing, the Marginal Cost of Labour, and Employment Variability." Discussion paper. London: Department of Economics, London School of Economics.

Feldstein, Martin. 1973. "The Economics of the New Unemployment." *The Public Interest,* Fall: 3-42.

Fethke, Gary, and Andrew Policano. September 1984. "Wage Contingencies, the Pattern of Negotiations, and Aggregate Implications of Alternative Contract Structures." *Journal of Monetary Economics,* 14: 151-170.

_____. 1986. "Timing of Negotiations and the Efficiency of Employment Contingent Contracts." Manuscript. University of Iowa.

Finseth, Eric. March 1988. *The Employment Behavior of Profit-Sharing Firms: An Empirical Test of the Weitzman Theory.* Senior Thesis. Cambridge, MA: Department of Economics, Harvard University.

Fischer, Stanley. February 1977. "Long Term Contracts, Rational Expectations and the Optimal Money Supply Rule." *Journal of Political Economy,* 85: 191-205.

Fitzroy, Felix R., and Daniel Vaughan-Whitehead. May 1989. "Employment, Efficiency Wages, and Profit Sharing in French Firms." Draft.

Florkowski, Gary W. "Profit Sharing and Public Policy: What Role Should the U.S. Government Play?" Industrial Relations, forthcoming.

Freeman, Richard B. December 1988. "How Do Young Less Educated Workers Fare in a Labor Shortage Economy?" Paper presented at the annual meeting of the American Economic Association.

_____. 1989. "The Changing Status of Unionism Around the World," in Wei-Chiao Huang, ed., *Organized Labor at the Crossroads.* Kalamazoo, MI. W. E. Upjohn Institute: 111-137.

Freeman, Richard B., and Lawrence Katz. September 1987. "Wages and Employment in the Open Economy." Prepared for the NBER Conference on Immigration, Trade and Labor Markets.

Freeman, Richard B., and Morris Kleiner. 1987. "Union Organizing Drive Outcomes from NLRB Elections during a Period of Economic Concessions." *Thirty-Ninth Industrial Relations Research Association Proceedings.* Madison, WI: Industrial Relations Research Association.

Freeman, Richard B., and Martin L. Weitzman. March 1986. "Bonuses and Employment in Japan." Working Paper No. 1878. Cambridge, MA: National Bureau of Economic Research.

Frisch, Ragnar. 1933. "Propagation Problems and Impulse Problems in Dynamic Economics," in *Economic Essays in Honor of Gustav Cassel.* London: Allen and Unwin.

Ghez, Gilbert R., and Gary S. Becker. 1975. *The Allocation of Time and Goods over the Life Cycle.* New York: National Bureau of Economic Research.

Gilman, Nicholas Paine. 1899. *A Dividend to Labor: A Study of Employers' Welfare Institutions.* Boston: Houghton, Mifflin, and Company.

Goldberger, Arthur S. 1964. *Econometric Theory.* New York: John Wiley and Sons.

Gomme, Paul, and Jeremy Greenwood. 1990. "On the Cyclical Allocation Risk." Working Paper 462, Federal Reserve Bank of Minneapolis.

Gordon, Robert J. 1982. "Inflation, Flexible Exchange Rates, and the Natural Rate of Unemployment," in Martin N. Baily, ed., *Workers, Jobs, and Inflation.* Washington, D.C. The Brookings Institution: 89-155.

_____. May 1988. "U.S. Inflation, Labor's Share, and the Natural Rate of Unemployment." National Bureau of Economic Research Working Paper No. 2585.

Gordon, Robert J., and Stephen King. 1982. "The Autoregressive Output Cost of Disinflation in Traditional and Vector Models." *Brookings Papers on Economic Activity,* 1: 205-244.

Gray, Jo Anna. 1976. "Wage Indexation: A Macroeconomic Approach." *Journal of Monetary Economics,* 2: 221-235.

_____. February 1978. "On Indexation and Contract Length." *Journal of Political Economy,* 86: 1-18.

Hall, Robert E. 1980. "Employment Fluctuations and Wage Rigidity." *Brookings Papers on Economic Activity:* 91-123.

Hall, Robert E., and David Lilien. December 1979. "Efficient Wage Bargains Under Uncertain Supply and Demand." *American Economic Review,* 69: 868-879.

Hamermesh, Daniel S. 1986. "The Demand for Labor in the Long Run," in Orley Ashenfelter and Richard Layard, eds., *Handbook of Labor Economics.* New York. North-Holland: 429-471.

_____. 1988. "The Demand for Workers and Hours and the Effects of Job Security Policies: Theories and Evidence," in Robert A. Hart, ed., *Employment, Unemployment, and Labor Utilization.* Boston. Unwin Hyman: 9-32.

Hamermesh, Daniel S., and Stephen A. Woodbury. June 1990. "Taxes, Fringes, and Faculty." Manuscript. Michigan State University.

Hart, Robert A. 1984. *The Economics of Non-Wage Labour Costs.* London: George Allen and Unwin.

Hart, Robert A., and Stephen A. Woodbury. June 1990. "Wages, Fringe Benefits, and Job Tenure." Manuscript. W. E. Upjohn Institute for Employment Research.

Hashimoto, Masanori. June 1981. "Firm-Specific Human Capital as a Shared Investment." *American Economic Review,* 71: 475-482.

Heckman, James, and Robert Willis. 1977. "A Beta-logistic Model for the Analysis of Sequential Labor Force Participation by Married Women." *Journal of Political Economy,* 85 (1): 27-58.

Hewitt Associates. 1985. *Salaried Employee Benefits Provided by Major U.S. Employers: A Comparison Study, 1979 Through 1984.* Atlanta, GA: Hewitt Associates.

_____. 1986. *Salaried Employee Benefits Provided by Major U.S. Employers in 1985.* Atlanta, GA: Hewitt Associates.

Hooper, Peter, and Catherine Mann. 1989. "Exchange Rate Pass-through in the 1980s: The Case of U.S. Imports of Manufactures." *Brookings Papers on Economic Activity,* 1: 297-337.

Horvath, Francis. 1987. "The Pulse of Economic Change: Displaced Workers of 1981-85," *Monthly Labor Review,* 110 (6): 3-12.

Huberman, Gur. January 1985. "Optimality of Periodicity." Manuscript. Center for Research in Security Prices, Graduate School of Business, University of Chicago. Revised version. Working Paper Series #138.

Huberman, Gur, and Charles Kahn. 1986. "Limited Contract Enforcement and Strategic Renegotiation." Manuscript. Center for Research in Security Prices, Graduate School of Business, University of Chicago. Working Paper Series #167.

Ippolito, Richard A., and Walter W. Kolodrubetz. 1986. *The Handbook of Pension Statistics, 1985.* Chicago, IL: Commerce Clearing House, Inc.

Jensen, Michael. Winter 1988. "Takeovers: Their Causes and Consequences." *Journal of Economic Perspectives,* 2: 21-48.

Jones, Derek C., and Jeffrey Pliskin. Spring 1989. "British Evidence on the Employment Effects of Profit Sharing." *Industrial Relations,* 28.

Jorgenson, Dale W., Gollop, Frank M., and Fraumeni, Barbara M. 1987. *Productivity and U.S. Economic Growth.* Cambridge, MA: Harvard University Press.

Keane, Michael P. 1990. "Sectoral Shift Theories of Unemployment: Evidence from Panel Data." Discussion Paper No. 28, Federal Reserve Bank of Minneapolis.

Keifer, Nicholas, and George Neumann. 1982. "Wages and the Structure of Unemployment Rates," in Martin Baily, ed., *Workers, Jobs, and Inflation.* Washington, D.C. The Brookings Institution: 325-351.

Kennan, John. 1986. "The Economics of Strikes," in Orley Ashenfelter and Richard Layard, eds., *Handbook of Labor Economics.* Amsterdam. North Holland: 1091-1137.

Kruse, Douglas L. 1988. "International Trade and the Labor Market Experience of Displaced Workers." *Industrial and Labor Relations Review,* 41 (3): 402-417.

_____. "Profit Sharing and Employment Stability: Microeconomic Evidence on the Weitzman Theory." *Industrial and Labor Relations Review.* Forthcoming.

Kydland, Finn E. 1984. "Labor-Force Heterogeneity and the Business Cycle," in K. Brunner and A.H. Meltzer, eds., *Essays on Macroeconomic Implications of Financial and Labor Markets.* Carnegie-Rochester Conference Series on Public Policy 21:173-208. Amsterdam: North-Holland.

Kydland, Finn E., and Edward C. Prescott. 1989. "Cyclical Movements of the Labor Input and Its Real Wage." Working Paper No. 413. Federal Reserve Bank of Minneapolis.

_____. 1990. "Business Cycles: Real Facts and a Monetary Myth." *Federal Reserve Bank of Minneapolis Quarterly Review,* Spring: 3-18.

Lazear, Edward P. September 1981. "Agency, Earnings Profiles, Productivity, and Hours Restrictions." *American Economics Review,* 71: 606-620.

_____. Spring 1990. "Pension and Defined Benefits as Strategic Compensation." *Industrial Relations,* 29: 263-280.

Lester, Richard A. April 1967. "Benefits as a Preferred Form of Compensation." *Southern Economic Journal,* 33: 488-495.

Levine, David. 1987. "Efficiency Wages in Weitzman's Share Economy." *Economics Letters,* 23.

Levine, Phillip B. 1990. "What Is Unemployment: A Comparison of Contemporaneous and Retrospective Measures." Mimeo. Industrial Relations Section, Princeton University.

Linneman, Peter D., Michael L. Wachter, and William H. Carter. October 1990. "Evaluating the Evidence of Union Employment and Wages." *Industrial and Labor Relations Review,* 44(1).

Long, James E., and Frank A. Scott. May 1982. "The Income Tax and Nonwage Compensation." *Review of Economics and Statistics,* 64: 211-219.

Lucas, Robert E., Jr. 1976. "Econometric Policy Evaluation: A Critique," in K. Brunner and A. H. Meltzer, eds., *The Phillips Curve and Labor Markets.* Carnegie-Rochester Conference Series on Public Policy 1: 19-46. Amsterdam: North-Holland.

_____. 1977. "Understanding Business Cycles," in K. Brunner and A. H. Meltzer, eds., *Stabilization of the Domestic and International Economy.* Carnegie-Rochester Conference Series on Public Policy 5: 7-29. Amsterdam: North-Holland.

Lundberg, Shelly. 1985. "The Added Worker Effect." *Journal of Labor Economics,* 3 (1): 11-37.

McClain, David. 1984. "The Inflation Deceleration: A Meltdown of the Core, or Just Luck?" Paper presented at the annual meeting of the American Economic Association, Dallas, Texas.

Maddala, G. S. 1983. *Limited Dependent and Qualitative Variables in Econometrics*. New York: Cambridge University Press.

Meade, James. 1986. *Different Forms of Share Economy*. London, England: Public Policy Centre.

Mellow, Wesley. 1982. "Worker Differences in the Receipt of Health and Pension Benefits: Extending the Analysis of Compensation Differentials," in *Proceedings of the Thirty-Fourth Annual Meeting of the Industrial Relations Research Association*. Madison, WI: IRRA: 16-25.

Mitchell, Daniel J.B. 1985. "Shifting Norms in Wage Determination." *Brookings Papers on Economic Activity*, 2: 575-609.

_____. 1986. "Union vs. Nonunion Wage Norm Shifts." *American Economic Review, Papers and Proceedings of the 98th Annual Meeting of the American Economic Association*: 249-252.

_____. Winter 1987. "The Share Economy and Industrial Relations: Implications of the Weitzman Proposal." *Industrial Relations*, 26: 1-17.

_____. 1989. "Wage Pressures and Labor Shortages: The 1960s and the 1980s." *Brookings Papers on Economic Activity*, 2: 191-231.

Mitchell, Daniel J.B., David Lewin, and Edward E. Lawler. 1990. "Alternative Pay Systems, Firm Performance, and Productivity," in Alan Blinder, ed., *Paying for Productivity: A Look at the Evidence*. Washington, D.C. The Brookings Institution: 15-99.

Murphy, Kevin, and Robert Topel. 1987. "The Evolution of Unemployment in the United States: 1968-1985," in Stanley Fischer, ed., *NBER Macroeconomics Annual 1987*: 11-58.

Murphy, Kevin, and Finis Welch. November 1987. "The Structure of Wages." Mimeo, Unicon Research.

Neumark, David. 1989. "Declining Union and Wage Inflation in the 1980s." Economic Activity Section, Division of Research and Statistics. Working Paper No. 96. Board of Governors of the Federal Reserve System.

Nordhaus, William. 1972. "The Worldwide Wage Explosion." *Brookings Papers on Economic Activity*, 2: 431-465.

_____. February 1988. "Can the Share Economy Conquer Stagflation?" *Quarterly Journal of Economics*, 103: 201-217.

Oaxaca, Ronald. October 1983. "Male-Female Wage Differentials in Urban Labor Markets." *International Economic Review*, 14: 693-709.

Oi, Walter Y. December 1962. "Labor as a Quasi-Fixed Factor." *Journal of Political Economy*, 70: 538-555.

_____. 1983. "The Fixed Employment Costs of Specialized Labor," in Jack E. Triplett, ed., *The Measurement of Labor Cost*. Chicago. University of Chicago Press: 63-116.

Perry, George. 1970. "Changing Labor Markets and Inflation." *Brookings Papers on Economic Activity*, 3: 411-441.

Poole, Michael. 1989. *The Origins of Economic Democracy Profit-Sharing and Employee-Shareholding Schemes*. London and New York: Routledge.

Prywes, Manahem. April 1989. "Linking Wages to Changing Output Prices." World Bank. Policy, Planning, and Research Working Papers, WPS187.

Ragan, Chris. July 1989. "Risk Sharing and Optimal Contract Duration." Manuscript. McGill University.

Rives, Janet, and Keith Turner. 1987. "Women's Occupations as a Factor in Their Unemployment Rate Volatility." *Quarterly Review of Economics and Business*, 27 (4): 55-64.

Rosen, Sherwin. January-February 1974. "Hedonic Prices and Implicit Markets: Product Differentiation in Pure Competition." *Journal of Political Economy* 82: 34-55.

_____. July 1983. "The Equilibrium Approach to Labor Markets." NBER Working Paper No. 1165.

Sawhill, Isabel. 1982. "Comment on Keifer and Neumann," in Martin Baily, ed., *Workers, Jobs, and Inflation.* Washington, D.C. The Brookings Institution.

Schroeder, Michael. "Watching the Bottom Line Instead of the Clock." *Business Week,* 11/7/88: 134-136.

Sloan, Frank A., and Killard W. Adamache. April 1986. "Taxation and the Growth of Nonwage Compensation." *Public Finance Quarterly,* 14: 115-137.

Solon, Gary. February 1984. "Estimating Autocorrelations in Fixed-Effects Models." NBER Technical Working Paper No. 32. Cambridge, MA: National Bureau of Economic Research.

Solow, Robert M. 1956. "A Contribution to the Theory of Economic Growth." *Quarterly Journal of Economics,* 70: 65-94.

_____. 1957. "Technical Change and the Aggregate Production Function." *Review of Economics and Statistics,* 39: 312-320.

_____. 1970. *Growth Theory.* New York: Oxford University Press.

Stokey, Nancy L., and Robert E. Lucas, Jr. 1989. *Recursive Methods in Economic Dynamics.* Cambridge, MA: Harvard University Press.

Summers, Lawrence. 1986. "Notes on the Share Economy." Discussion paper. Department of Economics, Harvard University, Cambridge, MA.

Summers, Lawrence, and Sushil Wadhwani. September 1987. "Some International Evidence on Labour Cost Flexibility and Output Variability." Working Paper No. 981. London: Centre for Labour Economics, London School of Economics.

Taylor, John B. May 1979. "Staggered Wage Setting in a Macro Model." *American Economic Review,* 69: 108-113.

U.S. Department of Labor, Bureau of Labor Statistics. *Employee Benefits in Medium and Large Firms.* (Various issues: 1981, 1982, 1983, 1984, 1985, 1986.) Washington, D.C.: Government Printing Office.

_____. 1988. *Labor Force Statistics Derived from the Current Population Survey,* 1948-1987, Washington D.C.: USGPO, August. Bulletin No. 2307.

U.S. General Accounting Office. December 1986. *Employee Stock Ownership Plans: Benefits and Costs of ESOP Tax Incentives for Broadening Stock Ownership.* GAO/PEMD-87-8. Washington, D.C.: U.S. General Accounting Office.

Vroman, Susan B. November 1988. "Inflation Uncertainty and Contract Duration." Manuscript. Georgetown University.

Vroman, Susan B., and Wayne Vroman. December 1987. "Wage Adjustments to Increased Foreign Competition." Paper presented at the annual meetings of the Industrial Relations Research Association, Chicago, Ill.

Vroman, Wayne. November 1984. "Wage Contract Settlements in U.S. Manufacturing." *Review of Economics and Statistics,* 66: 661-665.

_____. October 1986. "Union Wage Settlements, Incomes Policies and Indexation." Manuscript. The Urban Institute.

Vroman, Wayne, and John Abowd. 1988. "Disaggregated Wage Development." *Brookings Papers on Economic Activity,* 1: 313-338.

Wachter, Michael L. May 1986. "Union Wage Rigidity: The Default Settings of Labor Law." *American Economic Review,* 76(2): 240–244.

Wachter, Michael L., and William Carter. 1989. "Norm Shifts in Union Wage: Will 1989 Be a Replay of 1969?" *Brookings Papers on Economic Activity,* 2: 233-264.

Wadhwani, Sushil, and Martin Wall. 1988. "The Effects of Profit-Sharing on Employment, Wages, Stock Returns, and Productivity: Evidence from UK Micro-Data." Working Paper No. 1030. London: Centre for Labour Economics, London School of Economics.

Weitzman, Martin L. 1983. "Some Macroeconomic Implications of Alternative Compensation Systems." *Economic Journal,* 93: 763-783.

_____. 1984. *The Share Economy Conquering Stagflation.* Cambridge, MA and London, England: Harvard University Press.

_____. December 1985. "The Simple Macroeconomics of Profit-Sharing." *American Economic Review,* 75: 937-953.

_____. 1986. "Macroeconomic Implications of Profit-Sharing," in Stanley Fischer, ed., NBER *Macroeconomics Annual 1986.* Cambridge, MA: MIT Press.

_____. February 1988. "Comment on 'Can the Share Economy Conquer Stagflation?' " *Quarterly Journal of Economics,* 103: 219-223.

Weitzman, Martin L., and Douglas L. Kruse. 1990. "Profit Sharing and Productivity," in Alan Blinder, ed., *Paying for Productivity: A Look at the Evidence.* Washington, D.C.: The Brookings Institution: 95-191.

Williams, Donald. 1985. "Employment in Recession and Recovery: A Demographic Flow Analysis." *Monthly Labor Review,* 108 (3): 35-42.

Woodbury, Stephen A. March 1983. "Substitution between Wage and Nonwage Benefits." *American Economic Review,* 73: 166-182.

_____. (Forthcoming 1990). "Economic Issues in Employee Benefits." *Research in Labor Economics,* 11.

Woodbury, Stephen A., and Wei-Jang Huang. March 1988. "The Slowing Growth of Fringe Benefits." Paper presented at the Eastern Economic Association Annual Convention, Boston, Massachusetts.

_____. 1990. *The Tax Treatment of Fringe Benefits.* Kalamazoo, Michigan: W.E. Upjohn Institute for Employment Research.

Index